T0247578

UNDER A ROCK

ALSO BY CHRIS STEIN

CHRIS STEIN/NEGATIVE:
ME, BLONDIE, AND THE ADVENT OF PUNK

H.R. GIGER:
DEBBIE HARRY METAMORPHOSIS:
CREATING THE VISUAL CONCEPT FOR KOOKOO

POINT OF VIEW:
ME, NEW YORK CITY, AND THE PUNK SCENE

UNDER A ROCK

CHRIS STEIN

FOREWORD BY DEBBIE HARRY

ST. MARTIN'S PRESS
NEW YORK

First published in the United States by St. Martin's Press,
an imprint of St. Martin's Publishing Group

www.stmartins.com

Designed by Devan Norman

The Library of Congress Cataloging-in-Publication Data
is available upon request.

ISBN 978-1-250-28672-7 (hardcover)
ISBN 978-1-250-28673-4 (ebook)

Our books may be purchased in bulk for promotional, educational, or
business use. Please contact your local bookseller or the Macmillan
Corporate and Premium Sales Department at 1-800-221-7945, extension
5442, or by email at MacmillanSpecialMarkets@macmillan.com.

First Edition: 2024

10 9 8 7 6 5 4 3 2 1

FOR BARBARA, VALI, AND DEBBIE,

AND IN MEMORY OF AKIRA,

WHO IS IN OUR HEARTS AND WITH THE STARS

FOREWORD

Chris has asked me to write a word or two for his memoir *Under a Rock*, a "foreword," the sound of which also applies to our mutual sense of drive and desire to keep moving ahead creatively. The fact that he has asked me to write for his book makes me happy, of course, but somewhat overwhelmed, too.

The story opens in New York City, where Chris's mother, Estelle, gave birth to Chris at Harlem Hospital. Chris tells so many great stories: growing up in Brooklyn, going to school, his mom and dad, his friends and adventures, and all the memories of a kid leaving childhood little by little, then hanging out in New York City as a young adult, that are seriously funny and might even seem fictitious. But it's all real. A true story of a life that was allowed to evolve and go 'round the bend and back, and then take a somewhat unexpected shot at the moon.

With five years difference in age, we shared a lot of the same cultural influences. Our moon shot, or aim for the stars, was very different from the one Jackie Gleason would sometimes offer to his lovely wife, Alice (played by Audrey Meadows). He would say, "To the moon, Alice, to the moon," his fist raised in a manly salute. It was always funny. "Why I oughta" isn't on the tips of our tongues so much now, not to mention that moon shots are almost expected these days when regularly launched satellite deployments have become beyond normal.

But back then in 1973 and 1974, we took our first Blondie moon shot.

I remember clearly, exactly where I was standing, when Chris called me to suggest we reunite Blondie after a seventeen-year-long hiatus. There in the kitchen of my apartment on 23rd Street, I said, "No, are you crazy?" In fact, the only proviso I had after thinking overnight about doing Blondie again was that we create new music and not rely entirely on the hits from our catalogue. Creativity being the food of life made the prospect of bringing the band back a pretty exciting idea in spite of all the complications that would inevitably have to be dealt with. So then, once more, we aimed high and in the mid-1990s went to work on the second incarnation of our band.

Sometimes fate deals up a wild card. There's a lot to be said for one of these wild cards and from what I've learned over the fifty or so years of our friendship, Chris is a card from the unexpected deck. I've also learned to expect the unexpected. Growing up in Brooklyn isn't so strange but the very long leash Chris was given as a child astonishes me. I asked his mother what he was like as a child. She replied that Chris was the same person from the moment he was born that he is today. Quite a funny image for me to consider, for at the time, he was wearing high-platform pimp shoes, shoulder-length hair, spandex pants, and eyes dripping with black kohl eyeliner. However, Estelle was right: essentially, he is the same person I've known after all these years of living and loving and working with him.

We had both scrambled around the Lower East Side during the late '60s and early '70s, often going to the same concerts or shows or events but never meeting. When we finally did meet it was at the Bobern Tavern in the Flower Market district of Manhattan. I was singing in a trio called The Stilettos with Elda Gentile and Roseanne Trapani. Chris and his girlfriend, Elvira, came to the show, and afterward we met for the first time in the dark stairwell filled with the scents of plants and flowers mixed with the dust of perhaps one hundred years, which served as our dressing room just to the side of the stage. This was about 1972 or 1973. The two of them were dressed in a crossover mix of hippie glamrock fashion and much more black kohl eyeliner and drenched in patchouli oil scent.

A few weeks later we needed a bass player and Chris and I started what became a very long music and love relationship.

I'm not completely psychic, but sometimes we all get a feeling of what's to come. You'll simply have to take my word for this. Most of what we did went unrecorded, heard only by our small live audiences made up mostly of friends and a few drunks, and was eventually lost to the infinite particles of the universe. What we did was crackling with innuendo but then blew out like a puff of smoke in an era with no cell phones.

I can't say enough good things about *Under a Rock*. It's not in my nature to want to keep looking back nostalgically, but Chris has written a many-layered view with his tireless memory and I can only see a few places in our part of his story that may have been slightly different.

Reading about the early days, and all the things we did, and how hard we worked actually made me tired and dizzy when I first read some early pages. But it also gave me many wonderful feelings and refreshed remembrances that we shared as we flew headfirst on our fantastic "moon shot" on the good ship Blondie.

—Debbie Harry

THE CUP:
A DOWNTOWN MEMORY

One day I took a walk up Tenth Avenue, and at Thirtieth Street I saw a bottle lying at the edge of the curb that was unmistakably full of pee. Over the many years I have lived in this city I have seen bottles full of pee sitting on curbs all over town. I know from my friend Joe, who for years and years drove a yellow cab, that the bottles of pee come from taxi drivers. Taxi drivers aren't allowed to stop anywhere to pee, and they usually have twelve-hour shifts. So they pee in bottles and leave them by the curb. Looking at this particular one, I was reminded of an actual cup of pee I knew about once.

The cup of pee was noticed by Chris Stein one early November day as he walked past it. It was sitting on the granite ledge of a boarded-up window in an old industrial building on a street still more or less deserted. He'd lived in the city forever, so he instantly recognized it as pee. I don't remember why he told me about it but I remember him saying, "I saw a cup of piss sitting on a windowsill," and sort of giggling. Over the next little while he called every day to tell me that the cup of pee was still there, because every day he passed it on his way to the deli where he went to get coffee. Quite a few days later, Chris told me that the pee in the cup was starting to turn from yellow to a shade of amber. He was amazed that the cup of pee was undisturbed after weeks of sitting there.

Chris lived on Greenwich Street, right around the corner from the cup of pee. I liked visiting him, and I always thought his house looked like a museum after an earthquake. He had a glass case with a creature called a root demon in it and mirrors and masks and swords and paintings and junk he dragged in from outside and piles of books and sleeping kitties all over everything and plates of cat food and gadgets and guitars and skulls and a very messy kitchen.

We took lots of walks together during that time, and Chris always had interesting stories about certain old buildings and things that had happened in them. I remember him pointing out the building where the famous shirtwaist-factory fire had taken place with all the poor seamstresses trapped inside. And one day we walked by the building where the cup of pee was sitting on its granite sill before the boarded-up window. Chris was giggling as he showed it to me. He could hardly believe that the cup of pee was still there. But who would touch it? Would it just sit there forever?

It was around that time, in 1997, that my dad, Seaweed, came to visit me. He was a noticeable oddball. He had Tourette's syndrome. He didn't shout curses. What he did do was hum a little tune constantly and say *bump* over and over. He was born in 1922. He was very intelligent and he loved gangsters. He didn't have a lot of money, but he loved wandering around New York looking at the old buildings. I always put him in the Leo House, the Catholic hostel on West Twenty-Third Street, when he came to visit. They had an old hand-operated elevator then and sometimes the operator was a nun, which he liked very much.

Chris was away when my dad came, but he had told me, "Take your old man down to my place if you want." He knew my dad would appreciate it, and he did. He looked at Chris's skulls and books, he petted all of Chris's cats, and then in the basement, he looked at all the guitars lying around, and after a long humming silence, he said: "Are all these things in tune?" And he really wanted to know. We wandered up Canal Street and stopped in front of a Chinese fish seller where many different kinds of fish lay all over a big mountain of ice, and my dad asked, "What kind of fish is this?"

The fish seller said, "Rockfish."

"What kind of fish is that?" my dad asked.

"Grouper."

"And what kind of fish is this?"

"Perch. You want perch?"

And my dad said, "No, thanks. What kind of fish is that?"

He would have asked what kind of fish they all were if the fish seller hadn't turned away to help somebody else.

I told my dad the story of the cup of pee. Since it was right nearby, I asked him if he'd like to go see it. A look crossed his face as if he were about to say *What the hell for?* But he said, "Okay. Why the hell not?" So I took him around to the old building. And the cup of pee was gone. I could hardly believe my eyes. The cup of pee was no longer there. My dad didn't really care, but it seemed nevertheless like a chance missed, and he was disappointed. "I wouldn't have minded seeing it," he said.

These days it's usually the whole building that is gone suddenly when you go looking for something you remember. It seems that every other block has a big hole in it where something was and now isn't. Something old and quiet, some little old theater or two-story workshop or florist, and in their places new, very tall buildings are shooting up as fast as slum weeds. When I saw the bottle of pee on Tenth Avenue, it somehow, suddenly, looked old-fashioned.

I wrote the above in 2005, and since then New York has done even more shapeshifting, but somehow Chris has remained one of its constants. When I asked him just recently if he remembered the cup of pee, I knew before he answered that he would. You're either going to have a memory for all the eccentric little details of life or you're not, and Chris always did. His memory is like a vast catacomb of wonderful stuff where he can go and wander around anytime he wants.

—*Romy Ashby*

Romy Ashby wrote songs for the Blondie albums *No Exit* and *The Curse of Blondie*. She was the editor and cofounder of *Goodie Magazine*. She still lives in downtown New York City.

UNDER
A ROCK

CHAPTER 1

My parents met in the Communist Party in Syracuse, New York. This sounds more glamorous and/or terrible than it likely was. I never discussed it with them. I picture a bunch of pretty normal scholastic types sitting around a midcentury-modern living room in tweed jackets talking about the usual workers-controlling-the-means-of-production stuff while debating whose apartment the next meeting would be at. I have an old picture from this period of them on a couch, my old man, Ben, still with hair.

This was in the very early Cold War days, probably 1949, a few years before the Rosenbergs were convicted and executed. I don't think any actual spy craft went on in Syracuse and I'm fairly certain my mom and dad were only involved in the theoretical side and didn't blow up any factories. I'm not sure what sort of allure the Soviet system presented, as the failures and horrors of Stalinism were well documented by then. I get the excitement surrounding the Russian Revolution and I recommend watching *Reds* (1981), with Warren Beatty as John Reed, which provides some insight into this enthusiasm. In later years I found an old copy of *The Masses* in the garbage and Reed was indeed a great writer, but I digress.

My father had actually come from Russia when he was a little kid, maybe six years old. I was close to him but sadly I don't know any details of his history. I don't know anything about his parents or where he came from specifically. He had two sisters, Dorothy (Dottie) and Clara. We didn't at the time know when his birthday was. It was mentioned to me in passing that our last name was actually Langstein and Aunt Dottie had anglicized her last name to Langston while my father, maybe his father, went with Stein.

By contrast, my mother, Estelle (Stel) Busky, had a very large network of family—cousins, a sister—and her side is well documented. She was born in 1911 in New York before women were able to vote in the U.S. She was some sort of Armenian-Romanian mash-up but I think out of the whole crew, only my maternal grandfather may have been born outside of the U.S.

Anyway, my folks hooked up and presumably were married prior to my arrival. I missed being born on New Year's Day 1950 by five days and arrived at Sloane Hospital for Women, now Harlem Hospital.

My grandmother pressured them to name me Herman after my deceased grandfather. They didn't go for it and I suspect that the name Christopher was applied to enable me to skirt some of the anti-Semitism that they might have experienced, the times then being what they were. This was an unusual name for a Jew in 1950. My mother told me I didn't have a middle name and I've never used one. It was only after she died and I came into possession of my old birth certificate that I discovered to my chagrin that the middle name listed is Herman. I was very fond of my grandmother, so at least she got that.

I remember 1950s Brooklyn as positively rustic, trees and parks and run-down old properties in and about our neighborhood of Coney Island Avenue and Cortelyou Road. Coney Island Avenue was a big thoroughfare that was filled with the old round automobiles. Trolley cars on their steel tracks and sparking electrical overhead cables kept up a constant clatter. My father told me that prior to World War II, as trolley cars declined and were being replaced by buses, the old steel tracks were sold to Japan, which repurposed them into bullets that were fired at U.S. troops. I have no idea if this actually happened.

Our apartment was up a long flight over what I think was a corner drugstore. My whole life I've been in possession of old photos of me as a baby being held by my parents in this place. I remember being given a bath in a big enamel tub and sitting behind the bars of a crib. My memory of the apartment is of a huge dark shadowy space, the stairs to the street a vast cliff.

My father went to work and I hung out with my mother. We did mother/little-kid stuff. We had a gray cat that was named Elizabeth Noodle Soup. At some point Elizabeth had gotten her tail caught in the front door and from then on was possessed of a kinked tail. We had a big baby carriage that I'd ride in. One day we took Elizabeth Noodle Soup with us in the carriage, and near a park, she leaped out and was never seen again. I don't think I felt as bad when I was three years old as I do in retrospect.

Somewhere in here, the FBI came and talked to my dad about his evil Commie leanings. This was at the height of the Red Scare and he must have shit himself. I don't know if they came inside or just waylaid him in the hall. In later years he did tell me he "gave them the name of a dead guy" and they seemed happy that he had at least coughed up something. I really wish I'd pressed him for details on this but, alas, I didn't.

I wasn't aware of much music during this early period but my parents had a record player and I do recall them listening to Lead Belly. We got a TV. My parents were subject to capitalist influences. When it was turned on for the first time, there were seals on it barking. Black-and-white seals and they scared the hell out of me. I don't know that this has carried over as any sort of lasting fear of either seals or TVs but at the time it completely creeped me out. The other TV-related horror was a Buster Brown shoe commercial that had the signature dog in the shoe barking. I found this terrifying and would flee the TV's proximity during the times this would appear. I don't recall any other particular scary TV things from that period.

Downstairs from our apartment was a wonderful bygone TV repair shop run by a Mr. Daniels. Maybe this was where my parents got our TV. The great thing was that Mr. Daniels's store was filled with cats. The old wooden-console TVs were covered with languishing cats sitting in dusty sunbeams that fell from the big windows. I have these images of the store and cats in my head that are half memory and half dream.

Now that I think about it, a lot of my time back then was taken up with being scared of things. There was a polar bear in an orange juice advertisement in a store window that was particularly frightening.

My mother and me were in the basement of a Woolworth's department store in the neighborhood. I must have gotten separated and was wandering around in the uncaring aisles. Suddenly two things happened simultaneously. There was a pet section and an escaping parakeet or parrot began screeching furiously, and at that exact moment I rounded a corner and came face-to-face with a plaster mannequin that had half its head creepily caved in. I still remember this juxtaposition sixty-five years later.

The neighborhood was really no country for little kids and I didn't have any friends while we were there. I did make occasional chaperoned forays out into the streets and had some small interactions with local children, but the avenue was big and filled with traffic so I spent time with my mom at home watching TV. The two things I recall from that period of television are Winky Dink and the Holocaust. *Winky Dink and You* was an animated kids' show that was interactive. One would buy the Winky Dink play-set kit, which was a plastic press-on screen and crayons. The screen went on the TV and at a point in the show when Winky Dink (who was a little humanoid creature with a star-shaped hairdo) would get into a jam, the audience was required to draw connecting stairs, et cetera to help him move along. This of course led to thousands of kids all across the country scribbling on their actual TV screens with the supplied crayons. It was a minor scandal.

When I was born, Truman was president. The Second World War was fresh and I saw scenes of the bodies being bulldozed into mass graves on the TV. It didn't scare me the way the seals did and I'm not sure what I felt seeing these things at the time but I remember it very clearly.

Toward the end of our time there I was becoming more conscious. My mother invited some kid over for me to play with and we wrecked my room. We turned over everything that was turn-over-able and pulled everything onto the floor that could be pulled onto the floor. My mom asked me why I'd done it and I gave her some bullshit answer like "Mom, I just had to," which she thought was cute, and this approval possibly helped begin my descent into anarchy and chaos.

I was playing on the floor in a sort of hall space and must have knocked the wall and, lo and behold, the knock was miraculously returned from behind the wall. I never found out who was tapping back at me but they kept it up for a few days. I wasn't sure that it was a human source; I was more inclined to imagine a ghost or such.

My mother took me to visit some kids in the neighborhood at their apartment. It was dark and small with a bunch of brothers and sisters. There was a bass drum with some writing on it as a wall decoration that fascinated me. A mouse ran across the floor and the kids very cheerfully told me it was a fairy. Their parents had told them the mice were fairies. I think they knew they were actually mice, though. These same kids and I exchanged stories about our experiences with a local creepy guy called Mr. Go to Bed. I knew who he was and had been creeped by him too. When he would see any child, he would lean toward them and growl, "Go to bed!" That was his calling in life, aggressively telling kids to go to bed.

My mom put me in school. First a preschool, nursery-school type thing that was a big old house with a hard-packed dirt yard. I vaguely remember not wanting to be left there but eventually went along with the program. Beyond that I remember that I had a fringed yellow leather jacket that I pulled the fringes off and gave to other kids. Was this a metaphor for seeking popularity by distributing oneself? Regardless, my mother was annoyed because, while the jacket had come with spare fringes for repairs, I of course had pulled off way more than the few supplied as replacements.

A bit of time passed and I moved across the street to kindergarten in a public school. I recall a bit of this: Stel one day arriving late to pick me up, me freaking out, et cetera, but it was here that after a short while the school suggested that I skip kindergarten and go directly into first grade. My mother must have been chuffed with this but of course this upgrade was possibly the foundation for undermining any academic success I might actually have had for the next ten years.

My parents decided that we needed to relocate from our somewhat industrial area to someplace that was more conducive to actual childhood and social interaction. I went with them on some trips to look at rentals and we wound up moving to the bottom floor of a two-family house in Midwood a bit southeast from where we were in Flatbush. I had my own room but my parents made do with an area of what was a large living room space.

East Thirteenth Street between Avenues K and L was a tree-lined stretch of mostly two-story houses that were inhabited by middle-class working families. The whole area was a grid of lettered avenues and shady tree-lined numbered streets with the occasional named smaller streets on the periphery. On the corners of these long streets and avenues were apartment buildings, mostly six-story walk-ups, some with names, like General Grant or Evergreen or whatever.

At some point when I was littler I managed to write my father's name, Ben, on a piece of paper that he carried in his wallet. I somehow connect that with my always calling him Ben rather than Dad or Father. Even when I was a kid I knew this wasn't the norm and it would occasionally feel awkward, but he didn't mind and that's just how it went. There was a pull in two directions here, what's socially acceptable and regular against some inner impulse that wouldn't be overcome. I mostly called Stel Mom, though sometimes I used her name.

Ben's job was working for my mom's sister's husband's paint company, Vulcan Lacquer, as a bulk salesman. He would get large orders from other small corporate entities that he would go off daily and haggle with. Now I was able to go out on my own and simultaneously I began school in the new neighborhood, so my time alone with Stel was considerably less.

In spite of his Red leanings Ben was very old-school patriotic. He took me to see the launching/christening of the aircraft carrier USS *Independence*. As far as I can tell this was in 1958. It was a warm day and the ship was huge. I'd certainly never seen anything like it. Folding chairs were set up and there was an on-deck ceremony. The key speaker was Admiral William "Bull" Halsey. My old man proudly told me how much ass this guy had kicked during the war.

We would make trips to Coney Island and Brighton Beach in the summer. We took photo-booth pictures and I made an actual little record in one of those audio-recording booths that still existed unironically then. The recording was me ranting about my adventures on that particular day and I had the little disk for several years thereafter. I later on was surprised about the high pitch of my voice as a little kid.

My father had a story about getting stuck on the parachute-jump ride for two hours when he was younger. One hot day we waited in line at Nathan's. The old guy behind the counter was very enthusiastic, chanting

"French fries and salt!" as a kind of song. When I got up to the window he looked me in the eye and said, "French fries and salt! You ain't never gonna forget this!" I never forgot it.

I remember being the outsider in relation to the neighborhood kids for a while until I was gradually accepted and initiated in with some mild abuse. Mutual torment was the name of the game and a couple of times, Ben stormed out of the house to confront some attacker. He was a big guy so after a while things leveled out, though I did hear "Hey, your father's a tough guy." I was soon only subject to the regular day-to-day abuse of normal boyhood. Kids existed in a world of constant hazing, a perpetual state of having to prove some aspect of toughness or stick-to-itiveness that bordered on weird roles of dominance and subservience.

I fell in with a core group of boys who lived on the block. No girls. I guess there were some sisters around, but our clique was exclusively male. I still am in online touch with a few of these guys. This was all getting going around 1960, so a long way back now. Frankie and his two brothers, Johnny and Tommy; Eddie; Arthur; Donald, who was my next-door neighbor; Irwin; Bob; and George were all in this start-up community. Everyone was either Jewish or Catholic. George Wilson was the only Black member of the group. When one would meet someone new, one would almost immediately ask, "Are you Jewish or Catholic?" I don't think I was aware of any other religions in the world. All of these guys except for George and me were subjected to Catholic school, working toward eventually being confirmed, or Hebrew school, working toward being bar mitzvahed.

George and I would sit and watch the parade of our friends as they stoically headed off to "religious" lessons after regular school every day. We were aware that we were exempt from this particular struggle. George lived with his father, who was the super in the apartment building on the corner. I don't think his dad, Sam, was at all religious. Sam Wilson seemed like he'd seen a lot of hardship in his life and was a practical tough guy. My parents were also nonreligious, and George and me knew we had dodged a bullet, so to speak, as all of the participants expressed to us a lack of enthusiasm for their having to spend time with this stuff. I don't know if the others' parents were actually devout; I never heard any discussions of God or Jesus and I assume it was just what one did.

Things happened on the block; there were intrigues and endlessly shifting alliances. There were strange events, broken windows, dead cats and squirrels, a yearly savage snowball war with kids from another block, dummies thrown off the roof of the corner apartment building.

There was an adorable little kid named Donny on the block. He looked like the kid from *Jerry Maguire*, cuter even. One day his dad was sleeping on their living-room couch and Donny bashed him in the head with a frying pan. I don't think it was deliberate; it just happened. The poor guy came back from the hospital and would sit on his porch in a bathrobe, staring off. I guess he eventually returned to some semblance of normalcy.

A buddy was driving with his dad and they passed the scene of a car crash. The vehicle involved had knocked over a parking meter and my friend somehow convinced his father to put it in the trunk of their car and take it home. He put it in his basement where we went at it with hammers and screwdrivers for days. I don't remember actually ever getting it completely open but we managed to shake about seventy-five cents out of it.

We did a lot of hanging out in the basement and the alley behind the corner apartment building where George lived. One day the basement was suddenly marked with a fallout shelter sign and stocked with government-issue fallout-shelter supplies. We watched as big boxes of sealed crackers and K ration-type foodstuff quickly vanished. The boxes of medicine went first. Only big empty drums that were meant to be filled with water at the first sign of incoming missiles were left. People in the neighborhood cleaned it all out. It was a noble experiment, I suppose, but the basement had windows and wouldn't have provided much protection from a thermonuclear blast.

We were playing some sort of semi-violent tag in the same basement when Stanley Lefkowitz ran into a pole and split his head open. I really liked Stanley; he was a champion of the underdogs. He looked like a complete nerd but was preternaturally strong and could stomp anyone easily. He was bleeding profusely and we helped him back to his house and shocked family. His horrified mother said, "Why are you holding your head like that?" Stanley, to our considerable amusement, answered, "I saw Richard Burton do it in a movie!" You had to be there.

There was a period around the same fallout-shelter time that, during my walks home from school, the sky was painted the strangest colors that I have ever seen. I've often wondered if the vivid violets, purples, and odd green tinges of the early sunsets were somehow related to the nuclear-bomb testing that was a popular activity at the time.

On Avenue J there was a Carvel ice cream place that the kids would frequent. The lady who worked there was a big strong-looking person who spoke with an Eastern European accent. She had the numbers from one of the World War II camps tattooed on her left forearm. I'd seen other examples when I was young but she's the one I remember the most. It occurs to me that she always wore short sleeves.

School was PS 199, which is on Elm Avenue and is now named for Frederick Wachtel, who I'm pretty sure was the assistant principal when I was there. My memory of it starts at third grade. We had a very kindly older lady named Mrs. Monkelt. Mrs. Monkelt was a sweetheart and she didn't give us any homework. She would rest her hand on my desk, and on the side of a large gold ring she wore was a tiny engraved skull and crossbones. I conferred with some classmates who had also seen it and we had no solution to this mystery. In later years I realized it was some kind of memento mori thing, maybe a dedication to a deceased husband. Anyway, she was great. Then I went on to fourth and fifth grade.

My two daughters, Akira and Vali, both went to public school at PS 3 in Manhattan. Through it all I have been consistently astonished at the difference between the current New York school climate and what I recall of my own experiences. The schools now are bending over backward to be accommodating, polite, inclusive, and welcoming. Vali, my younger daughter, had Cynthia Sley, the lead singer of the Bush Tetras, as her fourth-grade teacher, for God's sake (hi, Cynthia). When Vali left middle school, she showed me a video of her and her friends walking down the street sobbing because they had loved it at school so much. It blows my mind.

My school life was like unto the ninth circle of hell. I had teachers who were full-on sociopaths, who shouldn't have been allowed to interact with other human people let alone children. It was amazing, really. Here I am, an old dude, and I'm still able to conjure up the horror of my relations with some of these alleged educators.

In fourth grade we had Mrs. Fendrick, who was straight up the Hollywood version of the guard at a women's prison. She was a brutalist. She would assign lots of angry homework and angrily expect it and then get angry about it. Parents would phone each other trying to figure out what to do about the terrified students. That was fourth grade.

We got word that our fifth-grade teacher, the first male teacher there, would be a Mr. Karras. We joked about his name because of course we all knew that character in the Mummy films named Kharis. Mr. Karras was worse; at least the Mummy was quiet. Mr. Karras was a full-on narcissistic sociopath. He would smoke in class. He stationed a kid at the door and if anyone approached, the kid was supposed to yell "Beethoven," which was a signal for him to extinguish his cigarette. The Beethoven position was very coveted within the *Lord of the Flies* class hierarchy that Mr. Karras had established. If an adult made it past the guard successfully, Mr. Karras would sometimes be stuck with a lungful of smoke, nodding instead of conversing until he was able to exhale surreptitiously into a closet or something.

Some blind students joined the class for a week. Mr. Karras read excerpts from "The Country of the Blind" by H. G. Wells. The class was divided into male and female halves with the occasional mixing for the sake of humiliation. I wound up in the last row of the girls' half for a while. A student who didn't know an answer would be made to stand while Mr. Karras said something like "Mr. Stein feels like he's in hell right now" to the rest of the class. He even got my parents to spring for some tutoring from him and he came to my house and was very charming and not horrible. At least when I asked him to be removed from the girls' section in front of my mother, he couldn't refuse. I wouldn't be at all surprised if Mr. Karras either died in jail or went into politics.

The whole environment was marvelously toxic. I remember two instances at "assembly"—you know, when everyone in school is gathered in the auditorium for whatever collective activity or lecture. At one, I think it was the dean, basically the school's adult bully, just going off on the whole student body. I have no clue what offenses inspired him to stand in front of us all screaming about the "rats" that he knew were in our midst, but his performance was memorable enough for me to retain its tone if not its context after all this time. The other incident was again in front of the whole school. This time the gym teacher was fed up with one of the more gangster-miscreant type of kids and grabbed this person and proceeded to bang his head against the wall while we all sat watching.

I'm pretty sure that PS 199 has moved on from medieval times and that these events aren't the current norm.

Across the street from the school were a corner soda fountain and an ancient-style penny-candy store. I remember a lot of bins of candy amid white-painted flooring and wood paneling. There was one particular round, blue space-themed candy that I consumed frequently before somehow discovering it was gum.

It seemed like every year at the beginning of school there was a hurricane, and in 1960 there was a serious airplane crash over Brooklyn. A midair collision sent a DC-8 falling onto Park Slope, where it killed six people on the ground along with all the plane's passengers. Everyone at school decided that had the plane been airborne for another ten minutes, it definitely would have hit PS 199 and killed all of us.

Sixth grade found me in the dumb, or special, class, since I had obviously done miserably the prior two years. I guess my lack of scholastic ability was predicated on basic indifference and daydreaming. My reading levels were always ahead of my grades but I somehow couldn't rally myself to be concerned about the rigors of learning stuff at school. Our new teacher was very nice, a Miss Foil; she was younger and sympathetic so that the final year of grade school passed uneventfully. Near the end of the year, as the weather got warm, I somehow found myself with my friend Mike Darden on the garden squad, which entailed picking up the occasional piece of paper in the grass around the building but mostly involved lying around in said grass and making trips to the candy store or soda fountain.

Michael Darden was a pretty close friend who had landed a small role in the film version of *The Miracle Worker*, with Anne Bancroft and Patty Duke. Michael and his pretty large family lived in a big old house that was located on a small street called Locust Avenue. Locust Avenue in 1960 was a dirt road. The existence of one dirt road at the time in Brooklyn indicates to me now that there were likely others around.

Really near to Locust Avenue was the Brooklyn NBC Studios. This was a complex of old movie studios; the main building, built as Vitagraph Studios in 1906, was bought by Warner Brothers in the fifties. NBC Studios were on the way to and from school and I would spend a lot of time going through dumpsters there. I found sets of cue cards that I would repurpose into all kinds of things but the real star garbage was the ton of colored lighting gels that would get thrown out. This stuff was great, big sheets of red, blue, orange, et cetera clear gelatin sheets. I would make simple things out of them but my mom would shine by using them to create these stained-glass-looking renderings of her drawings by fusing and embellishing with a soldering iron. I was always bringing her big piles of the gels.

I don't know how we found out but my friends and me somehow heard that Sammy Davis Jr. was going to be at the studio for a TV appearance. We went to the main entrance and hung out for hours. Sometime after midnight Sammy emerged in a tuxedo with the tie hanging open around his neck. He had an overcoat slung over his arm. He looked like he'd been working hard in classic Rat Pack fashion but when he saw us, he paused and smiled. He said, "How you doing, brother?" to George. There wasn't anyone on the street except Sammy and us. He remarked on us being out so late, then got into his limo and drove off. It was the first autograph I ever got. He was charming. George told me no one had ever called him "brother" before.

I'm not sure how I considered the realms of celebrity at the time, if I was aware of the rarefied sphere that some people existed in, people whose lives were conducted semi-publicly on TV and radio, but my buddies and I all certainly thought of Sammy as royalty.

In the summers for several years, my parents would make the pilgrimage up to a couple of Catskill locations in upstate New York where I would sometimes have weird quasi-sexual adventures with older kids I didn't really know very well. I saw a lot of animals and it was at these places that Stel really went at it with her painting. Stel developed a reputation as a kind of eccentric with other guests at these farms we'd stay at. She would take over some little shed that became a workspace. She was a terrific painter, an abstract expressionist and surrealist, and I had absolutely no fucking appreciation of what was going on with her and her work. She had been a window designer in the late forties in Manhattan and would sometimes do Lord & Taylor and other high-end stores. Once in later years she told me that she'd hung out with de Kooning a bit in the Village. I wish I had managed to hold on to more of her paintings.

One day on one of these Catskill trips my father came down to breakfast dressed in all black. I didn't know that he even had a pair of black pants. What was up? Marilyn Monroe had died. Ben liked Marilyn.

I moved on into junior high school (which no one referred to as "middle school" at the time) in the midst of great changes and social upheavals. These trends made their way down to my friends and me through the lens of popular culture. The influences of my early teenage years were wildly diverse but were linked by a dark humor and ironic worldview.

Stel had taken me to see my first movie in a movie theater when I was seven: *Witness for the Prosecution*, starring Marlene Dietrich, Charles Laughton, and Tyrone Power. This was a pretty weird choice for a little kid but I quite liked it.

My friends and I were all movie fanatics. We would take subway trips into the city to the big Cinerama theaters in midtown, Times Square in the pre-porn era. We went to see *Lawrence of Arabia* and *How the West Was Won* multiple times each. We were obsessed with horror movies, horror TV shows, and horror movie magazines. For Halloween I was regularly Dracula in a weird tuxedo thing Stel made and occasionally the Invisible Man (bandages, sunglasses). *The Twilight Zone* had started in 1959, followed a few years later by *The Outer Limits*.

I watched a TV host named Zacherley all the time. He hosted a very funky black-and-white show called *Shock Theater* in which he would insert himself, making jokes, into the horror movies. A character in an old film was looking through a pair of binoculars; cut to Zacherley in a terrible rubber monkey mask eating a banana. He was like Ernie Kovacs with horror content. Zacherley was directly aligned with Vampira and Charles

Addams. I still love Zacherley; he was a formative influence. William Castle was achieving great success with his gimmick-laden horror movies: tingling theater seats, monsters emerging from the screen, ghost viewers, et cetera. Probably because I had sent for things that were advertised in the pages of *Famous Monsters of Filmland* magazine, out of the blue I got an invitation to start a local chapter of the William Castle Fan Club. They sent me some membership cards and I recruited a couple of friends. Castle would have been right at home in the modern world of internet exploitation.

A couple of years earlier my friend Bob and me both went to our local theater, the Midwood, to see a double feature: *Terror from the Year 5000* and *The Spider*. *Terror from the Year 5000* scared us so much, we left before *The Spider*.

I must have been around ten; I was home with my grandmother overseeing me while my parents were out. I was flipping the TV stations and landed on the exact moment in James Whale and Boris Karloff's *Frankenstein* when the monster creepily emerges from the bushes and apparently drowns the little girl. That stayed with me.

It was still the tail end of the old Hollywood system and twice I got to see celebrities make appearances at local movie houses. Karloff, Peter Lorre, and Vincent Price came to the Albemarle Theatre for *The Raven*. Jack Nicholson was in *The Raven* too but he didn't show up and no one would have known who he was anyway. A year before that, the Three Stooges made an appearance at the Kingsway, which was a bigger space, and they did an impromptu performance on the stage, slapping each other around before *The Three Stooges in Orbit* played.

I did kid stuff. I built model cars. A certain 1958 Thunderbird I worked on found me getting pretty buzzed on glue fumes without knowing what was going on. Somewhere or other I dug up an antique phonograph. This was one of those self-contained nonelectric devices that was powered by a spring and driven by turning a handle. I stripped this thing down so I was just dealing with the motor and the crank handle. I would spend an hour watching it's pent-up kinetic energy, winding it up and letting it run down while attached to strings or wires that I'd fix to its spindle. Eventually it exploded while it was running and sprayed black grease all over the room that was impossible to get completely out.

Finally my parents got me a single-pickup Harmony Rocket electric guitar and a small Silvertone amp for Christmas 1962 when I was twelve. I remember being surprised that pushing the strings down on the frets produced more notes. I don't know what I'd thought; maybe that it only had six notes, I'm not sure. For about a year I played by pressing the strings with my thumb. I was enamored of Flatt and Scruggs and I think that when I saw Flatt playing a slide guitar, I mistakenly thought he was using a similar thumb technique. This was before I had heard of Bob Dylan. I was attracted to just the essence of the instrument, the mystique of the electric guitar. I had hinted around to my parents that I wanted one. Before the guitar, my old man had gotten me a dark blue snare drum that I beat on for a while.

I'd been walking past the apartment buildings on Avenue L, and looking into a basement window I saw a guy with a fancy electric guitar and a big amp that had lights all over it that looked very exotic and great to me. The other notable encounter was passing a gas station on Coney Island Avenue one night after dark and hearing an electric guitar being played in the depths of the garage, the low twangy notes definitely making a connection, evoking some immediate sense of mystery and adventure.

I had been somewhat of a music fan; I mean, everybody liked "The Loco-Motion," but I really hadn't focused on the Supremes or Shangri-Las. Things I now think of as brilliant struck me as kind of commercial as a kid. Novelty records had a heyday. "Monster Mash," the Chipmunks, "The Purple People Eater," "The Battle of New Orleans," et cetera. I'm afraid that at the time, I thought of "Leader of the Pack" as part of this genre.

Music was secondary to movies, and it was film soundtracks that led me into buying records before ending up as a music enthusiast.

West Side Story was a huge event. It's hard to explain to people what a big-deal part of the youth culture it was. It was everywhere. We would go to a showing and when Tony got shot, there would be actual crying and wailing in the theater that was a bit like the tears shed over the Beatles two years later. Maybe *West Side Story* led to a lot of young people becoming rabid music fans and helped open the doors for folk and pop music.

Ben's sister Dottie lived with her husband, Byron, downtown in the city and during this time, my parents would sometimes take me on trips to Greenwich Village to look around and socialize with them. I saw a little bit of the folk-music scene. This was still the beatnik era. My mother was very fond of a surrealist jeweler, Sam Kramer, who had a shop up one flight on Eighth Street. The doorknob was a brass hand that Kramer would put a glove on when the weather was cold. He used a lot of glass eyes in his jewelry. I liked that place.

My parents would also take me browsing in old bookstores and in the piles of military surplus on Canal Street. I remember whole bins of sword blades and trigger panels from battleship cannons. My father took me to Kaufman's military surplus on Forty-Second Street. He'd been in the Marines, somehow failed out of that, and finished his service in the army. He was stationed in the Pacific during the war. I don't know if he was in combat; he only talked about how beautiful some of the beaches were in that part of the world. At Kaufman's he bought me a Marine bolo, like a small machete, and a Fairbairn-Sykes British commando dagger that I still have. This was without doubt the start of my knife collecting.

In the expanded universe of junior high school I began making new friends who lived beyond the block. One kid, Jeff Hittner, whose family owned and ran one of Manhattans oldest car/truck rental services, and I would make forays into the city. One night we finished seeing a movie at the Garrick Theater on Bleecker Street, and instead of leaving through the street doors we went out a small fire-exit door that was located right in front of the screen. That door opened to a small alley that contained another door that opened onto some descending stairs and we emerged into the kitchen of the Café Au Go Go that was in the basement of the Garrick. Nobody said anything to us and we went into the club. This was my first live concert: Stan Getz, the great jazz sax player, and his band. It was a good place to start.

We went back to the Au Go Go a few times and even paid to get in. It was probably five bucks or less. I saw comedians and my first electric-rock-style band, the Blues Project. I really liked them. Al Kooper on keys, and I noticed that Danny Kalb, the guitarist and singer, played with metal finger picks, something I immediately was interested in. The Blues Project recorded a live album at the Au Go Go in 1965 but I think the show I was at was before that. I did eventually get a copy of that record and in the present time got to spend a day hanging out with Roy Blumenfeld, who'd played drums on the album and in the show that I'd been to.

I also got the first Beatles record. Think about this: When I was a kid in Brooklyn, *there were no record stores!* Now, there were definitely record stores around Manhattan, but in my neighborhood one would get records at gift shops or, in the case of *Meet the Beatles!*, at a local hobby shop that sold model cars and planes. I don't exactly know why I bought the record, if it was curiosity, irony, or wanting to hear more than what was on the radio, which at that moment was "I Want to Hold Your Hand" continuously.

I must admit that my first thoughts about the Beatles were overwhelmed by the massive media hype surrounding them. The hype preceded the music. I liked folk music and probably by then had the second Dylan record, and there was always the tendency among the folky crowd to disdain popular music. A live radio report from where the Beatles were staying at the Plaza Hotel: The streets in front of the hotel are filled with crowds of kids. The radio announces that Paul might be getting married. The crowd starts crying en masse. I could hear the sobs coming over the airwaves. I think this stuff fueled my early skepticism.

But when I finally got to sit around listening to *Meet the Beatles!*, I was pleasantly surprised. There was something about the forward motion and drive of the tracks that drew me in. I played certain tracks over and over. (My neighbors once complained to my parents when I'd spent a day playing "Lolita Ya-Ya" by the Ventures repeatedly.)

I had a little blue console record player, one of those things that's the size of a large hatbox. I also had an old Wollensak model 1515 tape recorder that my uncle, Stel's brother-in-law, had donated to me. I would make mix tapes of Dylan songs that I liked and listen to them late at night. I'm not sure how I figured it out but I discovered that I could hook external speakers to the speaker in the record player really easily. When I saw a discarded radio or TV on the street, I would pull the speaker out, and soon

I had a lot of them hung around my room. Just the bare speakers; I didn't put them in any kind of enclosures. Poverty hi-fi.

Junior high was bigger and more ferocious than grade school, or whatever you call it, was. More extreme hierarchies and generally more kids who aspired to a sort of gangster lifestyle. Rampant sexiness and cigarette smoking. This was early on, and kids who would undoubtedly embrace hippie stoner culture were then still enamored of the juvenile-delinquent position. The alpha boys went for the rockabilly Elvis-ish hairstyles, tight pants, and pointed shoes, and the alpha-girl contingent all wore those short white Courrèges go-go boots with the black heels. After-school fights were fairly regular ritualistic events, and in-school outbursts were fairly commonplace.

Andries Hudde Junior High School. Hudde was allegedly some influential early Dutch settler, but word on the street was that he was either a pirate or a horse thief or both and had been hanged, possibly on the very spot the school was built on.

I was deposited in this seething mass. Early on as we were all leaving a class, completely out of the blue and without any warning, some kid came up behind me and punched me pretty hard in the side of the head. Teachers observed this and the kid was led off, never to be seen again. Nobody said anything to me, but a friend shrugged as if to say Hey, *life in the wild, get used to it.*

Our homeroom teacher for the first half of seventh grade was a Mrs. Eisenberg. Mrs. Eisenberg was a tall brunette probably in her thirties who was absurdly hot. It was like a parody. She was the teacher from the Van Halen video. My father had recently started to bring me copies of *Playboy*-type "men's" magazines. I suspect he was trying to steer my sexuality toward what he considered a "normal" direction, though I knew that none of my friends' dads were supplying them with similar research materials, so the normalcy might be construed as a bit skewed.

In some biology or science class a student responded to a question about microscopic creatures in a pond with some comment about the "orgasms in the water." I was the only one who laughed, and the teacher gave me a bemused look. Regardless, I've always been grateful for the old man's contributions to my raging teenage hormonal life.

Mrs. Eisenberg was a constant distraction to the whole class. She must have had some inkling that she was constantly gossiped about. She drove herself to school, and reports said that she'd arrive in a different new car every day. I never found out more about who Mr. Eisenberg might have been or anything about her backstory, and her whole situation is just a pleasant school memory.

We had a math teacher named Mr. Radosche who looked like Phil Silvers. He was so profoundly hated that one day as he patrolled the cafeteria during lunch, some girl who had reached her breaking point in regards to his petty brutality and crankiness just flung herself at him and after getting him in a headlock proceeded to drag him around while the student body cheered and applauded. She was another one who was led off and never seen again.

It was 1963 and we were all in the cafeteria when odd rumors started to make the rounds. The PA system announced that we should all immediately return to our homerooms. Our homeroom teacher then was a Mr. Prenner who was an enthusiastic young progressive guy. We all got in our seats and he leaned on his desk and said, "The president's been shot. He's dead. Go home." That was it. The school let out amid a lot of chatter. On the street I saw Mr. Prenner and another young male teacher deep in heated conversation. I caught a bit of a phrase, something about "these times we're in," and I realized that these two guys were big supporters of JFK and that they were deeply affected by this event.

I walked home. People were crying in the streets. I bought a newspaper that had a big headline, "JFK Shot," but almost no information about what had happened. When I got to my house, my father was pacing back and forth in front saying, "Those bastards, those bastards." Then lots of black-and-white TV images for days, the funeral. People were sad. I'm not sure what I felt emotionally but I was aware of it all being a big deal. Bill Clinton came to Hudde in 1997 to tell the students not to smoke tobacco.

In the summer of 1964, New York was in the thrall of the World's Fair.

My buddies and me would take the subway up to Fifty-Seventh Street, where a special train would take an almost direct route out to Flushing Meadows Park in Queens, and we would wander around the vast grounds and observe all the examples of how our future would unfold in the modern science-driven age that we were residing in or at least on the cusp of.

Out of all the modernity, what remains with me are my memories of the tribal Watusi drummer squad that would play at the African Pavilion. I loved these guys. They would come out in long red robes and just go for it. They'd do a fifteen- or twenty-minute set, take a break, and come back and go at it again. Sometimes my buddies would leave me there and then retrieve me before heading back to Brooklyn.

Also at the fair was an elevated bucket-cable-car ride that traveled between two of the pavilions. We would go in a bucket and drop pennies off the side. The buckets passed over a Moroccan-style "exotic" bazaar, and the object was to drop a penny on a large brass tray. This was successfully accomplished at least once, the tray producing a loud clang and people nearby all looking around in confusion. The drummers and the pennies are my main memories of the fair, that and my amazement when I heard that almost all the pavilions were going to be pulled down after the thing concluded.

Junior high dragged on. I had one English teacher who I really liked, an older guy who was very happy about what he was doing. It was kind of like Bernie Sanders excitedly extolling the virtues of socialized medicine except it was *Catcher in the Rye*. I had one memorable triumph in a science class that I was generally underperforming in. We had to do a term project. I was visiting my buddy Frankie down the block and his little brother John had a paper-making kit, the kind of "educational" toy that one would find in a hobby shop. He let me have it and I made a lumpy sheet of paper using the wood pulp that was in the kit. I wrote a couple of paragraphs about the process that were pretty much copied from the booklet that came with the kit. I pasted the homemade paper on a larger sheet with *This paper was made with the method below* on it and stuck it all together. The teacher, who generally ignored my mediocre science-ing, went crazy. He held up my thing and announced to the class that this was the way to do a project. I got an ironic A+.

After hours of practice I figured out how to play the guitar part from the Animals' "House of the Rising Sun." Another milestone.

My mother encouraged me to take the test to get into Mensa, the organization for smart people. I think she'd seen an ad in a magazine. Per the protocol, I took the test twice, once in my room and once at their supervised location. It was pretty easy and borderline fun. The Cattell IQ test is mostly logic. I have no math abilities. I remember one question that I liked: *Letter* is to *message* as *bullet* is to (a) *gun*, (b) *death*, (c) *soldier*, (d) *war*. And the answer is probably *death*, because the bullet delivers death as the letter delivers the message. Stuff like that. I got a good score both times and became a member. My mother told me that the testers were surprised that a thirteen-year-old kid was among the group taking the test. Stel obviously thought that getting in would be affirmative and encouraging, and it was an ego boost, but it also helped with my disdain for schoolwork, providing a foundation for considering myself smart enough to give less of a fuck than I already did. I'm sure if I took the same tests now, I would no question be proven to be way dumber than I was at age thirteen.

We moved to another house on East Thirteenth Street, one block north between Avenues J and K. Another ground floor in a two-family but with one more room for my parents. I started high school and things kicked up considerably.

My new room was in the rear of the house with a window overlooking a small weed-covered backyard and a beat-up wooden garage that I don't think I ever set foot in. I painted the walls of the room gray and the ceiling red, a motif that was inspired by some military uniform that I thought was cool. I hung all my speakers around and hooked up the blue record player. By this time, I had a Hofner single-cutaway Club bass and an Ampeg B-15 amp. I would play bass along with records and the radio for hours.

Jerry White was a DJ who played folk music on WJRZ, which came out of Newark, New Jersey. This was an amazing source and there was something a little clandestine about it; it was very different than listening to the regular aboveground radio.

I stopped getting haircuts and began classes at my local high school, Midwood. Midwood alumni included Woody Allen, Ramblin' Jack Elliott, the folk singer, and a bunch of notable sports guys who I'd never heard of. I think Woody came and spoke at some alumni events while I was still there. I don't remember much of my freshman year, and my father died suddenly the following summer.

He was a big guy and he smoked incessantly. He'd been hospitalized with stomach ulcers when I was smaller and I think he'd had a previous heart attack. I was in the bathroom. A call came in, and my mother told me through the door that she didn't think Ben was coming back. She went out. I think delivering the news like that was just poor judgment on her part in the heat of the moment, though various psychiatrists suggested otherwise in later years. I've tried to come to terms with this and not cast any blame in her direction. She was really rattled. I didn't know how to react. I found some whiskey and got a little drunk because I was aware of the Hollywood solution to the death of a loved one. It didn't help, but I got to sleep.

It was Sunday and Ben had gone out to get some bagels and such and the moment he entered a bakery on Coney Island Avenue, he fell over and was gone, the victim of a massive stroke. It was July 18. I knew that Holden Caulfield's brother had died on the same date.

Ben and I had been close. He'd take my friends and me to parks and on outings. He was a frustrated writer. He wrote odd poetry that was overly complicated and was rejected when he submitted it to different periodicals. He'd been some kind of labor organizer after the war, and when I was younger, I saw but don't have now a couple of old newspaper columns about the labor movement that he'd written. He and I went to a bike shop and he got me a bike that was equipped with a banana seat and long handlebars. This was really early for this kind of modification and the bike only lasted a few weeks before getting stolen from the front porch. Ben tried hard to be a good dad.

A week later I was home by myself and got a phone call from another relative telling me that Ben's brother-in-law Byron, Aunt Dottie's husband, had also died. When I told Stel, she just sighed and sat down. Ben's sister and her husband had been very close to my parents. Byron was a surgeon but they were great borderline bohemians who lived in the Village, listened to popular music, and went to the local coffee shops and clubs. I remember dancing the twist with Aunt Dottie to the Chubby Checker record in their apartment. Dottie had been a real beauty but had developed some degenerative muscular disease that slowed her down and left her very thin.

They were charming people but some faction of Byron's family took over the situation and I never saw Dottie again.

I got a suit for Ben's funeral. A lot of people we didn't know showed up, guys he had played cards with in Prospect Park. Ben got a military burial and the rest of the summer was a numb blur.

CHAPTER 2

started meeting other kids, even girls. My set of friends expanded. I met two guys who lived around the block on East Fourteenth Street, Barry Goldman and Simon Somers. These two were totally into music and had guitars and we began occasional jamming in basements and living rooms. I was pleased to discover that Simon was responsible for a tag I'd been seeing on the local streets and subway for about a year. The tag was *Who is Zev?*, which had some autobiographical component that related to Simon's middle name. He really did a good job of coverage; it was all over the place. He also would tag the line *Earthmen, we are laughing at you.* Barry, Simon, and myself started going into the city and hanging out in the West Village, around Washington Square Park and in the MacDougal Street youth-scene milieu. (The subway was fifteen cents all throughout my childhood, finally going up to twenty in 1966 amid great outcry.) Somewhere in this period we played in the basement of a church in Brooklyn for some gathering, and that was technically my first time playing in a band on a stage. I can't imagine what material we played; probably just blues. I don't think anyone sang.

The MacDougal Street scene was magical. It was the beginning of the whole thing. The street was filled with kids every day. People in the neighborhood produced a campaign that centered on the catchphrase and sentiment *Stop the circus on MacDougal Street.* It didn't matter; the flow of kids was inexorable.

The place my friends and I gravitated to was the Figaro Café's basement. Figaro was one of several old-school bohemian coffee shops that were in the area. It was at the epicenter, the southeast corner of Bleecker and MacDougal. The very unfinished cellar was devoted to a kids' hangout. One would buy a fifty-cent soda as a cover charge and sit around listening to a small PA that played a lot of Rolling Stones music. Little metal tambourines were available for you to bang on the beat-up tables in time with the music. The basement was as bleak as could be imagined, gray stone and brick walls, maybe one or two posters, dim lighting, and a wooden board that acted as a bar or counter. Somehow this all translated to an exotic and mysterious environ. Figaro is still there in the current timeline but the basement street entrance has long been sealed up.

This was *December's Children* culture, lots of huddling in chilly black-and-white doorways. The uniform was generally jeans and army wear. Lots of old army jackets and the omnipresent peacoats were de rigueur.

A new friend I'd made, Jessie Cohen, another guitar player who had figured out how to overdrive his small amp to get that sustain, helped really sell me on the glory of the Stones. Jessie had an older sister, Emily, and some of her friends were in a band called the Resurrections. These guys had found a place in Brooklyn where they were able to record a direct-to-disk-type record. From whatever master they had, they managed to produce a few copies, one of which Jessie had acquired. We worshipped the Resurrections' scratchy-sounding album with a fierce devotion. Something about its clandestine unavailability combined with it actually being pretty good made us into a tiny, enthusiastic fan base. I guess the Resurrections qualified as garage rock. I made a tape that I'd play at home. I still remember most of the songs.

I don't recall buttons or badges or whatever you call them—pins with slogans and images—much before the MacDougal scene. They had always been around as political endorsements and advertisements but not so much as purely tokens of art or personal style. They came to exist in somewhat the same space that internet memes now occupy. There was a little closet-size storefront on MacDougal called the Big Store run by an older man named Mark. The Big Store sold almost exclusively posters and buttons, and some of the buttons became wildly popular to the point where to be hip, one had to sport one or more of them. I don't know how into *Lord of the Rings* anyone really was at the time but FRODO LIVES in regular and Elvish script were big ones. Another was a simple red-and-black-on-white geometric pattern that became known as the "LSD Dimension Button." On the street there was an older guy whom we knew as Mother Hive. He sold his own buttons that were required wearing: MOTHER HIVE'S PIF CLUB, followed by a chapter location—GREENWICH VILLAGE CHAPTER, BROOKLYN CHAPTER, and so on. PIF had multiple meanings: "Pig Is Fat," "Pot Is Fun," et cetera.

The scene was home to numerous characters possessed of a variety of street names. Action and his brother Re-Action; Spade Steve; Russian George; Mortician George; a guy named Pinky who looked like John Lennon a little. Josie and Little Bit were a very sketchy pair who would corner kids, allowing Josie to grab them in their nether regions.

Mortician George hung out with my group from Brooklyn and it turned out he was part of a band situation called the Morticians. Barry, Simon, and myself briefly filled out their ranks. Mortician George was George Cameron, a drummer. George and his bandmates were a little older than us and I think it was with these guys that we jammed one afternoon at the Night Owl Café. The Night Owl was known as the start-up location of the Lovin' Spoonful and Jerry Jeff Walker, who wrote and sang "Mr. Bojangles."

We did one gig at a barbershop with the Morticians. I have no idea where it was; I think in the city. We played a couple of their songs that I vaguely remember. The Morticians then picked up some non-teenage members, got some funding, changed their name to the Left Banke, and recorded "Walk Away Renee," which became a massive hit song.

We would see notables around the area. I saw Jimi Hendrix carrying his guitar and walking purposefully on MacDougal Street a couple of times. Richie Havens was a Washington Square staple, frequently playing in the park. I saw the guys from the Lovin' Spoonful around, and we would cheer them since they were the local heroes. I recall Joe Butler waving back enthusiastically.

Barry was friends with a very tall kid whose very bohemian parents had named him Dürer. We knew him as Dury. He and I were on Eighth

Street one day when we saw Keith Richards emerge from an upstairs fur shop carrying two big shopping bags. He got into a cab, which proceeded to slowly drive down MacDougal Street with us walking slightly ahead of it. We passed two random girls who were moving in the opposite direction and told them, "Keith Richards is in that cab." The girls sneered at us. As we neared the corner past the park, we heard bloodcurdling screams coming from behind us as these girls saw Keith.

I was really unhappy at school as my junior year began. I just didn't like it. My father dying was a deep shake-up that I wasn't really aware of, and maybe such a large personal event cast the petty machinations of school life as an even greater source of annoyance to me. My fear of maniacal teachers was submerged in the greater cosmic dread that my dad's death had created in me. I started acting out a little, belligerently telling a teacher, "I didn't do my homework," as if that were some revolutionary battle cry. I wore sunglasses a lot, and while the standard school look (school fashions were super-conformist) was a navy-style blue peacoat, my friends and I found junk surplus stores in Manhattan that sold khaki-colored army coats that were similarly tailored. The departure from the peacoats was anarchistic in the scheme of things. I weirdly became aware that I was the recipient of more female attention than I was used to. I started getting a couple of gray hairs around this time, and a strange girl stopped me in the hall and cheerfully asked if she could pull one out of my head.

This was 1965 and one must remember that there was no bridging group, like skateboarders, that was an intermediary sect between jocks and hippies. The lines were very sharply drawn: kids who were attached to sports and the "normal" approach to the day-to-day versus a small group of hippie types.

So it was no surprise when the school dean rounded up a few of us, maybe four boys, brought us to his office, and told us that we were out of school until we got haircuts. The fucking guy actually told us that he was very worried that we'd be crossing the street and our hair would blow in front of our eyes and we'd be hit by cars. He really said this. (My hair wasn't very long; maybe a bit below my ears.) It was a little amazing to me even then.

I remember feeling very liberated as I walked home from this meeting with the dean. I was fully prepared to just leap into a dropout black hole and fall into the final frontier of existential freedom, whatever that might be. There must have been a day or so of sitting around listening to records before I got a phone call from the school. It seemed to be someone with greater authority than the dean and they spoke to me personally rather than asking for Stel. The offer was this: If I came back to school, I wouldn't have to take gym. I don't know how I responded and I might have been aware that at that very moment, court cases were being litigated over whether telling a student to get a haircut could be construed as an infringement of the student's civil rights. The Midwood High School deep state wanted no part of this problem and I guess they knew that almost nobody liked gym.

I hung around the house for a few days and then my mother intervened by finding a cheap private school that I could attend.

Quintano's School for Young Professionals was right across from Carnegie Hall on Fifty-Sixth Street above a Bultaco motorcycle store. The "campus" was a dance studio on weekends: big mirrors and the ballet barre all around the room. It cost around four hundred bucks a year and the focus was strictly academic, no frills. The object was to get you through high school painlessly. It was aimed at kids who were actually in showbiz. Patty Duke, Diane Lane, Sal Mineo, Tom Finn from the Left Banke, Steven Tyler. Johnny Thunders, Sylvain Sylvain, and original New York Dolls drummer Billy Murcia also went there. When I was there, one of the girls was a dancer on *Hullabaloo*, a musically inclined TV show, and one of the boys was a jazz guitarist who did gigs at Trader Vic's. Although the thrust of Quintano's was these professional kids, the majority of students were a bunch of miscreants like myself who had escaped the real world.

I loved it. It was awesome. Mr. Quintano, who was in charge of the whole thing, was a sweetheart. The teachers, a lot of old Broadway types, were sympathetic and not cranky. We could sit on the motorcycles in the store downstairs and go to Central Park for lunch breaks. I even liked taking the long subway rides from Brooklyn to Fifty-Seventh Street and back again.

I'd seen Andy Warhol and his entourage on TV, I guess on *The David Susskind Show*. I remember being particularly taken with Jackie Curtis, who was very clever, pretty, and anarchistic. I went to an event at Carnegie Hall, the Sing-In for Peace. I see it credited (September 24, 1965) as one of the first, if not the first, anti-war concerts. The folk and rock worlds were still a little split at this point; there was a lot of chatter about rock music being somehow "less pure." (This all came to a head at the Newport Folk Festival that year with Dylan "going electric," Dylan's manager Albert Grossman and archivist and historian Alan Lomax supposedly getting into a fistfight backstage, Pete Seeger threatening to cut the power lines with an ax, et cetera.) I remember Joan Baez being a little apologetic as she announced she would sing a "rock and roll song" dedicated to Lyndon Johnson. She sang a bit of "Stop in the Name of Love" by the Supremes, and the crowd went wild, the rock and folk people seemingly joined in bipartisan approval. I think the Fugs played too.

At the end of the long show the audience was filing out and I was at the base of the stairs in the front when suddenly the crowd parted like the proverbial beige sea and there in the gap was Andy. He was accompanied by a gorgeous tall model who was wearing an oversize football jersey. Warhol's hair was bright silver and he had on that signature brown leather bomber jacket. He was from the future; everyone else was still back in 1965.

I didn't make it to Newport that year but the following summer, myself and a kid I didn't even know that well got bus tickets and succeeded in attending the folk festival.

Newport, Rhode Island, is a quaint, bucolic little seaside town that's not that far from New York City. Starting in 1959, every summer, a bunch of hipsters descended on it. People all gathered in the streets at the center of town, kids my age, teenagers, and exotic older people who were on the periphery of the Kerouac/Beats nomad scene. Lots of acoustic guitars. We got sucked into a party at some house where, for the first time, I had a couple of hits off a joint. There wasn't much psychic effect but I did get a little hungry.

At the actual festival I saw a couple of sets by Bukka White in a very intimate setting—not much of a stage, just chairs and a small platform near the main stage. After the controversy surrounding Dylan and Butterfield the previous year, I was pleased to see the Lovin' Spoonful totally accepted and the recipients of rapturous applause during their set. I still have the program book from the festival and it's filled with ads for guitars and microphones. The pull was strong; it was obvious where things were going.

One night back in Brooklyn, Dury showed up at Barry's house with a nickel bag of weed and we all got stoned to the point of hysteria. It was very funny and interesting. Dury's face seemed to detach and hover in front of his head. We sat around laughing for hours. The next few days involved figuring out how to procure more pot. Somebody knew somebody who knew somebody who was a dealer of sorts in Manhattan. We would go to this guy's big loft that was right off Cooper Square and his girlfriend would come to the door and sell us those little yellow paper bags of weed for five bucks each.

Then, finally, to really kick off the era, someone got hold of some acid and a group of us all went to Jessie Cohen's house to see what was what with this stuff. Jessie lived with his parents and older sister, Emily, in a really big prewar Brooklyn apartment that was decked out with amazing artifacts that Jessie's father had brought up from Mexico. I don't know what else his dad did for a living, but he would go down there, buy fantastic antique religious iconography, and resell it in New York. So there we were, watching old Catholic icons, crucifixes, and paintings all sort of breathing and possessed of secret auras and energies. I recall one of the group settling down with a pen and a yellow legal pad, telling us he was going to write out the solution to the universe. He filled a lot of pages with diagrams and text but I don't remember what any of it said or looked like.

Drug procurement developed into a group activity. Angles were investigated. Sources detected. We would get word of what might be described today as a pop-up shop, only one that sold weed. Everyone would chip in some funding and one or two would be sent out to make the buy. Somebody heard about a dude selling hashish in Manhattan, and Barry Goldman and me collected a few hundred bucks and took a trip to the Village where this cowboy guy and his girlfriend were holed up in the Hotel Albert. It seemed like neither of them had left the tiny room, which was littered with pizza boxes and beer bottles, for days. He had a suitcase full of hash in the closet and we bought a couple of ounces.

Another appointment somehow got made and a kid, a total stranger, showed up at my house in the middle of the night in a raging snowstorm to sell us some acid that looked like it was made by a pharmaceutical company rather than in a garage.

We got wind that one of the neighborhood gangsters, Junior, could sell us some pot. Junior (Tony) Sirico and his brother Carmine were local legends, and wildly exaggerated tales of their adventures would sometimes reach us. They allegedly hung out at Artie's downstairs pool hall on Avenue J. We went to meet him with fifty bucks. He took the fifty, punched me on the chin, and ran off. No weed. This was the same Tony Sirico who went on to play Paulie Walnuts on *The Sopranos*. He was the real deal. There's no hard feelings; it was just business. I'm sorry I never got to meet up with him and discuss the old days.

My mother was very sympathetic to my friends and my situation. She didn't want me running around the streets like a complete maniac. She was still affected by my father's death and liked having people around, so the result was that my friends and I would congregate at my house. I painted the walls of my room black and touched them up with designs done in fluorescent paint. The idea of the black room was that the walls would recede, leaving one in a pseudo-void, given the right conditions.

One morning I woke up to find that my face and neck were covered with a partially dried and partially wet substance. My friend had told me he'd had a nosebleed in his sleep once and I briefly assumed that was what was going on. I was very surprised to see that I was covered in black paint. There was no sign of a container anywhere and I never figured out how it got on me.

I found a car's big chrome bumper on the street and propped it up in the room as a sculpture that was gradually covered with ephemera. I found even more old speakers out in the world in trashed TVs and radios and dragged them home to hook up around the room. Finally I had a big red plastic letter N from a movie marquee on the wall and when someone would ask what it stood for, I got to say, "Nothing."

The house became notorious in the neighborhood. People came and went at all hours. People I knew brought friends and my circle grew. We jammed in the basement that was partly filled with Stel's larger paintings.

I never paid much attention to the little newsletter that Mensa sent around but there was some kind of contact list available through it and eventually I did hear from one other member. This guy must have been smart since he figured out that I would turn out to be a kindred spirit. I'm not sure what this intel might have been based on. Maybe I had a bio that said something about music. An older long-haired guy, he showed up in a lived-in-looking station wagon with his own weed. He said he'd been traveling around the East Coast getting in touch with other Mensa members. But he had a Vox Super Beatle amp with him that he brought into the living room; he plugged an acoustic guitar with a pickup into it and proceeded to spend a half hour making tonal feedback. (My buddy Bob had gone to see the Beatles at Shea Stadium, where the sound system was composed only of a lot of these amps in rows along the baselines. Bob said he could barely hear anything over the screaming.) The monolithic amp stayed in the living room for a couple of weeks until this guy came and picked it up and continued his journey.

School was winding down. Quintano's had been great. By this time, students made regular lunchtime trips to smoke pot in Central Park and though I don't recall much of an actual graduation event, I vividly remember an acid trip I took that began at school one day in the middle of a snowstorm.

Jessie met me at school, where I had already taken what acid I had. He was pissed off that he didn't have any but accompanied me on a subway ride downtown anyway. The snow was descending earnestly and the city was white and silent. We got on the subway as I was peaking, and the car buzzed with etheric currents. There was wet mud all over the floor of the car but almost no people. We got out downtown and a block or two from the subway came upon two girls dressed in black who were involved with scooping snow off a car with a black umbrella surrounded by whiteout conditions, an indelible image. We made our way through the dunes to the deep West Village, where we successfully located the headquarters of Timothy Leary's League for Spiritual Discovery, an old storefront on Hudson Street. It was draped with dark fabrics, and a few people hung around, incense burning, Indian traditional music playing, all the trappings. The West Village back then retained most of the atmosphere and physical structures of years before when it was exclusively a dock/seaport area. The old elevated West Side Highway was still in use, throwing the streets below into shadows.

I'd spent time with a copy of *The Psychedelic Experience,* the trip manual based on *The Tibetan Book of the Dead* that Leary had written with Ralph Metzner and Richard Alpert. It made for perhaps a more introspective approach to tripping than just running around being fucked up. I did do some meditation and looking inward, along with running around being fucked up.

For a while I sat in the league's storefront next to a guy who was working on a drawing. He was an accomplished artist and was doing a self-portrait with colored pencils. He was wearing a string of multicolored metallic beads around his neck, and the seated Buddha-like version of himself in the drawing featured the same beads expanding out of the page and seeming to merge with their real-world counterparts. It's a small detail I've carried around. (It did occur to me at the time that the guy doing the drawing was in all probability very un-stoned, as he was exhibiting too much control and fine-motor skill, but I could be wrong.)

Bob Fass was a DJ on WBAI radio. He had a popular sort of underground show called *Radio Unnameable.* One night he started talking about what a great time he'd recently had at JFK Airport, just grooving around in the International Arrivals Building. The subtext seemed obvious: that he meant he had been totally stoned. He named a date in February when people should go out to the airport for this big celebration known as the Human Fly-In. A group from the block got in the only car, my friend Jack's. (Growing up in Brooklyn with the subway and occasional friend with a vehicle, I didn't learn to drive for thirty-seven more years.) We all took acid and went to the arrivals building. It was a freezing night and there wasn't much air traffic but a few thousand stoner hippies descended and sat around playing acoustic guitars with the standard incense-burning and tambourines. It was very cheerful and I wandered around looking at the archetypal paisley shapes that formed in the random patterns of stones embedded in the marble flooring. I noticed that Muzak accompanied me everywhere in the building. I went up to an old guy who was mopping some floor space in an empty corridor and asked him where the music was coming from. He was obviously amused by my intoxicated state and very seriously said, "It don't come from nowhere."

After that my friends and I made several evening trips out to JFK Airport on our own. The TWA building that still looks like some midcentury sci-fi invention was a favorite location.

The human be-in in Central Park on Easter Sunday of 1967 was the next big event. This got a lot of pre-publicity; there were these great Peter Max flyers all over the place, and unlike the fly-in, which was a bit more spontaneous, the Central Park gathering was looked forward to by many.

I went alone and was in the middle of a few thousand people who had assembled in Sheep Meadow in the park. My memories of it are very selective and positive. Watching people dancing and communing, costumes, and again the usual acoustic guitars and incense, I had a great time. Today seeing old footage of the be-in, I'm amused by all the guys who look like Gene Hackman in *The Conversation* throughout the crowd: suits and ties, pretty conservative styling that isn't a part of my tunneled magical memories. In actuality, the hippies were way outnumbered by uptown New Yorkers, people who lived around the park.

But the cultural floodgates were opened; it was inescapable. Be-ins started up all around the country. The city changed its tone. I started hanging out on the Lower East Side more than in the West Village. Jessie's older sister, Emily, moved to a one-room apartment there that was twenty-four dollars a month rent. We visited her. We went to a bar on Avenue B between Tenth and Eleventh Streets called the Annex where we could get beers even though we were seventeen. I didn't really like beer but it was something to do on an afternoon. The first head shop, called the Head Shop, opened on East Ninth Street followed by the Psychedelicatessen on Avenue A.

One day while walking near Cooper Square we noticed a little old storefront with some odd plastic flowers and a big ornately silver-framed mirror in the window. There was no sign or indication of what the place was. We watched our reflections for a minute and then went through the door. Inside was a long bar with a bartender and three people sitting there. The mirror was see-through from the inside so these people were just sitting there drinking and watching other people pass by and occasionally looking at themselves.

The Dom, later the Balloon Farm, then the Electric Circus, was a great old Polish hall on St. Marks Place, right in the middle of things. I saw the Grateful Dead play to about fifty people: a group of teenage girls just sitting on the floor in front of the stage politely listening. There was a bigger turnout for Sly and the Family Stone there. After every song, they'd play the same four bars of "Pow Wow the Indian Boy" as a weird coda. It was some musical inside joke that the band was sharing. Andy took over the Dom with silver balloons and some of his *Exploding Plastic Inevitable* shows, which featured the Velvet Underground. I didn't see the Velvets there but one afternoon I wandered in on their opening act, the Spike Drivers, doing a sound check and was happy to see the guitarist using finger picks.

A couple of newcomers appeared at my house in Brooklyn: Joey Freeman and Dennis McGuire. Dennis was a fantastic photographer who'd landed a scholarship at the School of Visual Arts based on a pretty small portfolio. He studied with Garry Winogrand and apprenticed with Diane Arbus. Dennis got me really interested in photography, him, and also seeing *Blow-Up*. Dennis lived nearby but his friend Joey lived out in Sheepshead Bay.

Joey arrived first, having met some of my friends at possibly the same Easter be-in in Central Park. Joey had long blond hair, the longest hair of anyone. When he was thirteen he became fascinated by Warhol, and he put on a suit and went to the Factory to interview Andy for his school paper. Andy liked him, and Joey wound up doing odd jobs at the Factory and for Andy. When Andy was still living with his mother, Joey would be the one to go to Andy's house in the morning to wake him up. We got Joey stoned on pot for his first time and he went very crazy laughing and yelling about seeing the "pussy bunny" coming for him while insisting that everyone in the room was in fact the "pussy bunny."

There were always people at my house. Jamming in the basement was ongoing. One afternoon Joey appeared and told us that the opening act for the Velvets had canceled and did we want to go and play in the city.

I really liked the first Velvets record at the time. In the midst of all the cheerful hippie music being promoted, here was this dark brooding album that dealt with heroin and angst.

We were all on board with this and got on the subway with our guitars and made our way to a place called the Gymnasium on East Seventy-First street, an actual gym that was also used for shows. Andy had an in with whoever ran the place, and the Velvets were there for an extended period working on their sets and material.

We were walking down the block to the venue when we were approached by a bunch of kids who spotted our guitar cases. "Are you the band? We got tired of waiting." "Yeah, we're the band."

There were very few people there, maybe twenty, and with Joey's help we got word that the Velvets would be okay with us using their amps and drums. We had a brief meeting on the stage with Maureen Tucker, who said we could turn her bass drum upright—she played it on its side like a timpani—and without much of a sound check, we just went ahead and played. Our singer was a guy named Jim who played harmonica, and another dude named Sonny played saxophone. We did about a half hour of blues-rock stuff, like Willie Dixon's "You Can't Judge a Book by the Cover." We didn't really know what the hell we were doing and the echoey acoustics of the big room were daunting. I wasn't used to dealing with natural reverb and slap-back; we were always playing in basements and living rooms. But when we were done somebody approached and said, "Oh, Andy thought you were fabulous!," which was gratifying. We never saw Andy; he was up in a balcony area doing the lights.

Watching the Velvets was quite a teaching moment, as they incorporated the echo of the hall into their very loud and forceful sound. (Over the years I've come to appreciate that the place one plays in is as much a part of the overall sound as the PA system or amps.) They were fantastic. I've heard that during these Gymnasium shows, they developed "Sister Ray" for the first time.

A couple, each holding one end of a chain, was doing a slow dance on the floor in front of the band. I'm pretty sure it was Mary Woronov and either Gerard Malanga or Ronnie Cutrone. There was no way then to appreciate the historic context but I thought it was all very cool. I went back to the Gymnasium about five years ago with a BBC news crew and it's still exactly the same.

The year progressed and the hippie ethos took hold of the U.S. and most of the Western world. The title of the upcoming Beatles album was either leaked or released and I heard a DJ breathlessly and with great fanfare announce the strange title *Sgt. Pepper's Lonely Hearts Club Band* on the radio. It felt like the whole country was waiting for this one record to come out. My friend Greg had gone to Vietnam. He was on a ship and wasn't in that much physical danger but he missed the '60s apex. I wrote him a few letters trying to explain.

The "San Francisco as youth destination" cultural movement took hold and I was intrigued. As the school year ended and the Summer of Love approached, I found out that my friend Eddie's brother and some of his friends were planning to drive to California. These guys were older, in their twenties, but I managed to book a space in their car for fifty bucks or whatever they thought my contribution should be. So four of us in a beat-up vehicle with a glove compartment filled with pre-rolled joints hit the road.

The trip was leisurely but we avoided much sightseeing, just plowing ahead. We stayed in cheap old motels and the occasional actual hotel in a bigger city. In St. Louis on a warm evening we all wound up at a party at some stranger's house that was strung with Christmas lights, of course smoking weed and listening to music. My three road partners left and I stayed behind for a bit longer. When I eventually left in the middle of the night I realized that I didn't have the slightest idea where the fuck I was. I wandered around tree-lined streets for an hour or so and miraculously stumbled on our hotel. The guy I was sharing a room with wanted to know where I'd been.

We stopped at a drugstore in Amarillo, Texas, and one of the guys went in for snacks while we relaxed in the car in the parking lot. A local cop spotted us and came up to the car and looked through the window. He was the total package: mirror shades, white shirt and badge, cowboy hat, and a pearl-handled revolver on his hip that he kept his hand on. He said, "Your long hair makes people around here nervous. When you leave here, don't stop again till you're out of the state or you're gonna be in a jail cell." When

Eddie's brother got back with some sodas and potato chips he had to ask why we all were shaking. We were happy to get to the New Mexico state line.

We got to LA after four, five days. It was the weekend of the Monterey pop festival. I should have made an attempt to get there but I was anxious to get to San Francisco and I didn't give it much thought. The rest of the guys' whole plan was to stay in Los Angeles and chase girls. They found a monthly furnished room in a motel-style place and moved their stuff out of the car. What they didn't have was sheets and pillows and towels, so we all drove to an actual motel and rented a room and stole all the sheets and pillows and towels. They told me I was welcome to stay but after a night, they took me to the bus station, gave me a bunch of the pre-rolled joints, and said goodbye.

The bus ride up the coast is long, beautiful, and relaxing. Lots of scenery; clouds falling onto hills by the ocean. I got into San Francisco at night and right as I stepped off the bus, a hippie-style girl walked up to me and stuck an orange slice in my mouth in semiofficial greeting.

I walked for a few blocks and came upon a party in full swing on the lower floor of one of those Victorian houses that are all over the city. "Lucy in the Sky with Diamonds" was blasting, people were coming and going, and I just walked in. A couple was doing a very organized ballet-style dance to the song; a group that was watching surrounded them. I found my way to a kitchen area and began talking to a guy as we sat there. I offered him a joint and we soon were best buddies, and he said I could come and crash on the floor at his apartment in Haight-Ashbury. (This was a bit of a culture shock, as I'd never heard the word *crash* used to mean "sleep" before.) I stayed with him for a couple of days while looking around a bit before running into a girl I knew from Brooklyn on the street. She invited me to stay with her in a communal situation at another Victorian house in the Haight. I went and they gave me a basement room to myself. I went to the local free store and got a can of free white paint and painted one of the walls, which sort of never dried because it was oil-based paint. I passed an old movie theater that had been hosting some sort of political event. All the glass was broken in the cases around the outside of the lobby and I pulled a big red-and-white-striped piece of the flag out of one of the cases and brought it back to hang on the sticky wall. It didn't have any stars, just the stripes. There was a window in the room that some very specific variety of bug used as a graveyard so the sill was always strewn with these bug corpses.

The commune had a vague cultlike hierarchy; there was a leader guy who seemed well off and lived on the top floor with his girlfriend. The rest of us descended in rank to me in the basement with the dead bugs. If it was indeed a cult, it was a very inclusive one, as there was a very diverse group. It even included a token gangster dude with an old-school greaser hairdo who looked like he'd just been released from jail. He told us that shooting heroin while tripping was the ultimate experience.

I spent a lot of time walking around on Haight Street. It was filled with young hippie tourists like myself. It was a magical environment. There was a merging of these modernist sci-fi and deco and Old West themes all overlaid with do-it-yourself spirituality. Stores along the street all had "meditation rooms" with low lighting and cushions. I bought a bunch of the early posters and mailed them back to Brooklyn. The place was attempting to forge its own language and style, and the graphics and store interiors all shared similar motifs. One day at the house several people came in all buzzed and enthused about having seen George Harrison arrive at some store on Haight Street.

The local radio was dedicated to its role as part of the psychedelic milieu. There was one station that used a terrific morphing series of hallucinogenic sounds for a call signal or tag. The sound of a train would blend into dogs barking and then into car sounds and finally into music, all very seamlessly. It was a revelation that what I thought of as corporate was trying to pitch itself as part of the counterculture.

I saw the Grateful Dead play in Golden Gate Park. The park was right at the end of the street and was like a giant sink that masses of kids spilled into. I asked a girl what the popular local bands were. She gave me an incredulous look and said, "Big Brother," in a tone indicating she pitied me for not knowing who they were. I spent an afternoon sitting in the free clinic, accompanying someone with some malady.

I met a pair of very street-savvy kids who were around my age and we started hanging out. These guys were like Dickens characters and knew their way around. At my communal living space there was a bowl of acid on the mantel of the communal living-room fireplace. My two friends came back with me and after a couple of visits had consumed most of the LSD in this bowl. People at the house were displeased and told me, "That was supposed to last for weeks." These guys had some tolerance.

One night late we were walking on Haight Street when we saw a pickup truck with a group of people slowly driving by. A kid began running after the truck, and the people in the back shouted encouragement and reached out to pull him up. Once the kid was dragged into the back of the truck, the people threw him down and started stomping on him mercilessly while the truck picked up speed and drove off. Did we really see that? Of course, we were tripping heavily. We were appalled and my two friends' composure cracked. The atmosphere was getting heavier. The Haight-Ashbury scene for all its innocence was surrounded by predatory darkness.

I don't know if I hitched or went with someone in a car, but I took a trip to Sausalito, where I wound up staying with some guys on an old riverboat that had been converted into a nightclub called the Ark. These guys were in a band they called Phananganang. I have since found a little info about Phananganang and even a couple of recordings on YouTube. They did gigs around the Bay Area till 1970, 1971, opened for Quicksilver Messenger, the Dead, et cetera. They were looking for a lead singer/guitar player but I wasn't confident enough to do the singer part so we just hung around and jammed on the club stage while I was staying there.

One night there was a big party going on in the nightclub on the Ark. We were upstairs when an older guy holding a case of beer knocked on the door asking if he could take a shortcut through our living area to the club below. Phananganang's leader was a guy named Ross, and in no uncertain terms he aggressively told this guy to go around and take the longer scenic route. I saw some of the other band members looking uncomfortable and when the guy left, someone said to Ross, "Man, that was Boz Scaggs."

I got back to San Francisco and ran into another friend from the Mac-Dougal Street scene, Spade Steve. Steve was a flamboyant and very likable energetic kid. Someone had given him an old station wagon and he told me he was going to drive back to New York and did I want to come along. Of course I was down with this spontaneous plan and the next day we set out in the old beat-up station wagon. Steve was driving. We got onto the Bay Bridge and naturally the car just gave up and died. Luckily it broke down next to a little alcove off the main road so we pushed it in there and just left it. We walked back to San Francisco and I didn't see Steve again for a few years.

I'd been out here for around three weeks and I felt like it was time to go back. I made it to the bus station and got a ticket to New York. At the bus terminal I met some more kids who told me they were living on a ranch and said I should accompany them back there, that it was a really great scene. I changed my ticket to wherever they were going. While we were hanging out sitting on the floor I noticed one of the kids behind me pointing at me and making stabbing gestures. I remembered the guy in the pickup truck getting stomped on and told them I was going to the bathroom and I changed my ticket again. The guy in the ticket booth glared at me. I don't know if that kid was just fooling around but I thought it might be a good idea to avoid any complications.

The bus ride was peaceful and took around four days with no stopping except to change drivers. Uneventful. My primary memory is of a nice older lady sharing her lunch with me, some fried chicken that was wrapped in tinfoil. Back in Brooklyn I picked up where I had left off, getting stoned and jamming.

David Ludwig was a kid I'd been aware of since junior high. He'd been at Hudde too, a year ahead of me. He was an über-freak. He had long hair before anyone else did and he'd come to school in strange medieval garb that resembled armor. I once saw him in the halls of Midwood with what looked like a large shield slung over his shoulder. On one trip home after school he got on the bus with a big bouquet of daffodils and proceeded to hand them out to all the girls. He said it was for his birthday. The amazing thing was that he was never murdered for these strange behaviors.

My friends and I were frequently set upon for having long hair in the neighborhood. I eventually had to call in a favor from one of my older crew. Philip Crean was a big, very tough Irish kid who I had been close to in my pre-stoner days. He had a single conversation with the guys who would terrorize us as we walked to the subway on Avenue J and they backed off and didn't bother us again.

But David was so otherworldly and confidently indifferent that he was left alone. We were finally formally introduced by a mutual girlfriend and we became friendly. We took some very memorable trips in his room at the top of his parents' house. Here I was definitely imprinted with a lot of musical motifs as we sat around during all-night sessions. A lot of psychic events that were intangible and indescribable. Small separate occurrences that would seem to be interconnected on some grand historical plane while listening to the Incredible String Band's and Blue Cheer's albums. I had a lot of adventures with David, whose name gradually morphed into Dove and finally Robin, where it is today. We spent a month or so in Vermont near the Goddard College campus in a country-style farmhouse where we took acid every day for a week and heard rumors of how the big tobacco companies had copyrighted all the weed names, like Panama Red and Acapulco Gold, in preparation for eventual legalization. One night as we were yet again in the throes of chemically induced euphoria someone arrived with the message "There's something in the barn!" There was a large barn on the property and we approached armed with kitchen utensils. We got close and suddenly the whole wooden wall seemed to shake from within as if some great creature were flinging itself against it. We fled and never found out if it was Bigfoot, a bear, or just a particularly violent raccoon.

My mother coerced my usually cheap uncle, her brother-in-law, into springing for my first year at the School of Visual Arts. It's located on Twenty-Third Street in Manhattan and after the summer, the one that saw me going to Newport, I started the daily commutes and began art school.

This was yet another whole group of people and things. One standout was my friendship with one of my teachers, Bill Tapley, who taught color theory. Under his instruction we explored opposing colors and values. He was also the master of gradation painting, fading one color into another seamlessly. He got a gig painting the uptown-headquarters playroom of Bert Stern, the renowned photographer who was known for the last photo session with Marilyn, among many other iconic images. Bill mapped out the whole thing very carefully and hired me to paint a bathroom. The idea was that the area outside the bathroom was a certain shade of blue while the bathroom interior was the opposite shade of intense orange so going

in or out would theoretically make one's eyeballs explode with the disso-
nance and contrast. It was really hard getting the orange color as dense
and precise as Bill wanted it and he told me he'd had to touch it up a little.
Except for a few odd things, I often credit painting Bert Stern's bathroom
as the only job I had outside of show business.

The Vietnam War was in full swing and we heard about a big protest
that would take place in Washington, DC. Tapley organized a road trip to
DC and the class made hundreds of little flags to hand out at the protest.
We tore white bedsheets into rectangles, silk-screened each with an orange
Day-Glo eye-in-the-triangle Illuminati motif, and glued them to dowels.
We got in his Volkswagen and he drove to Washington.

My first serious girlfriend, Debbie, came with us. I was really crazy
about her but it ended badly, with her father wanting to murder me. Sometime after this event she and I were sitting in Sheep Meadow in Central
Park when groups of young people started attacking park-goers. Martin
Luther King Jr. had just been killed and there were outpourings of dismay and spontaneous episodes of violence around the city. We were surrounded by a group of kids. There was a little shoving and I thought we'd
get our asses kicked but one of the kids said, "Wait, these guys are hippies,"
and another asked me if we wanted peace. I said, "Sure, we want peace,"
and they all left us and went and beat up some guy in a suit a few feet away.

It turned out that the DC demonstration was in front of the Pentagon. The flags were well received and we gave them all away quickly. We
wound up right in front of a stage that had been set up in the midst of the
huge crowd, and we watched as Allen Ginsberg and the Fugs attempted
to levitate the Pentagon with lots of chanting and incense. Abbie Hoffman had explained that the demonic symbolism of the five-sided building
called for an exorcism. I'm not sure how far off the ground they got it
before we started getting whiffs of tear gas and left the scene. Norman
Mailer got arrested.

When I wasn't in school I kept making frequent trips down to the East
Village. The Village Theater/Fillmore East was a favorite destination. My
friend and I discovered that by climbing over a metal door into the rear
alley, we could get in through a fire door. I think this is how we wound
up seeing Big Brother and the Holding Company's first public New York

concert at the first Fillmore event. They had done one concert earlier at the nearby Anderson Theater for the Hells Angels.

I'll always remember how excited Janis got when the audience went wild after the band's first number. It was like she hadn't known what to expect and she seemed genuinely happy at the positive response. After a while we got to the front of the house and managed to sit under the stage for the remainder of the show. We came out after the gig and were sitting on the front of the stage when Janis emerged, drained a bottle of Jack Daniel's, which she tossed in our direction, and collapsed into the arms of a guy dressed like an Orthodox rabbi who had been waiting in the wings. A few days later I was walking on St. Marks Place when I saw Janis arm in arm with the actor Michael J. Pollard and another guy coming toward me. She actually stopped and listened to my enthusiastic fan babble for a minute before smiling and continuing on.

During this period my appearance was extra-freaky. I had very long hair and would wear things like tight purple-and-white-striped women's pants and a weird Elizabethan-style red satin vest with ruffles that I'd stolen from a vintage costume store. The Lower East Side was still a very funky neighborhood that was closer to a hundred years prior than to even thirty years in the future. My friends and I were always actively seeking odd antique fashions. We found an old storefront junk clothing place near Avenue C that was run by an old couple. There was nothing in this place except piles of old clothes on the floor. You would go in and dig through these dusty heaps. I found an old motorcycle jacket that might have been from the forties or fifties. They asked for five bucks for it. I never wore it in the late sixties. In spite of my odd fashion choices, I was still bound by some cultural conventions and stuck to the hippie aesthetic.

I was always going to events. I can barely remember all of it. I saw Jim Kweskin and the Jug Band play with Paul Butterfield at Town Hall. (Geoff Muldaur of the Jug Band was how I really learned to appreciate Bukka White.) I saw John Cage do a show in which he sat in an overstuffed easy chair that was wired up so that whenever he moved, crossed his legs or whatever, the movement would be accompanied by an electronic sound. I saw the Living Theatre at Hunter College. These guys were so provocative that arguments and fights broke out all over the auditorium. Nobody used the term *triggered* back then. At the same auditorium at Hunter I saw what might have been the first U.S. appearance of the kid guru Maharaj Ji, who was thirteen years old or something and already had a whole cult going. The Grateful Dead and the Jefferson Airplane did a free concert in the Central Park bandshell that I made it to.

I passed by the Fillmore one afternoon, tripping yet again and wearing a long black priest's cape. I noticed that the doors were open and I walked in. A band was onstage playing . . . well, making noise. I went down to the front and saw that it was Frank Zappa rehearsing the Mothers. But it was interestingly weird, as the band members were all playing horns and it seemed like none of them were actual horn players; they were just producing random sounds with a bunch of trumpets, trombones, and such. Frank was patiently conducting them, seeming to be attempting to get some organized rhythm out of the grunts and squawks. I climbed up onto the stage and looked around. Their gear was dense and all over the place and had funny little features like small bells and shakers that were attached to music stands and wired up.

When I saw the Mothers back in the West Village at the Garrick, they would do a bit where the music would stop and someone would run out onstage and drop a big coil spring, which would make a *boing* sound and become a part of the song. Someone spitting on the stage filled another gap in a song.

I looked around a bit until a gigantic roadie dude emerged from the wings and indicated that I should get off the stage. A massive guy like a biker, with long hair and a beard. I jumped off and sat in the first row. But then Zappa, who'd obviously been following the action out of the corner of his eye, dropped his hand by his side and beckoned me back on the stage. He did it so that the big guy didn't see. I climbed back on the stage and the roadie reemerged and again silently gestured that I should retreat, which I did. This happened another two or three times; it was very Charlie Chaplin. Finally the guy was miffed and he pointed to the exit and I left. Bands will occasionally prank and torment crew members; maybe this fell into that category.

As summer approached, a bunch of my friends planned to go out to California for another season. I think this may have been my first plane ride anywhere. The airfare then was around seventy bucks coast to coast. I traveled with a girlfriend who I'd met at Visual Arts. That relationship ended the minute we got to Berkeley, where everyone else had already set up camp.

I don't know exactly what the logistics were but my friends from Brooklyn had rented a big house on San Pablo Avenue right near to the Bay Bridge. The house is gone now, replaced by a self-storage place and a bait-and-tackle store.

There were a lot of people staying there, about ten to fifteen, and there were always a lot of cars parked in the big front-yard area. There was a free store right across the street. We would get old T-shirts and the occasional odd item there. At one point they had a big box of antique cylinder records. I took one and punched a hole in it to use as a joint-smoking device. A day or so later the cops showed up at the free store and carried off all the old cylinder recordings. We couldn't figure out if they were stolen or if this was just some power trip/redistribution of valuable objects that the police thought were better out of the hands of the radical underground. The political climate in Berkeley was complicated and volatile, the groundwork being laid for the big People's Park confrontation the following year that was put down by then governor and former movie actor Ronald Reagan. Reagan actually called the UC Berkeley campus "a haven for Communist sympathizers, protesters, and sex deviants." He had a way with words.

The summer was initially pretty relaxing; I made a couple of trips into San Francisco but mostly stayed in Berkeley. We saw some advertisement for a local concert and strangely wound up in a high-school parking lot with about twenty others watching Steve Miller. Some of us were stoned in San Francisco one afternoon and when passing a newsstand we saw the headline "Kennedy Assassinated." Everyone had the same flashback reaction: "Didn't this happen already?"

One day a friend of a friend arrived at the house in a borrowed blue Mustang and asked if anyone wanted to go for a ride. A couple of us went. We went tripping in some nearby hills and the whole thing was very peaceful and organic and I felt young and healthy. We came back to the house after several hours while still in a hyper state. We pulled into the driveway and were taken aback to see several police vans parked and the front of the house was crawling with uniformed cops. We backed out as quickly as possible; I feel like the whole in-and-out episode only took ten seconds. We stayed away for a few hours and returned after dark. Somebody had somehow gotten ratted out for selling some pot, and the cops had put in an appearance and raided the place.

They had tossed the house pretty completely, had busted a few people and taken some items, among them my wallet with my ID that had been in a drawer next to where I was sleeping. This resulted in trips being made back and forth to the local courthouse/police station and me going along. I thought I'd attempt to get my ID back. I knew I had two tabs of acid in a guitar-string envelope in the wallet but for whatever lack of judgment I proceeded with this mission. I was directed to the office of some cheerful detective guy. His desk was covered with examples of confiscated illegal drugs: balls of hashish stamped with weight marks and a really big bottle of assorted colorful pills. He told me to come back in an hour and when I came back, he waved the guitar-string envelope at me and said they had to hold me for that. He seemed a little apologetic but I still found myself in jail overnight. Another kid who was in my cell told me he had almost snuck some acid in but that the cops had found it. I didn't think it would have been a good idea to trip out in jail, however. I got off. I don't think they had much of a case, the offending items not really having been in my possession, but whatever happened, the judge let it go.

With others having been arrested in the raid and elsewhere, our group made several more trips to the courthouse. One day we were there, waiting for someone else to deal with the scales of justice. We were in a second-floor hallway that had big windows overlooking a courtyard. Suddenly the yard below filled up with police in riot gear, all very energized, banging their batons on the ground and generally stomping around getting ready for some confrontation that they were about to be deployed to. One of the cops looked up and flashed us an ironic two-finger peace sign, which my friend Jack Finkelstein responded to by holding up a middle finger. The cops didn't take this well and a few of them came running up the stairs, one of them yelling that he would "clean house" if there were any more antics from us.

Now, in our group was a tall thin Black guy named Joe and he glared angrily at a young Black cop who was pretty much his height and size. These two stared at each other as if on opposite sides of a deep canyon. When the cops turned to go down the stairs, this young officer was the last to leave, and Joe, having some sort of spontaneous overwhelming mood of final disdain for authoritarianism, kicked the cop down the stairs. I couldn't believe it. No one could believe it, and everyone immediately started yelling at him, *"Run . . . Joe, run!"* He had a head start and took off, followed by the fuming cops in hot pursuit. We saw him a few hours later back at the house. Apparently once he'd gotten outside and been pursued for a block or so, strangers in a passing car assessed the situation and let him hop in and drove him away.

A week later I got busted again for stealing a can of crabmeat from a supermarket. I found myself in front of the same judge, and in exchange for reducing the charge to "malicious mischief," I told him I was going to immediately return to Brooklyn, which I did. Miraculously, I've managed to stay out of the hands of the law ever since, but I wish I had copies of my mug shots.

CHAPTER 3

The house in Brooklyn was a borrowed-time situation. The neighbors complained about the noise produced by us playing instruments and records; the cops came by a couple of times; and I think the place was considered a den of iniquity by people on the block. One night a very old guy in a bathrobe who lived next door lost it and attacked our front door with a hammer, smashing a series of holes into the wood before being led away by relatives. He pretty much destroyed the door. I was sorry that we'd instigated his cracking up but I only became aware of most of the complaints after the fact. I didn't know this guy and I certainly didn't know he was so close to the edge.

So we got kicked out. I'm not sure how this eviction was carried out, if the rent was raised or some lease clause was in dispute, but we had to leave.

Stel found an apartment on Ocean Avenue, a wide street that runs for a long way north–south through Brooklyn. The stretch that this apartment was in was pretty industrial, with rows of large multifamily dwellings. The whole moving deal was pretty sad. A lone old guy with a truck showed up and helped us load the truck with as much of the house contents as possible. This was where most of Stel's paintings were abandoned, left in the basement with other artifacts from my childhood that I should have kept. I have a small amount of her paintings and drawings, but so much was lost. It's always been a sore spot for me, especially as I get older. I was able to recruit several large friends to help drag things up the four flights to this new place. One of these guys went back to the old house and was looking around in the basement when someone called the cops on him and we had to smooth things over and tell the police that he had permission and wasn't a burglar.

I realize now that leaving the blocks where I spent most of my childhood must have affected my psyche. The apartment itself was big enough but the neighborhood felt darker and more closed in. I still maintained relationships with my friends but the communal-stoner situation was gone. I did meet various new neighbors, including the proprietor of a bleak local head shop called Farty's Eden that was hidden away near the Avenue H subway station. I had no conception or consideration that I was experiencing addictive or destructive behavior. The drug use caught up to me.

I of course caution people to be careful with psychedelic drugs obtained on the street because you really have no fucking idea what you're actually taking. Something advertised as LSD can be a cocktail of weird chemicals. This plus my inner emotional turmoil—not really processing my father's death, being uprooted, and feeling generally exposed—made for a lot of tensions I wasn't aware of. The war and the draft were hanging over everyone's head, and 1969 was on track to be a very stressful paranoid year. I began having actual psychotic breaks that included auditory hallucinations—voices and odd sounds—and distorted thoughts. I had a lot of misadventures, getting into fights and bothering strangers. Wandering around the Lower East Side, I decided that the buildings were in fact a kind of set, a facade that I could get behind if I found the right route. An overheard phrase from somebody on the subway, like "Be careful," would become a direction of deep cosmic significance.

What I can see now as a lot of metaphors were things I was taking literally. Like others, I had a fractured relationship with the Beatles' *White Album*. In my case I wasn't hearing commands but I'd hooked onto the idea that every time the record was played, it was in fact a live version that came from a psychic link to the four Beatles, that the poor Beatles had to somehow reproduce the record mentally each time anyone anywhere dropped a needle onto a copy. I imagined them being woken in the night and having to run through the tracks in their respective heads. I worried about their well-being, having to deliver millions of mind concerts in much the same way Santa Claus distributed toys. This was connected to an idea that the *White Album* was different every time it was played or heard.

My mom was extremely worried and got me to go to a few therapy sessions but I tended to think that any adults I met with were government agents of some sort who were observing me.

After I arrived home with a cut on my head and slept for close to twenty-four hours, Stel got me into a taxi and took me to a facility in the city. I found myself at the Bernstein Institute, which was part of the Beth Israel Hospital campus in downtown Manhattan. This place had recently established inpatient rehab and psych wards and I was a perfect candidate. I spent the first week in solitary in a locked, windowed room being observed. I don't know that anyone informed me of where the hell I was but it mightn't have sunk in anyway as I was too far gone. My thought patterns were really confused. I remember following streams of associations as if they were actual reality. Looking at the gold lock on the room made me think of soldiers (medals) and cigarettes (Old Gold) and these random thoughts solidified into representing the outside environment, not just my tumultuous mental state. It was as if my inner voice were a separate entity that was keeping up a dialogue with me (an element explored by Julian Jaynes in *The Origin of Consciousness in the Breakdown of the Bicameral Mind*, which I recommend. Another book that to me does a great job of portraying this type of skewed mindset is *The Ordeal of Gilbert Pinfold* by Evelyn Waugh). This tangential thinking was combined with a tremendous fear and anxiety, so all told, I was a complete mess.

Thorazine is a pretty crummy drug that causes blurred vision, shakes, and sleeplessness. It is an effective antipsychotic, though. I was freed from solitary and loaded with Thorazine, but for a while I was still in the throes of hallucinations and misconceptions about where I was. As I wandered the corridors of the ward, I thought all kinds of oddball stuff was going on, like for days I was sure that I was on an airplane.

Gradually a lot of the delusions wore off or were shed and I was left in this depressed limbo situation. I became aware of people around me. I made friends with a young orderly who told me he'd been a photographer for the *National Enquirer*. At that time the *Enquirer* was dealing more with mayhem than celebrity. He said he'd be sent on assignment to shoot a car crash or other mid-level disaster and when he delivered the pictures the editor would compliment them but then encourage him to "get in closer" and provide more gory detail next time. This continued until he had a nervous breakdown and wound up working in the mental-health field.

The ward was coed and now that I think about it, I realize I only made friends with fellow inmates who were women. There were a few male background characters that I don't really remember but I fell in with a group of girls. My hair was a long mess, and pretty early on in my stay these girls gave me a semi-successful haircut. This resulted in a bit more acceptance. There was one guy who referred to me only as Hippie, but after I had a trim he started using my name. This was the only time in my life that I ever smoked cigarettes. There was a very beautiful and elegant older woman who I would sit in the dayroom with smoking.

I was still being followed around by trailing hallucinations and strange thought patterns but they were gradually diminishing. The Thorazine treatment was a trade-off—instead of distorted thinking you had blurry vision and a clouded perception. My doctor there told me that my schizophrenia was likely a lifelong condition. I felt like this was a lousy diagnosis. Even then I thought that my confusion was more related to drugs than to any lasting innate mental disorder. Shock therapy was administered to some of the older patients and I saw a few incidents of unwilling participants being dragged, struggling, into sessions and emerging unconscious. This didn't make for much faith in the overall treatment plans at the facility and it was very creepy.

They started taking those of us who wouldn't try to escape out on field trips. I recall sitting on a park bench eating vanilla ice cream and seeing the wild color palette that was a result of hallucination and bright sunlight, the ice cream various shades of purple and violet. We went to a local gym or YMCA for some exercise. I was sitting in the locker room waiting to leave and I must have looked somewhat discouraged because a guy approached me and asked if I was okay. I told him some of my situation and he proceeded to deliver a very positive and enthusiastic pep talk that I still remember the spirit of, if not the exact words. He said his name was

Garland Jeffreys and that he was a musician. I always appreciated those few minutes.

I met a girl there who left a week or so after my arrival. Vicky had been in for a suicide attempt and she came back to visit me as I got more clearheaded near the end of my stay. I got out after three months and started dating Vicky. She'd been seriously injured in a bad workplace accident and as a result of the insurance settlement, she had an income and could pay for her therapy and NYU tuition. We decided to find an apartment together. Somehow we were steered toward the manager of a building on First Avenue. Vicky was Polish and British and cute and had a Polish last name, and she charmed this guy into surrendering a fifth-floor walk-up that he'd been using as some sort of clubhouse for him and his friends. The super of the building approved of us due to Polish nationalism. We moved in, and this was my first New York City apartment.

As a result of being crazy and then hospitalized, I found myself the lucky recipient of various benefits. The Division of Vocational Rehabilitation offered to send me back to art school, and the city was going to give me welfare. In 1969, when I first got there, the apartment's rent was around ninety dollars a month. (The old lady next door paid forty-five.) I discovered that I was eligible for survivors' benefits from Social Security as a result of my father having been the family wage earner. When this came through, the guy from Social Security called me and said they were sending me around two grand and that I could "buy a lot of pot." He actually said that.

As the summer of 1969 approached everyone began hearing about this upcoming big music festival that was going to take place in upstate New York in or around the town of Woodstock. There was a lot of hype leading up to this event, so of course I sent away for tickets, which I got in the mail. Vicky was down on drug use and because of that I had long periods of relative sobriety. As a result of my being a ward of the state, as it were, I also saw a couple of counselors and attended group-therapy sessions that I don't remember anything whatsoever about. One of my social-worker counselors was into astrology. She did my chart and told me that I had cracked up as a result of Neptune conjuncting with something or other.

Vicky wouldn't go to the festival with me since she assumed there'd be people getting high all over the place. I went by myself. I didn't take anything; I just went to the Port Authority bus terminal and got a ticket. Extra buses had been added and a long line of very enthusiastic kids were enthusiastically waiting to board. Someone came in and held up a newspaper headline: "Traffic Snarled at Hippie Fest." This was greeted by wild cheers. It was miserably hot in the Port Authority and a girl climbed on her boyfriend's shoulders and proceeded to hold the flame of a Zippo lighter under one of the sprinklers on the low ceiling. The sprinklers all went off, getting everyone in line wet. Within a few minutes firefighters appeared wearing helmets and heavy rubber coats, carrying fire extinguishers, and looking annoyed.

As soon as the bus pulled out, probably two-thirds of the fifty-odd passengers pulled out joints and lit them. The bus filled with smoke. The driver must have had a tolerance, since he got us there safely after a couple of hours in the stoned night.

I disembarked on a country road that was filled with endless lines of people walking in both directions. I asked a guy where to hand in the ticket that I had and he just shrugged. The fences and any kinds of checkpoints were long gone or lying flat. I made my way to a hill overlooking a big brightly lit stage area and saw Joan Baez finishing her set. It was all very fairy-tale and twinkling lights.

I might have slept but I don't remember where or under what conditions. The next day was sunny and warm and I started looking around. The atmosphere was so cheerful that I wasn't concerned about being on my own. There were wooded areas that were inhabited by different scenes and hippie-style encampments. I found the Hog Farm commune, where they were feeding people en masse, and ate a lunch of beans, rice, and seaweed. I saw a guy standing around yelling, "Get your mescaline!" Only he was pronouncing it "meskewleeen," and for some reason I thought that was charming and I've retained that little memory.

I found my way back to the dusty road as the music was starting up and amazingly ran into Jessie, my buddy from Brooklyn. We hung around briefly and before he left he gave me a bright orange tab of acid that I immediately took. Forty-five minutes later, I was tripping pleasantly and lying by the side of the dusty road watching the streams of people pass by. A large contingent of my Brooklyn crew very casually walked by and said hi—Eddie Greenberg, whose older brother I had driven to California with, and a bunch more of the usual suspects from the neighborhood, guys I played music with. I was quite relieved; these guys had a van and a campsite, and my path to returning to the city was clear.

Somebody pointed out a flag with a *J* on it—for Avenue J—that was at the end of a pole in the midst of this vast sea of people. We made our way through the crowd. Seeing the movie the following year gave me more of an idea of how huge the thing actually was. Canned Heat as the first rock band of the afternoon bumped up the crowd's energy, and the day wore on. We saw some of Creedence and Janis before making our way to the van area. I heard the Jefferson Airplane in the distance as I was falling asleep.

Through it all, I kept thinking, *This should be going on regularly.* Mostly I was imagining a kind of permanent ongoing festival rather than a load of individual ones, but the idea was in the same ballpark.

Another funny thing was the guy who was doing the announcements from the stage—"Don't take the brown acid," directions to the medical tent, et cetera—was a kid I'd been friendly with in high school. Neil Miller had reinvented himself as "Muskrat." Neil would come to school in a neat shirt and tie. I remember we talked about jazz a lot.

It rained. Mud. A water truck arrived and distributed its contents; an ice cream stand gave everything it had away; I found a leather vest by a fence that I wore for years; I ran into my old girlfriend Debbie; Alvin Lee played some really long-ass solos.

Finally it was Sunday. I don't know why Sha Na Na was on the program. Nothing against Sha Na Na but it was an odd act to put on, especially next to last. I often wonder if anti–Sha Na Na sentiment contributed to the diminished crowd size on Sunday afternoon. The sea of abandoned mud-covered sleeping bags was exposed. It was the only time I saw Hendrix. I was very close to the stage. When he came out he looked around at the crowd and said, "I see we meet again," which I thought was amazing.

Later I heard "The Star Spangled Banner" as we were walking around. We drove back to Brooklyn.

Vicky and I decided to go to Europe during the Christmas break. She had relatives in the UK and Poland, and we would trek around and visit them. The first stop was London and I made trips to the house on Powis Square in Notting Hill that was used for Nic Roeg's film *Performance*, the head-quarters of the Process Church of the Final Judgment, and Kensington Market. Vicky's aunt lived on the Isle of Man. The Isle of Man in 1969 was in all probability unchanged from what it had been like during the war and before, it was a magical windswept place that was stunningly beauti-ful. The aunt lived in a little group of flats that were near a series of docks. It was all obscenely picturesque; she had a water pump in her kitchen sink rather than a faucet.

We made a day trip to the Witch's Mill that was in Castletown, the island's former capital. The Mill was a museum of sorts that had been es-tablished by one Gerald Brosseau Gardner who was a practicing witch and the first person to write openly about modern witchcraft in the UK. The place was on the edge of a barren heath and was fraught with atmosphere. The actual mill was a big ruin of a tower, a shell, where a group of local witches had, during the war, established a magical cone of power to thwart German invasion plans. It must have helped. Gardner, who was born in 1884, had died a few years earlier in 1964 in Tunisia, and the museum and collection was rather dusty but still amazing. Over the years I've become quite a fan of Gardner.

One night right before we left, while we were driving on a dirt road through some hills, the old car's headlights illuminated a group of young girls walking in their school uniforms, and the fleeting temporal image has maintained space in my head forever.

The next place we went was Czestochowa, Poland, where Vicky's un-cle and family lived. This was accomplished by a longish train trip that began with the ride from London to Prague. I think I was vaguely aware that the Soviet Union had invaded Czechoslovakia the year before but I wasn't prepared for the tension that was all pervasive in the city. As we were getting off the train two men in very cliché secret-police trench coats dragged a younger guy off the crowded platform and nobody paid any attention, or didn't want to act like they were. This sort of thing was probably both very normalized and fear-inducing for the locals.

Prague now is a major party town but back then it was very shut down. We were at some small hotel. The bellboy offered to exchange money for us, offering a rate that was way more than what we'd get at a local bank. We were approached at least twice on the street by strangers who'd pinned us as Americans and implored us to give them our addresses in the U.S. so that they could somehow use them as references to leave Czechoslovakia. We were there on Christmas Eve and wanted to find a simple restaurant. Nothing was open. Long empty streets were lined with beautiful, closed antique buildings and shops. One of the people back at our hotel had recommended a place where we could go, so we found our way to a banquet hall and paid a small amount to get in and get dinner. We were dressed in typical backpacker style, jeans and sport jackets. I had my long hair tied back but long hair was still an anomaly here in Eastern Europe and I kept getting odd looks from people. I'd seen only one other young guy with long hair anywhere on this trip; he'd been some kind of janitor at the big train station in the center of town. So we found ourselves seated at a fancy table in a room of much older people, all of whom were dressed very formally in suits and brocaded gowns. My impression was that this group had saved all year for this event that we'd just used Yankee dollars to infiltrate easily. It was surreal; they had a fixed menu of weird things, creamed herring and the like, that was far removed from what we were seeking.

Last, another train ride to Czestochowa, a small city in southern Poland. The streets looked like some frantic infrastructure building project had been abruptly halted in the midst of construction, leaving unfinished roads and parks and raw blocks of flats everywhere. Vicky's uncle and family were charming and their apartment was a neat contrast to the chaotic unfinished exterior of the building it was in. There were five adults living there: the uncle, his wife, their two children, and a grandmother. It wasn't that big an apartment. The daughter was beautiful, looked like Anna Karenina. I gave her a Rolling Stones tongue pin I had and she wore it while we were there like a brooch. When we showed the uncle a current picture of Vicky's dad he said, "My God, he's so old!"

They hadn't seen each other for twenty years or so. (We took pictures of them all and back in New York when we showed Vicky's dad one of his brothers, he said, "My God, he's so old!") The uncle told us that Vicky's dad had been a partisan during the war and had blown up a Nazi airstrip and planes. He'd never mentioned anything about this to Vicky.

We made a pilgrimage to see the Black Madonna at Jasna Gora monastery, which, being as it was Christmas week, was packed with devotees. The Black Madonna might have been painted by Saint Luke on a table from Joseph and Mary's house. The monastery was one of these places where the stairs were worn down from centuries of feet coming and going. We saw part of a very somber and beautiful Mass. We spent New Year's Eve 1970 in Zurich and came back to New York.

I really started to enjoy art school. I had great teachers; Malcolm Morley, Alex Hay, Mel Bochner, Emily Wasserman were all heavyweights in the art world. I even had an electronic music class with Steve Reich, which found him attempting to get us interested in building our own simple sound-producing oscillators. He tried to get me to play a simple rhythm in some odd time signature at one point but I was hopeless and he gave up.

This was during the onrush of trends in conceptualism and minimalism in the art world and some of my friends presented themselves in extreme and radical expression. My buddy Henry Frick palled around with Vito Acconci and produced some fantastic performance-based pieces. Henry set up a big galvanized-metal tub filled with water in the Twenty-Third Street lobby of the school and came in every day for a week, took off his clothes, and lay naked in the water as his fingertips shriveled. He got several hundred deceased crickets from a medical-supply house and pinned them individually in neat rows to a large board in one of the classrooms right before a class began. My particular favorite took place on a very warm day. Henry had obtained an uncured freshly skinned animal hide from a slaughterhouse somewhere. I guess he bought it. He came into school, got undressed down to his briefs, took this thing out of a plastic bag, and draped it over himself. Underneath this wet, glistening, grotesque blanket he held a transistor radio that was tuned to an R&B station. He wandered the halls of school with a few flies buzzing around him while being avoided by horrified students.

A class that somehow attracted a group of like-minded people was the single video-production class. Sony had brought out a line of prosumer stuff in 1967, portable reel-to-reel video decks, and the school invested in a bunch of them. Our teacher was a very jovial guy named Bill Creston who lived in a great old loft that was over Billy's Topless bar on Sixth Avenue and Twenty-Fourth Street. Bill had been a taxi driver and painter in New York City before becoming a filmmaker. The video-production class was the first one ever at Visual Arts. We made the most of the Sony Portapaks, as they were called, running all over the city shooting and doing on-camera skits.

Visual Arts then had several buildings, and one was on East Twenty-First Street. This old warehouse was adjacent to the New York Police Academy on Twentieth Street. The rear of the school overlooked the cops' exercise yard and there was occasional taunting back and forth. There was a little bad blood between these groups at the time, seeing that SVA was filled with radical dope-fiend hippie artist types. There was a police supply store on the same block and they began selling little enamel pins with a picture of a pig in a police hat that had the words PRIDE, INTEGRITY, GUTS around the edge. The pig pins only went so far in co-opting, as the students bought a lot to wear ironically.

So when we shot a video of my friend Bob Rosen walking out of the school building naked wearing only shoes and socks and holding a briefcase, it wasn't much of a surprise that he barely made it a few paces onto Third Avenue before being arrested. Bob was back in video class the next day and told an anecdote about how he had spent the day in jail in a blanket and explained to the judge that he was "doing an art project" and how the guy following him in court who had stabbed his mother told the judge that he too was "doing an art project." I think there was an annual police cadet/art student softball game somewhere but I never pursued it.

A lot of pot smoking went on at SVA. There was a somewhat unused stairway that was behind the cafeteria where people congregated to get stoned. Someone had decorated the walls with giant murals of rolling-paper packages—E-Z Wider and the Rizla man, et cetera. One of my other friends and video partners, Jody Terzo, actually made a couple of summer trips to Kabul, Afghanistan, where he would smoke a lot of hashish. There were no Russians or Taliban there in 1970. Jody and I discovered that across the street from school, up one flight in a loft, there was a photo-poster place. This was one of many places that advertised in magazines and newspapers "Send in your photos and have them made into posters." So people would send in snapshots and these guys would rephotograph them, then make large black-and-white paper prints and return them to the photographer. The thing was, the rephotographing produced large-format negatives that *they would throw out!* In front of this place daily were big black trash bags full of images from all over the country that ranged from the mundane to the weird and personal. We would drag these bags back to the school darkroom and make contact sheets from the strips of negatives. Generally the images fell into one of several categories: sports, cars, birthdays and children, and sex. The sex stuff was the most interesting. People were sending nude pics of themselves, their wives, girlfriends, boyfriends, et cetera to be blown up. Some of these images were completely grotesque and we would ponder about why someone would want to hang a large version on a wall. We wound up with stacks of these behind-the-scenes pictures of America's psyche. Jody hand-tinted a lot of them. It was art.

I found the conceptual art movement a bit unromantic, so even though I was in the fine arts program I drifted more into photography. I remember a classmate doing a project that entailed Xeroxing the same image repeatedly until the final result was a blank piece of paper that he handed in and got an A+ for.

The Division of Vocational Rehabilitation, in an effort to make me into a taxpayer, was not only paying my tuition but also giving me five hundred dollars a year for supplies. In my freshman year I used the money for paints and standard materials but the next two years I used the whole amount to buy photographic paper and spent a lot of time printing images. Me and a couple of friends set up a darkroom in the basement of the Twenty-Third Street building. I brought my enlarger there. I discovered that the darkroom was right next to the school's large phone circuit board so it was easy to bring in a telephone and hook it up. Joey Freeman would come in and spend hours talking to his girlfriend, who was out in California.

The school had its own darkrooms and it was just a matter of walking around the corner and bringing back chemicals to our darkroom. I don't remember if I ever asked anyone at the school about using the room but the darkroom stayed in use for my junior and senior years. From 1970 to 1973 I did a lot of street photography. I just wish I had shot even more film then, as I had no idea what would happen to the city in years to come.

My relationship with Vicky deteriorated and she moved into her own apartment in Manhattan Beach in Brooklyn. I would take occasional subway rides out to the end of the line and visit her. Kingsborough Community College was right there and I had some friends who went there and grew weed on the grounds of the old abandoned naval base that overlapped the school campus. I spent a lot of time wandering around and taking photos in this necropolis-like derelict miniature city that was the remains of the base. I shot a series of self-portraits of me standing in the rubble wearing a parachute with a grass skirt around my neck.

I hadn't heard from Vicky in several weeks when I got a phone call from her brother saying she had committed suicide. The last time I spoke to her she'd seemed okay. I spoke to her mother at length. She attempted to be comforting even though she was very sad herself. I spoke to her therapist, who said there was nothing that I could have done, but I couldn't help wondering how much our breaking up might have added to her depression. I was young and I shook it off as best I could. I think about it more now. I wish she'd gotten more help. I felt guilty for a long time and I don't know if I could have been more supportive, if I missed some signal or action that might have changed the outcome.

CHAPTER 4

There were bulletin boards in the lobbies of the school buildings. All kinds of things were inscribed on sheets of paper that were displayed in this public forum. A flyer resulted in one of my buddies getting some kind of small part-time job. Once he asked me if I wanted to make some money and accompany him and I agreed. We went to the huge loft of some older lady sculptor that was located near Madison Square Park and the Flatiron Building. This place was filled with Louise Nevelson–like constructions and endless rows of shelves that held metal and wood elements. She must have been in this location for many years and her collection, of course, bordered on hoarding. She was getting this stuff "organized" prior to moving to another location. It was brutal and I quickly realized that my friend just wanted someone to share his suffering and have some company during his tedious employment. We spent an afternoon moving heavy ancient barrels of iron rods and planks of wood in seemingly random rotation from one spot to another in Kafkaesque futility. At the end she gave me twenty bucks and implied that we could have worked harder. I wanted to murder my friend. He was too polite to quit outright but I didn't go back. This might qualify as another actual job I had, though to say it was in the "real world" is questionable.

I started noticing flyers on the bulletin board for musical events and bands. I kept seeing ones for something called the New York Dolls. Whoever was supporting them was pretty aggressive with their flyer application.

Then I saw a review for the Dolls in the *Village Voice* that was very positive and claimed that the singer was like unto Mick Jagger. Everyone was crazy for the Stones at that point. "Brown Sugar" was the background song for everything. A friend covered his apartment in silkscreen images of Jagger he'd made at school. A couple of years before in 1969 my pals from Brooklyn had waited overnight for tickets to see the Stones at Madison Square Garden. They landed a bunch of seven-dollar seats for the Friday matinee. This was the concert that Jagger introduced by saying "Welcome to the breakfast show!" when he came out, the one that's featured in the Maysles Brothers film *Gimmie Shelter*. It was fantastic. Maybe this detail of lead singer comparison is what convinced me to go to this place called Mercer Arts Center to see the New York Dolls.

I should interject that I was still actively pursuing some kind of musical endeavor. I went to band auditions that I would see advertised in the back of the *Village Voice*. I would travel to the Bronx on the subway and be in a living room with a few kids with guitars and drums and jam with them for a bit and then when I was leaving I'd meet some kid who was arriving for the next audition and I'd exchange phone numbers with him and then never call. I went to one in Brooklyn that was in some guy's parents' closed restaurant. This particular group was deep into heavy metal stylings. I jammed with these guys for a while and they were very enthusiastic and told me how we were going to rule the music business and become huge celebrities. I called the lead singer a few times but I never could get him on the phone. His mother would answer and say he was sleeping and after a while I gave up and never heard from them again. They had given me a lift to the subway station, though. Also around this time Tom Verlaine came to my apartment. I don't know how we connected. I think he had just recently arrived in the city and we jammed a little and I heard a couple of his songs. He had long hair and I actually don't know if he was calling himself Verlaine at this point. He called me once after that about a band situation but I didn't follow up. Both Tom and Richard Hell have told me that I auditioned for the Neon Boys but I don't remember that at all. Though I told them both I did recall, out of politeness. This is telling since Richard has written that I was deemed "too nice" to be in their group. It all worked out anyway.

Mercer Arts Center was a little place buried on Mercer Street near the border of the West Village. It had started out as someplace to screen video art, having been founded by early video pioneers Steina and Woody Vasulka. It was an exciting avant-garde environment that was divided up into gallery and boutique spaces as well as a couple of rooms where bands could play. The biggest room held around two hundred and was named after Oscar Wilde. This was May or June of 1972. (In keeping with the theme of small-town incestuousness, David Johansen, who was the afore-mentioned singer of the New York Dolls, had appeared at my house in Brooklyn a few years prior when he was dating a girl from my group of friends.)

The band opening for the Dolls was a group called the Magic Tramps and I was drawn to them. A couple of friends and I had been wandering around the Lower East Side months earlier and we went into a bar on the Bowery called Hilly's. The Magic Tramps were playing and I remembered Eric the singer. The band featured a violin player and I liked their mate-rial. Eric Emerson was larger than life and exuded a strange mix of child-ishness and confident machismo. They closed their show with a rousing version of the *William Tell Overture* that Eric yodeled over. It was a crowd-pleaser. There wasn't any security and I just made my way backstage and met the guys in the band. Then I must have returned to another of their shows with a camera and taken pictures because I showed them to Eric. Whatever the sequence of events was, I became friendly with Eric and the band and began hanging out at Mercer Arts regularly. I felt like I'd landed someplace familiar.

The Magic Tramps came to Visual Arts for a photo shoot with some upscale studio lighting that was available at the school. The shots were good and I took them to Eric's apartment. He was living with Jane Forth and their infant son Emerson Forth Emerson. Jane was very elegant and sophisticated. Both of them were Warhol superstars and had appeared in several of Andy's films.

I was regularly hanging with the Tramps and accompanied them on an out-of-state trip in the capacity of roadie/entourage to Connecticut or someplace equally exotic. They had a gig at the local weirdos' bar, a mix of a variety of sexual persuasions in attendance. The Tramps maintained a sort of mystical approach to their stagecraft and on this particular night they had lit candles on all the amps. During the show right at a high point, great-looking guitar player Kevin Reese backed up just a little too much toward one of those candles. He had a large Afro-style hairdo and these guys were wont to use a bunch of makeup and hairspray, which at this moment acted like an accelerant. Kevin's hair dramatically caught fire with fairly large flames leaping off the back of his head. It took him a minute to realize what was going on. I've seen a lot of rock and roll moments but this was up there. He just shook his head until the fire went out and kept playing with smoke pouring off his singed hair. They didn't miss a beat and the audience went insane.

After the show, of course, everyone was invited to some local's house for the obligatory wild party. We had two vehicles. I was in a van with the equipment and another roadie/entourage guy whose name was Phanor. Wayne Harley, the bass player, drove the van, and the other four band members were in an orange Karmann Ghia that Eric was driving. There might have been a few more cars, and this small caravan pulled out of the bar's parking lot. The van and the Karmann Ghia were going pretty fast when Eric started playing chicken with Wayne and the van. We were in a kind of rural area and I watched wooden phone poles rushing past the van's right window. I was sitting cross-legged on the spare tire that was between the two front seats. Phanor was in the passenger seat. Pretty quickly I knew this wasn't going to end well. We went faster and I watched one pole and then another go by and I thought, *We're gonna hit the next one,* and that's exactly what happened. We plowed head-on into this wooden pole at about fifty miles an hour. The pole was embedded in the middle of the windshield. I flew into the dashboard and only chipped my front tooth. Phanor was crumpled into his seat with a cut on his head and the passenger-side door had to be pulled open by a group of the guys who had now pulled up. Eric looked at my broken tooth and said it was a new look for me. Meanwhile, Wayne had staggered out of the driver's seat and although he looked okay, he began saying he couldn't remember anything. I've not really seen anyone with amnesia before or since but this sure seemed like it. He kept looking at his driver's license and wondering where his girlfriend was. It was decided to take Wayne and Phanor to a local hospital while the rest of us either went on to the party or back to New York. I opted to go back to Manhattan. I don't remember how we got back. Later I was told that Wayne, although seemingly intact, had in fact hit his chin and sustained a deep gash that required sewing up. They had gone to some small local emergency room and their appearance must have been surprising to whoever was helping them. Wayne's beard was dyed green, for example. The two guys got patched up and proceeded, bruised and battered, to this party, where they were greeted with enthusiastic cries of "The band is here!" I spent a month or so with a lopsided grin until I finally went to a dentist to have my tooth filed into shape. The dentist was across the street from Mercer Arts and got me buzzed on nitrous oxide, which I didn't like that much; it made me quickly hungover.

I was still in touch with my friends from Brooklyn and I got a call that one of the old gang, Barry, who I'd been in bands with, had joined the Hare Krishnas. My other friends were concerned that he'd been somehow brainwashed and they recruited me to join them on a trip to reason with Barry at a Krishna temple in Brooklyn.

I'd had a little cult experience up to that point. Much earlier I had found myself at a lecture in a very fancy uptown town house given by someone from something called the Unification Church. There were about twenty people gathered in a big room that had great floor-to-ceiling windows. The lecture was vaguely clever. The guy who gave it demonstrated very succinctly that the Bible unequivocally showed that the Messiah was imminently going to appear in Korea. The arrival of the Korean Messiah was backed up by a lot of quotes and passages from both Old and New Testaments. I don't know if anyone bought this stuff but a few years later when Reverend Moon, the Korean arms dealer, showed up as the head of the Unification Church, I had to give them props for sneakiness. I also took the initial Scientology test but got bored and left before I finished. I got calls and letters from them for about a month before they got bored and gave up.

We got to the temple and had Krishna lunch, which was a lot of very sweet vegetarian stuff, and we did get some time with Barry. He'd had his head shaved and was a sort of Krishna prospect. He told us that the men and women weren't allowed to sleep in the same areas, were discouraged from having sex except to have "Krishna kids," and that he was put off by the macho ass-slapping antics that took place in the men's locker room. But every time we got him alone, we would quickly be surrounded by a bunch of cheerful acolytes whose obvious function was to keep us from reasoning with Barry. I saw Barry many years later when he had gone on to become a swinger or something, and he told me that although the experience had made him more centered and peaceful, he still felt like he'd wasted ten years. He told me that when he had become full Krishna he'd run into our old friend Dury in Washington Square and approached him. Dury hadn't registered that it was Barry right away but when he did he "screamed and ran off."

My friend Joey Freeman was a great source of meeting new people. He must have picked up some laws of freak attraction as a result of his associations with Andy. He'd gone to a variety show called the *Palm Casino Review*, which led us to meeting a lot of people who we dealt with for years to come. Benton Quinn was some displaced Southern aristocrat who'd fled his home situation. Fayette Hauser was one of the original Cockettes. Caroline Thomson was a friend of Vali Myers. I'd seen flyers around the West Village for a movie about Vali but I wouldn't meet her for years.

Joey was hooked up with a partner, his friend Howie from Brooklyn. The two of them became very successful weed dealers. Joey's girlfriend made a trip to Israel with a smuggler who paid all her expenses. The smuggler created some big sculptures that he filled with half a ton of Lebanese hashish. He sealed them with polyurethane and successfully shipped them to the U.S. He gave Joey's girlfriend several pounds as a gift. This might have inspired Joey and Howie to take a hash-buying trip to Paris later on. They replaced the chocolate in a box of candy Easter eggs with hashish, in the same tinfoil wrappers, and then mailed it back to the States. Their endeavors paid off and they were able to rent a nice-size loft in Hell's Kitchen that they called Sphinx Studios.

Joey and I videoed a party at the Canal Center Rest, which was a dive bar on Canal Street. I'm not sure how this place became a preferred hangout, but by 1972 it had a whole spectrum of members of the hipster art/music scene getting cheap drinks there, together with old beat-up semi-homeless guys from the neighborhood. We hung mics from the ceiling in the bar that were hooked into the video deck. The place was packed by nightfall and we did a longish interview with Bebe Buell, who had just arrived in New York and was gorgeous, in the middle of this pandemonium.

Joey and I fell in with Fayette and her friends Gorilla Rose, Screaming Orchid, and Tomata du Plenty. These four would do comedic drag-based skits that Joey and I would video on the ancient Sony reel-to-reel machines. I had previously (some of the things I'd shot at Visual Arts were played at the station) discovered the existence of Manhattan Cable public-access television. Cable TV was in its infancy, and in their wisdom the FCC or some other organization had declared that all cable stations had to provide at least one channel that was devoted to public offerings. However . . . almost nobody had cable TV in Manhattan at that point and even fewer people bothered to submit tapes to Manhattan Cable. I guess this blank TV space was intended for civic-town-meeting stuff but we worked very hard on something called *Hollywood Spit* and then brought the tapes in to be played. Because of all the free airtime, the people at the station would just replay whatever we gave them until we came and picked up the old tape and gave them another. Some of these episodes must have run ten or more times, being broadcast out into the ether. Somebody must have seen it but I can't recall any audience feedback.

The shows themselves, I think there were four or five all told, were pretty lively, with some singing, a lot of comedy, and an overall noir approach that was enhanced by the black-and-white video aspect. We would shoot in and around Joey's loft with a lot of action on the roof. There was a lot of preparation, makeup, and costume adjustment; the preparation-to-actual-taping ratio was extremely skewed. Unfortunately a fire in Joey's loft resulted in the tapes being destroyed and all I have left are still images. Joey said that the fire department stole all their cash and weed too.

Somebody, I can't remember who, had lent me a Teac four-track reel-to-reel tape recorder and I was always keeping various small musical projects going through everything else. I really loved the Teac. I'd fooled around with tape recorders since the midsixties but the ability to overdub was terrific. I would travel to my friend Pete the drummer's house in Brooklyn and get him to play drums along with me playing rhythm guitar parts. I'd record these jams and vaguely organized pieces on a cassette machine then I'd go home and overdub bass and more guitar. I got Eric to sing and yodel on a couple of tracks. The four tracks would be bounced onto a cassette, sometimes recorded back onto the four-track. The finished things were pretty low-tech but I really enjoyed the process.

If one (of many) generalizations can be made as to the difference between early seventies New York City and its current incarnation, my comment might be "It was less commercial." New York was closing in on its final form as party-town tourist central. Every block now seems to have a boutique hotel that acts as its own club and gathering spot. Visitors flood the streets; human traffic is everywhere in vast quantities.

In 1972 the city was relatively empty. It felt to me like there was more of a focus on work and the day-to-day normal comings and goings of regular inhabitants. In and around this facade of vague normalcy, the various freak cultures that were based on shared affinities in sex, art, and music wove themselves throughout society without much actual overlap. There was not much gray-area fringe culture that was represented by something like the current "hipster." The fringe groups lived in their own spaces and stayed fringe; there was very little integration except at nodal points like Andy or Max's. There was nothing in SoHo, nothing. One bar that served hamburgers was it. All the action went on in the old lofts. The Artists in Residence program was a city-regulated program that allowed working artists to live in commercially zoned spaces. SoHo was filled with AIR signs and plaques all over the old factory and iron front warehouse buildings. I was at a party at someone's huge ancient loft and a whole side of the place, an area the size of a two-room apartment, was packed with dusty old burlap sacks that were filled with equally ancient fabric scraps that were left over from the days of light industry and just never removed.

The city was in the last days of its time as a center for these light industries. Printing and garment manufacture, which used to fill endless acres of floor space in lofts all around Manhattan, was in decline in the seventies. One summer Howie inhabited this great space on Sixth Avenue and Twentieth Street right across from the church that would later become the

Limelight club. This place was called Zoom Studios but beyond being some semi-rich guy's playroom, I couldn't tell what kind of "studio" activity went on there. Zoom Studios was on the second-floor corner and had amazing huge rounded windows. The place came with a very nice long-haired cat, but the poor cat's fur was so matted that it had trouble moving around, and when we trimmed its fur and liberated it, it went crazy and ran all over the place. If nothing else in life, I at least helped that cat. The place had sleeping loft areas wherein one's face was in proximity to the ceiling. The trouble was that at eight o'clock every weekday morning, a massive printing press on the floor above would start up, making rest impossible, but other than that Zoom Studios made for a nice few weeks.

I don't think I felt the same desperation, the "fear of missing out," in regard to nonsocial events. The pull to go see a movie or watch a TV show was self-imposed, not external. Advertising was always brutally powerful but I don't think it had its hooks in so deep back then. I remember when I saw the first GAP/American Apparel–type store, I was amazed that clothing I associated with thrift shops and junk stores was being elevated and stuck in a giant picture window and presented as wildly desirable. These places were actively pushing clothing that, if received as a Christmas present, would require a polite, if fake, "Thank you." Advertising is like a TV pundit. If you yell something loud enough and with enough conviction, people will go for it no matter how inherently bullshit it is.

I kept hanging out at Mercer Arts and because of Eric I started occasionally going to Max's Kansas City, which was a sort of nightclub restaurant near Union Square. I met a girl named Elvira that I started dating. She had a young daughter who I was fond of and I would sometimes watch her while Elvira worked. Elvira had been a girlfriend of Billy Murcia, the original Dolls drummer who had died of an overdose in London. Billy dying was something I heard about frequently. People had held him in high regard for his cheerful attitude and bouncy playing. Elvira and Caroline Thomson knew each other and were friends of Vali's. Caroline even had fine facial tattoos like a Berber tribal woman that Vali had done for her. Their style was radical and included wild red-hennaed hair. Carol was a little more hippie-gypsy and Elvira was closer to proto-Goth. An early date we had was going to see this poet, Patti Smith, read at Le Jardin, a night-club that was in the basement of the Diplomat Hotel on West Forty-Third Street. She was great and after reading she brought out Lenny Kaye, who played an electric guitar while she sang. I left thinking she should really have a band.

Because of the leaning toward glam in the rock community, I was already wearing eye makeup at the time and I'd gotten pretty good with application. Elvira helped me with personal styling and I started using kohl on my eyes that was just black. I traded the old motorcycle jacket I had gotten years before for a pair of knee-length green high-heeled boots that I wore a lot. I had very long hair and I appreciated the disdainful looks my appearance would get from people on the street and subway.

The school year was winding down. Holly Woodlawn and Jerzy Kosinski both came and spoke to the students. Holly, of course, was the Warhol superstar and Kosinski was the brilliant writer whose breakout novel, *The Painted Bird*, described the horrific brutalist and possibly autobiographic adventures of a young boy in World War II Eastern Europe. I shot a nice photo of Holly and I asked Kosinski if writing *Painted Bird* was at all painful. He indicated that he had transcended the superfluity of the trappings of the flesh and wasn't bothered by emotional connections to things like seeing murder. I thought he was pretty cool.

I somehow got into a position where I was able to recommend that the Magic Tramps play at the end-of-year school party. They did in fact get the gig and I introduced them wearing an antique white Palm Beach–style suit that my friend had found in yet another junk store.

Eric and Jane stopped living together and Eric asked me if he could stay with me for a while on First and First. Up to this point the neighbors in the building, in spite of my weird appearance, probably didn't think much of my outsider status. With Eric as a new roommate, all this changed. There was a lot of late-night coming and going. There were a lot of visitors. Eric got a lot of dates.

When I first moved in, there was a whole building behind ours. It was abandoned and was the site of a shooting-gallery type of drug repos-itory that included a lot of people frequenting the place after dark. The rear building was just a few feet away from my windows and I would see candles burning at all hours. One night I was awakened by a general cacophony. The rear building was burning flamboyantly. The apartment was bright orange and got hot. A few weeks later, Godzilla-like machines arrived early in the morning and began smashing what was left of the building's shell. I didn't watch much TV and this was very entertaining. I then gained a great unimpeded view of Houston Street and the little park area that was behind my building.

Eric would show up at three in the morning in this area behind the building and yell up at our windows, "Throw my works down! They're in the drawer by my bed!" All the lights in the building would go on and there would be an overall sense of grumbling and cursing. One night it was just the two of us in the apartment. It was probably around two in the morning. I was in the kitchen in the front when I heard Eric yelling, "Chris! Chris! Come check this out!" I ran to the rear and looked out the window. The rear of our building was right across Houston Street from Katz's Delicatessen. There was a guy who was throwing a big steel city wastebasket against the big plate-glass window of Katz's. As we watched, he bounced it off a couple of times till finally he used enough force to get it through, making a huge crashing hole. He climbed through the hole and was inside for five or ten minutes. When he emerged he was carrying a large box that was filled with salamis and who knew what else. Staggering under the weight, he rounded the corner and disappeared down Ludlow Street. At this *exact moment* a cop car pulled up and two cops jumped out and shone their flashlights into the hole. If they had looked around the corner, they might have seen the guy but he made it to steal salamis another day.

I wrote a song with Eric that was really just a blatant copy of the Velvets' "Waiting for My Man," which for me is one of the great rock and roll tracks. Eric did some throwaway lyrics about going uptown and being high, and there was the song that was then titled "Tripping." I went with the Magic Tramps to watch them play at some bar in upper midtown. It wasn't very crowded and I'm not sure if the guys from the band knew that a writer from the *New York Times* was there. Then, while the band was playing, in walks Lou Reed with a small entourage. Lou sat down right in front of the stage and oddly yelled some suggestions to the Tramps while they were playing. He really liked Larry the violin player and would call for him to come forward. I got to know Lou in years to come and I wish I had asked him about Eric, but I didn't. I don't know what their relationship was. There was some contention about the back of the first Velvets' album cover. The photo was of the Velvets at the Balloon Farm and behind them, as part of the slide show, was a giant projection of a picture of Eric displayed upside down. Eric made a stink about wanting to get paid for this use of his image and I think they changed subsequent pressings. Anyway, when the small column about the show came out in the *Times*, the writer had conflated our "Tripping" song sounding like "Waiting for My Man" with Lou being there and wrote that Lou had written the song for Eric. I had arrived!

I did one of a few shows with Eric where I played in the band. It was on July 22, 1973, on a ferry that had been hired. Eric, the Jackie Curtis Review, and Manhattan Transfer. Manhattan Transfer was very popular at the time and were the headliners. Fayette's brother Tim Hauser was coincidentally one of the members. The ferry floated around for about three hours while the performers did their thing on a little stage under some stairs. Eric did two sets. I played guitar on one and bass on the second. We all had costume changes. During our second set nobody would turn off the light over the stage, so I smashed the bulb with the peghead of the bass. It looked much more dramatic than it sounds. I assume the ferry was used in daytime to move people around and I'm not sure how many events like this took place, but the story went around that the Hells Angels later had a ferry party that included throwing a few people overboard and this contributed to these proceedings being halted.

Elvira went to London and asked me to join her. I appeared at British immigration with my usual look: long hair, eye makeup, green boots, and one of those old Japanese reversible silk Sukajan bomber jackets that was really beat up. The customs people kept me for a half hour while they went through all my stuff. They even read a couple of letters I had with me; I suppose they were looking for some connection to crime syndicates and/or drug references.

By some cosmic alignment, Elvira was staying with friends in a flat around the corner from Powis Square in Notting Hill. It was a basement place, and the small backyard was adjacent to the backyard of the house used in *Performance* where Jagger's character, Turner, lived.

I think it was around this time that I found out that the *Performance* house was only used for exteriors; the interior scenes were filmed elsewhere. I was disappointed but still impressed by the proximity to this sacred landmark. The neighborhood then was still pretty rugged, similar to the way it's portrayed in the film. I spent time wandering around Portobello Road. On a couple of occasions I passed Brian Eno on the street and we looked at each other, since we were the only men wearing eye shadow. Elvira knew Lemmy, then a pretty big star from Hawkwind, and we met him in a pub for drinks. He was very gracious and friendly. In later years I asked him if he remembered meeting me and, always a gentleman, he said he wasn't quite sure.

There was a lot going on in London. The last time I was there I'd just been passing through; there was a nice difference living there, even for just a couple of weeks. We heard about a show that had recently opened up on King's Road. It was called *The Rocky Horror Show* and starred this Tim Curry guy. It was awesome and campy and extremely minimal. I don't recall any sets, just costumes and the music on a bare stage. The "Time Warp" was a pretty catchy song.

I went to a concert at the Roundhouse, which was a funky old railway building that had been used to turn trains around. The band was three or four guys in monks' robes who came out carrying massively smoking incense censers and played some combination of Gregorian folk and metal. I have no idea what they were called.

We would make treks to Kensington, to the Kensington Market and to Biba. Biba was an over-the-top very lavish and trendy location that was kind of like if Studio 54 was a massive Goth department store. It was decked out in exotic deco styles and filled with peacock feathers. Tens of thousands of peacocks must have given their lives for this environment. Biba had its own furniture, clothing, and makeup lines and I was quick to pick up on the severe makeup. I wasn't that much of a cosmetics expert but I was pretty sure that in America, one couldn't find a coordinated palette of green makeup—that is, green face powder, green blush, green lipstick, and green eye shadow—all in one place. At least you couldn't in those days. I got a couple of small black eye shadows that lasted for years. All their packaging was very severe and cool: shiny black containers with gold writing and deco design elements. There was even a theater in Biba's where the Dolls had played earlier in the year.

Over the years I've come to appreciate the vast difference in the relationship between vehicular movement—that is, traffic—and people in London and New York City. In New York, people meander casually in front of cars, at times possessed of a vaguely threatening manner, as if to say *I dare you to drive toward me. I'm walkin' here* sums up the New York approach to the pedestrian ethos. In New York and in America, there is the concept that the pedestrian has the right-of-way. It's like "innocent until proven guilty" or "the customer is always right." There are no pedestrians in London, only potential victims. I have asked if the "pedestrian has the right-of-way" rule applies in London and been laughed at. When crossing the street, even if one isn't a Yank befuddled by the misdirection, one takes one's life in one's hands. I don't mean to cast aspersions on London drivers—they're in a hurry, I get it—but I know more people who've been hit by cars in London than in New York. Maybe all this is just the result of disorientation. I know I've been repeatedly saved by those little LOOK LEFT/LOOK RIGHT signs painted on the ground at crosswalks in the UK. After one such day of traffic-dodging, I returned to the flat only to find out that I'd missed a trip to Eno's house to smoke hashish.

That year, 1973, was also the first year that Trinidadian community activist Leslie Palmer was the director of the Notting Hill Carnival. Apparently he gave the festival a big boost, getting sponsorships and including electric reggae bands. Under the motorway that crosses Portobello Road, it seemed like an infinite number of fantastic reggae bands were set up and playing every day. I remember more than one group doing great versions of "Mustang Sally." It was eye-opening. I'd heard "Stir It Up" by Johnny Nash but that was about it and I don't know if I'd even heard the term *reggae* before. Suddenly being inundated with a lot of this fresh form in this full-blown party atmosphere was great.

It was challenging to discover new music in those days. A thing that would happen occasionally would be my turning on a radio halfway through a new song I liked and not being able to find out what it was until

I heard it again. This happened to me with Joni Mitchell's "Sisotowbell Lane," which haunted me for weeks. Similarly I heard about a third of Dr. John's "I Walk on Gilded Splinters" on the radio and it took quite a while to figure out what it was. My only reference for reggae music was aspects of what I heard in Dr. John. In London I collected some reggae records that I brought back to New York with me.

Finally, before departing the UK, a group of us attended a concert that was at something called the Crystal Palace located on Sydenham Hill in southeast London. Lou Reed was headlining a show with Golden Earring, Jeff Beck, and others. The Crystal Palace Garden Party was a very early version of the now common one-day festivals that happen all over. It took place in a woodsy park. The odd thing was that the stage, in a big band shell, overlooked a little lake and was far from the audience. Lou came out and his band was very pumped up and aggressive. He did some old Velvet's songs and some from Transformer. Not long after the first number a girl in a long black evening gown jumped in the water and began wading and swimming toward the stage. Immediately she was followed by a lot of others. It was a warm day. I later heard about Keith Moon dressed as a pirate paddling around the same lake in a rowboat and serving tea to people near the water's edge during some show he was doing the year before. The people who got to shore by the stage were led to the sides by security.

I went back to New York. I'm not really sure where I got the money for airfare.

The city was always straining. It was still years away from the great becoming that would kill all the neighborhoods and produce a homoge-nized version of what had been. Really rich people didn't live downtown. The Lower East Side was a dense jungle. This was even before the drug epidemics that would bomb the place and result in empty blown-out ten-ements. It was still pretty sketchy, though.

I came out of my apartment building one sunny day and ran into a kid I knew from the streets. He was a guy who might have been border-line homeless but still maintained a carefree style. He was dressed in the height of non-fashion: old mismatched clothing that had a sort of biker-outlaw sensibility. He was carrying a small battle-ax, the kind that would be a decoration in some den or finished basement, and wearing a big cowboy hat. He said the ax was for self-defense and that he'd discovered a treasure deeper in the Lower East Side that I would find intriguing. I took a few photos of him and put my camera away back upstairs.

The year before, my art-school buddy Bob Rosen and I were entering my building and were followed in by a couple of guys who wanted to rob us. They brandished knives and got Bob's watch and my (the same) camera. As they were leaving they said, "Pull your pants down!" and we figured we'd have to fight them to avoid getting stabbed in the balls. But the pants thing was just to give them a head start in the ensuing chase. We pulled up our pants and ran after them as they went around the corner onto Houston Street. As fate would have it, there was a security cop right there, not even a real NYPD cop, just a guy who was a kind of hired watchman for the relatively new building on the far side of the little park behind my apartment house. I yelled something at the cop and he too gave chase. He caught up to one of the kids on Ludlow Street and grabbed him by the shoulder. The kid slipped out of his jacket and my camera, and the cop came walking back holding the jacket and camera by its strap. They got Bob's watch, though.

So now I wish I had taken my camera with me when I went to see this kid's treasure but at the time I was cautious about it getting stolen. (Actually, this same camera, a Pentax, was finally stolen from the apartment. I never figured out exactly how. It had been near the front door that I probably left open at some point.) We proceeded farther into Alphabet City, past Avenue C, which was far in for me, past the abandoned buildings and burned-out cars, until we finally got to what this guy thought was so worthy of exploration. It was just a ground-floor empty apartment in a semi-wrecked building. We climbed in through a wide-open window, and the image of my friend crouching on the windowsill has stayed with me as a mental photograph. Somebody's life had been majestically demolished. The apartment was full of stuff but every bit of it had been broken, pulled down, pushed over, and made unrecognizable. We dug around in the rubble for a while but didn't find anything interesting.

Looking back, I think it all seems so remarkably ancient. I don't know what I was aware of. The city maintained itself around me; systems were in place that affected everything. Being on welfare was like a little part-time job. Occasionally a check would go missing or get stolen from the mailbox, and getting it replaced would involve hours of effort. On Fourteenth Street there was an exceedingly bleak New York City Human Resources office that was always filled with people waiting to see caseworkers. The caseworkers were always bored and impatient and seemed to provide the minimum of service. I don't know what I expected for free. Everybody put up with the oppressive atmosphere of this place, though, sitting on the gray metal folding chairs for an hour while waiting for another bored impatient person to call your number.

Another issue I had was with my bank. I didn't ever have any money beyond whatever was left over from welfare after paying bills, so I only had a checking account. Since there was no such thing as an ATM machine, I was always cashing checks for ten bucks or whatever and the people in the bank started to complain and told me to open a savings account. It wasn't too professional on their part.

A benefit I got from proximity to Eric besides meeting people was getting into Max's easily. Mickey Ruskin opened Max's in 1965 and it quickly rose in stature as an "art bar" and general celebrity hang. The proximity to the Warhol factories added to the mystique. At the time the area on lower Park Avenue was pretty empty. I always liked hanging out in the back room. There was this great Dan Flavin neon sculpture in the corner that gave everything this reddish cast that added to the seediness. The walls were covered with squares of rough dark gray carpeting, and when the room was eventually renovated and the carpeting thrown out, I got a bunch from the garbage that I put on walls in various locations that I lived in.

Mickey pretty much single-handedly developed the "velvet rope" style of admissions to the place. I think he had gotten into too many fistfights with people wanting to get in, so by 1973 they were selective about clientele. But Eric had the run of the place; everyone liked him, and all I had to do to get in was say, "I'm Eric's roommate." One evening I went in and I heard the dull throb of live music coming from the room upstairs. A staircase in the middle of the club led up to a small concert room. (I was at a Silver Apples show there even earlier. I'd met Simeon Coxe someplace; maybe the West Village scene.) I went in and the Stooges were in the middle of an energetic set. Iggy was shirtless, and his blond hair and gold shiny pants made him look like a human torch as he zipped around the small stage.

I got into crazy stuff with Eric. He asked me to meet him at Anton Perich's giant loft that was right on the corner of West Broadway and Prince Street. Anton was a photographer and filmmaker who documented a lot of the Max's and general downtown scene; he videoed everything. Anton also had a public-access cable TV show up and running.

When I got there I walked in on Eric and a guy named Jimmy being recorded by Anton. Jimmy never wore a shirt. He was a tall, good-looking dude with very long hair, and even in the dead of winter he would arrive at Max's with no shirt. There was a small crowd watching them. What might have started out as some friendly horseplay between these two had quickly devolved into a semi-violent altercation. Eric was sometimes armed with a gold-painted bullwhip but Jimmy was also wielding a bullwhip, and the two of them went at it with the whips for a while until they both rushed each other. I was watching a monitor as they crashed into the camera. It was very dramatic television. My memory of it is awesome. Anton has a YouTube channel but that's not on there. I think I asked him about it over the years but he probably has a million videotapes.

The Southern Hotel on Lower Broadway contained the old Winter Garden Theatre where in 1864 there was a production of *Julius Caesar* starring John Wilkes Booth and his two brothers. The theater burned down in 1867 and was replaced three years later by the Broadway Central Hotel, also known as the University Hotel, which for a time was the biggest hotel in America. It was very grand but, by 1970, it was a run-down dive and home to a lot of run-down individuals who were living on the fringes of the run-down cityscape.

Back in Brooklyn years before, one of my former girlfriends began dating an older guy who was seriously nuts. He dressed like Lee Harvey Oswald and was all about being pursued by the CIA and generally being spied upon. He told me that if one came home every day and threw up in the same spot, the floor would dissolve. I wondered about this in relation to what happened next. Directly behind the Broadway Central was the Mercer Arts Center. On the evening of August 9, 1973, the hotel gave up the ghost, killing four residents. It collapsed "like a stack of pancakes," as people say, and took Mercer Arts with it; great clouds of dust billowed all over the streets. The story that circulated then was that the Magic Tramps were rehearsing at Mercer at that moment and had to run the hell out clutching their instruments as plaster rained down around their heads. I don't know for sure if this really happened but it is a cool story.

I didn't watch much TV, but one day I was looking at a New York City tourism commercial that was shot in the Statue of Liberty. Some out-of-town family was ascending the endless spiral staircase and briefly passed a *TAKI 183* graffiti tag on the wall behind the stairs. I saw this as outlaw culture creeping into the mainstream. Maybe something would happen. The *Billboard* top 100 song chart for 1973 had "Papa Was a Rolling Stone" as number 100 and "Tie a Yellow Ribbon Round the Ole Oak Tree" as number 1. Times were tough. I appreciate how fucking primitive things were now that humanity has become an integrated circuit. I'll repeat: 1973 was closer to a hundred years prior than to thirty years hence. When I was a kid, the subway had woven wicker seats and those white enamel loops that you'd hold on to. The evolution of phone booths—from the ones with wooden doors and seats to more industrial steel things that were made to thwart destruction.

Earlier that year it was as if all the denizens of Max's and Mercer Arts turned out to see David Bowie descend onto the stage at Radio City Music Hall to do a very long show that questioned some of the tenets of celebrity. Joey's partner Howie had gotten front-row-balcony seats. Salvador Dalí was allegedly in attendance. Although the glitter movement was full steam, the Dolls, Iggy, Suicide, and others were waiting in the wings, indicative of something else.

ME SHOOTING AT CB'S AT THE END, FINAL WEEK.
(PHOTO BY EDDIE SUNG)

STILL LIFE IN THE FIRST AND 1st APARTMENT, 1972.

(PHOTO BY CHRIS STEIN)

ON TOUR WITH VIDEO GEAR.
(PHOTO BY LYNN GOLDSMITH)

FROM LEFT TO RIGHT: CHRIS, IGGY POP,
JIMMY DESTRI, DEBBIE HARRY, AND MARK HAMILL.
(PHOTO BY LYNN GOLDSMITH)

**DURING *PARALLEL LINES* SESSIONS
AT THE RECORD PLANT, NEW YORK CITY.**
(PHOTO BY ALLAN TANNENBAUM)

SELF-PORTRAIT, FIRST AVENUE APARTMENT, 1971–72.
(COURTESY OF THE AUTHOR)

ME IN POLAND, CIRCA 1970.
(COURTESY OF THE AUTHOR)

ROOF OF MY 58TH STREET APARTMENT FOR
NEW MUSICAL EXPRESS, WHICH WE REFERRED TO
AS "ENEMY"—(NME—GET IT?)—HENCE THE GRAFFITI.
WE'D ACTUALLY GOTTEN TO THE NED KELLY
MUSEUM ON A TRIP TO AUSTRALIA.

(PHOTO BY ALLAN TANNENBAUM)

GODZILLA, KING OF THE MONSTERS.
(PHOTO BY ALLAN TANNENBAUM)

THE LOFT ON GREENWICH STREET, NEW YORK CITY.
(PHOTO BY ROBIN PERINE)

ROOF OF THE RECORD PLANT, NEW YORK CITY.
(PHOTO BY MARTYN GODDARD)

DEBBIE AND ME BEING LIGHTLY ASSAULTED BY MILTON BERLE AT SOME TELEVISION AWARDS CEREMONY.

AS SOON AS WE CAME OUT ON STAGE, UNCLE MILTIE GRABBED MY FACE AND GAVE ME A BIG KISS ON THE LIPS.

(PHOTOS BY RICHARD BOCKLET)

JOHN CASSAVETES SHOOTS BLONDIE AT
THE WHISKY A GO GO IN LOS ANGELES, SEPTEMBER 1977.
(PHOTO BY SAM SHAW)

**FIRST AND 1st DOWNSTAIRS
FROM THE APARTMENT, 1972.**
(PHOTO BY CHRIS STEIN)

CONEY ISLAND, 1971.
(PHOTO BY CHRIS STEIN)

Nation, which starred Wayne and Cherry Vanilla. That was a grand success and Andy asked Tony to adapt and direct Andy's first play, *Pork*. *Pork* was based on phone conversations between Warhol and superstar Brigid Berlin. It ran in New York and then did an extended run at the Roundhouse in London, where David Bowie among others attended. *Pork* was another success and Tony returned to New York where he wrote and directed a play called *Island* that again starred Wayne County, Cherry Vanilla, and the up-and-coming Patti Smith. After all this, Tony was absorbed into MainMan, a management company formed when entrepreneur Tony Defries took over management of Bowie. MainMan was unique in the 1970s music world, as it combined management as well as films, records, and production. It was an early model for what now is standard in the music industry. MainMan oversaw production of Bowie's *Hunky Dory* and *Ziggy Stardust* and Lou Reed's *Transformer*. MainMan's influence and connections in the downtown music scene were second only to Warhol's during the early seventies.

Ingrassia was a great asset. He directed the girls to get in touch with the emotional content and consider the technical aspects secondarily. Debbie and I were friendly for a month or so, but the attraction was mutual and when, much to Tony's annoyance, we both arrived late to a rehearsal together, everybody knew that we had hooked up.

I was crazy about Debbie. We started hanging out together most of the time. She was living in New Jersey near where she worked at a hair salon and would commute back and forth in a blue 1967 Camaro. She struck me as very together, with a car and job, as compared to my scattered situation. I was still benefiting from welfare and food stamps and occasionally hitting my mother up for some funding. Debbie, however, had a stalker ex-boyfriend who was bugging her with the usual male terrorist tactics—lots of phone calls, showing up unannounced, et cetera. He called my apartment looking for her and I think me answering the phone put him off. Debbie decided to move back to Manhattan, and Roseanne and Tony helped her get an apartment in their building on Thompson Street. I helped Debbie move her stuff and I met her parents, who had shown up also. I had been interested in seeing them, expecting a very exotic older couple. When we were driving back to New York I asked her what was up, as those two people looked absolutely nothing like her. That's when I heard about her having been adopted.

Debbie settled into Little Italy and I spent days walking between our two apartments. My route along Houston Street took me past what were then empty lots and broken-down buildings. Debbie would go to work in the mornings and I would frequently return to my apartment. I would pass a particular chain-link fence that was on the northeast corner of Houston and Bowery, and one day, I'm not sure why, I noticed a note stuck in the fence. I've always been attracted to little things that carry on in the fringes of our secular existence. I looked at the note. It was written on paper-lined tinfoil, the kind that's inside a pack of cigarettes. It was semi-coherent with a bunch of numbers and a message written in pencil. Also, it was dated! I kept it. The next day there was another note. Every day, another note was carefully placed in the fence. I soon had a collection of them. Many were written on pages torn from a small spiral notebook as well as on the cigarette papers. A theme emerged: This fellow, Andrew Creechy, and his niece Vernice were owed various sums by the government and Social Security. The numbers that were written were supposed to be Social Security numbers, but they were always different. Maybe the notes were hyperbolic. The actual writing would have a few formed words, a half sentence, and then it would trail off into an approximation of writing that was more like drawings. After I had a lot of these things I started thinking that I was not following the prime directive. By interfering with this eco-system of the notes and the guy and the fence, by removing them, I might be perpetuating his note writing, causing him to think that the notes were being delivered. One day I thought I saw an old dude putting a note in the fence. Was this the elusive Andrew? I ended up with a hundred or so notes, I still have one glued in a notebook.

The Exorcist had just come out and we went to see it with Roseanne and a few others. Roseanne's Catholic upbringing didn't go well with the film and she was so freaked out that Debbie and me sat up with her all night. Soon after, she left the group and was replaced by a very gorgeous girl named Amanda Jones.

I was in Debbie's apartment one afternoon when she came back from work at the salon in New Jersey and I saw that she had dyed her hair blond.

She said they hadn't had many customers and she and her friend and coworker Ricky had gotten bored. She had it slicked down; it looked like Twiggy's famous haircut.

One night we were in the back room of Max's when Elda came in very excited. She said she had just come from a bar downtown where she had seen a band who were "dressed like old men." This was, of course, referring to Television playing at CBGB's.

We did a gig opening for Television and at the end of the show it seemed like every guy in the place surrounded Debbie. We walked home and were set upon by a big guy who forced us at knifepoint into my apartment, tied us up in different rooms, raped Debbie, and stole a bunch of stuff. All these years later and I still want to kill this person; not a good feeling.

Friends were supportive; Eric and Tony made some bad jokes that were weirdly comforting. We never bothered with the cops and we did our best to just move forward. Was danger and violence more normalized then compared to currently? I knew a number of girls who'd been assaulted. Horribly, there was a prevailing "goes with the territory" attitude.

After that we spent more time at Debbie's apartment and less at mine. The Stillettos did more shows at CB's opening for Television and did a big show at the 82 Club on East Fourth Street opening for Wayne County. The atmosphere at the 82 was more upscale than CB's. It was an old basement drag club that had seen its heyday in the 1950s and '60s when it was run by members of the Genovese crime family. It wasn't really an LGBTQ club, as the patrons were generally straight, but the performers were men in drag and the staff were women in male drag. By the seventies it had passed its glory but had become popular amongst the members of the downtown new music scene. The Dolls did a great show at the 82 that found them all wearing dresses. The atmosphere was fantastic: mirrored walls and plastic palm trees that had survived but were falling into decay. In a rear area was a wall of yellowing framed photographs of old-school celebrities posing with performers. I was entranced by a picture of Abbott and Costello standing next to a very tall drag queen who was dressed in the height of showgirl glitz, complete with a giant bejeweled feathered headdress. By the time we all were there, the manager was a very tough older woman named Tommy who covered the door and presumably kept order. Tommy would usually wear a man's white dress shirt. She sported a blond pompadour hairstyle and generally seemed like someone you wouldn't want to mess with.

A friend, photographer Bob Gruen, brought UK journalist Chris Charlesworth to the 82 Club gig. Chris became entranced with Debbie and sent Bob's pictures of the Stillettos to *Melody Maker* to accompany an article about the New York band scene. This may have been our first bit of UK media coverage.

On Halloween of 1973, the Dolls played a big show at the ballroom of the Waldorf Astoria hotel. I didn't attend but the story I got was this:

The Dolls were always late getting onto the stage and this night, the doors opened an hour later than what was advertised. This was the first, and probably the last, rock concert to occur at the Waldorf and the freaky glitter concertgoers mixed awkwardly with the hotel's bourgeois guests. I'm not sure what other acts participated, but Eric, tripping heavily and wearing a pair of gigantic white-feathered angel wings that someone had made for him, showed up and was allowed to perform a couple of numbers, accompanying himself with an acoustic guitar, before the Dolls came on. Eric would do these stream-of-consciousness songs that were partly improvised that would lyrically evoke his surroundings, what he was thinking, et cetera. Of course, once he got going he wouldn't vacate the stage in spite of being signaled to wrap it up from people who were watching in the wings. Eventually Mike Quashie, who was working with promoter Howard Stein, went out onstage to persuade Eric to leave. Quashie was known as the Limbo King and was associated with Hendrix and Lou Reed, among others. Eric, who was absorbed, didn't want to get off, and a struggle ensued. Eric hit Mike over the head with his guitar, smashing the instrument to bits, and the crowd went wild. Eric was pissed and stormed off the stage. He grabbed the girl he was with and left. He pulled her into her car, a blue Mustang, and started rapidly downtown. He made it into the Holland Tunnel and started speeding madly toward New Jersey, bouncing off the walls. Here you can picture sparks flying wildly and blue paint being scraped. The cops had been alerted and were waiting for them in Jersey City with guns drawn. Then comes the scene where the police yell, "Exit the vehicle!" and watch as this guy wearing giant angel wings and covered in gold glitter gets out and stands there with his hands up.

Eric wound up in jail in New Jersey, and back at the Waldorf during the Dolls' song "Frankenstein," Johnny Thunders grabbed one of the pumpkins that was decorating the stage and threw it in the air—it came down on David Johansen's head. The show was a great success.

Eric had previously met Edgar Winter's ex, Barbara Winter, at a party and gotten her phone number. Barbara was a friendly girl who Edgar paid alimony to. Eric called her and she bailed him out.

The Stillettos continued doing shows into the summer of 1974, frequently opening for Television at CBGB's. CB's then was a bit like owner Hilly Kristal's apartment if it had happened to have a bar and a stage in it. I think he actually had an apartment nearby but he would sometimes sleep at the club. I recently came upon an article from the *New York Times* of May 18, 1895, headlined "Burglar or an Astral Body," wherein a cop passing by the window of a "wholesale liquor store" on "315 Bowery" thought he saw the figure of "a seven year old boy, with a big shock of hair" trying to break into a safe. It doesn't say how anyone concerned, the cop or the writer, knew this person was seven years old. Eight more cops were summoned and they surrounded the place. When the owner arrived and opened the store, of course nobody was there.

Many years later, CBGB's, at 315 Bowery, was still a very eccentric environment. There were old overstuffed easy chairs and small sofas at the edges. A bookcase in the front had some old, odd titles and military manuals. There was a pool table in the rear and, for a time, a large, inflated raft hung from the ceiling. The stage was a small set of wooden platforms that was covered with red shag carpet. I've heard that Eric helped build the stage. The walls were layered with history. On the side opposite the bar were these little horse-racing murals that could have dated back to the twenties or thirties, when the place was some kind of sports bar. All around were bigger-than-life-size photographs of old vaudeville stars like Fanny Brice. At the end of the bar there were more modern murals that portrayed some of the denizens of the bar sitting around drinking or passed out at the tables. In later years Hilly told me that these paintings were done by a local woman artist and depicted some of his early patrons, who he knew by name. Hilly also had two dogs, big insect-like creatures, Salukis or Borzois or something. They would wander around slowly and contribute to the rarefied atmosphere. I don't think anyone was aware that OMFUG, the CBGB subheading, stood for "other music for uplifting gormandizers," meaning ravenous eaters of music. I, like most, assumed it meant "original music from the underground," which seems not to be the case. The CBGB font referencing the Hells Angels one was obvious, though, and I vaguely remember a few of the Angels hanging around early on.

Debbie and I got roles as extras in a full-on Hollywood movie. Well, it was really this mediocre vanity project that somehow had landed a substantial cast. It was called *Deadly Hero* and starred James Earl Jones and Don Murray, who is known for his part in *Bus Stop* opposite Marilyn. Lilia Skala, who was the head nun in *Lilies of the Field*, was the female protagonist. In the movie, she is a musician, and in the opening sequence she is conducting a big Broadway-style show that I guess is supposed to be like *Hair* but is just a shapeless montage. We were in the rock-band section along with Tomata, Kieran Liscoe (Kieran was an early CB's regular who had a self-named band. He might have been how we got the gig. Kieran later got us a show at the Pride parade, which I believe was the first time a stage was set up at the end of Christopher Street), and at least one other guy from the scene who I didn't know but whose face was painted silver. This rock band was somehow playing along with a full orchestra; there were dancers, acrobats, the whole nine yards. This was shot at the Lucille Lortel Theatre on Christopher Street in front of a full audience. It went on for a few days.

So James Earl Jones is a burglar, and after the performance he breaks into Skala's house but he's very polite as he steals her stuff. Then Don Murray, who plays the cop, shows up and murders Jones, who was about to surrender and was harmless anyway. Skala witnesses this and as Murray is hailed as a hero, she is racked with guilt. Murray is a sociopath and he stalks her and in the big showdown on a farm somewhere, she impales Murray on the metal stand that protrudes from the bottom of her cello, killing him—the end.

I think this may have been the first time I met Michael Sullivan, who was also an extra. Mike is an old friend of Debbie's and he appears in several of the later Blondie videos. Mike once was filming a World War II scene on the roof of his building and a neighbor called the cops after seeing a very realistic cardboard machine gun that he'd built. A SWAT team showed up but they didn't lecture Mike; they were just relieved not to be dealing with an actual machine gun. The stylist on *Deadly Hero* was murder, and Debbie had her hair shoved inside a man's cap. She had these big metallic stars stuck on her eyes and was a bit unrecognizable. There was a moment when they were shooting some headshots, and after she pulled off her hat I heard comments of "Wow, she's beautiful." I had told them I could do my own makeup so I wasn't subjected to their attentions. Anyway, it was the most we'd ever gotten paid for anything, a few hundred a day plus lunch. We aren't credited; there isn't even a band credit, just one for "dancers." The director, Ivan Nagy, was a convicted bookie and went on to do a bunch of porn movies out of LA, including titles like *Anal Angels 2* and *Naked in 60 Seconds.* You can see *Deadly Hero* for three bucks on Amazon, I think.

Eric left the First Avenue apartment and moved into a big loft on the corner of Park Avenue and Twenty-Fourth Street with Barbara Winter. It was a great, really large space and the Stillettos did a few rehearsals and photo shoots there. Amps and drums were set up and Eric encouraged late-night sessions. Odd musicians would occasionally be recruited from the streets and various area clubs. One night somebody brought along this guy who he had met in a bar or something. This person was very normal-looking, was dressed in one of those polyester disco shirts, and he had a brand-new Fender twin amp and a brand-new Telecaster with him. Sort of very average, heavyset dude. A jam commenced and the guy just sat there holding his guitar and listening. Then when we got to a peak in the jam, a high point where everyone was on the same wavelength, this anonymous guy came in with just an amazing, impossible guitar line that elevated the whole thing to some cosmic Zen level. The rest of us were knocked out but kept playing. But this guy's part was distracting and the jam deteriorated. The guy just waited until it came back together and then he did it again! We were dumbfounded. Eric would pause his stream-of-consciousness vocalizing to listen. This happened a few more times and then that was it and the guy dragged his gear out and disappeared into the night.

Late loud jamming and parties also enhanced Eric's relations with lo-cal law enforcement, with the police being called by the neighbors. Word reached us one afternoon that Eric and Barbara, obliviously stoned, were screwing in front of one of the large windows that overlooked Park Avenue. The loft was on the second floor and it was lunchtime, so crowds of observ-ers gathered on the streets below, blocking traffic. The cops' pounding on the door finally distracted Eric.

Eric living in relative luxury was causing him to get bored and some-what crazy. He bought a tattoo machine and worked on himself and any-one he could coerce into getting a tattoo from him. Barbara got him an expensive Nudie white suit and I saw him at a club late one night with that suit in shreds hanging off him. He'd gotten into a fight of some kind. (Eric told me he'd once gotten into a fight with Brian Jones over a girl.) He was also using too many drugs.

On Debbie's birthday, July 1, the Stillettos did a show, opening for Eric and his band Star Theater and the Dolls at something called the Bacchus Rock Palace on West Forty-Eighth Street. The girls sang some backup for the Dolls. Shortly after, Debbie, drummer Billy, bass player Fred Smith, and me left the Stillettos. The trio situation was too small to contain all the styles and ambitions of three leads and the group went the route of other girl trios with one member emerging.

We did at least two gigs at CB's under the somewhat unfortunate name Angel and the Snake, which derived from an illustration I found in a magazine that depicted a girl who looked a bit like Debbie with a snake draped around her. The illustration, a realistic drawing, made for a good flyer if nothing else.

I knew this kid Tommy from Mercer Arts who had a band called Butch. I ran into him somewhere and he said, "I heard you found a place to play downtown," meaning CBGB's. He said he had a band called the Ramones, and I wondered if they were a Latin act. Both the Angel/Snake gigs were with the Ramones and the first show on August 16 was the first time the Ramones played CB's. Also on the show was the crew from my old cable-TV days, Gorilla, Tomata, Screaming, and Fayette, who did a skit called "Slaves of Rhythm." Gorilla wore a clear plastic tuxedo that was made out of a shower curtain.

The Ramones were totally awesome even in their very raw state. We immediately became die-hard fans and went to several showcases they had at a rehearsal space called Performance Studios. The Performance Studios stage was tiered, with three or four steps in front. At one Ramones show, Joey sort of fell in slow motion but kept singing in an upside-down position. They would do these very precise super-short songs that might have been construed as parodies if the songs themselves hadn't been so great. They sometimes stopped in the midst of a song and discussed and argued some aspect of it. This evolved into a bit after a while that they seemed to do for fun, but pretty soon they were playing all the way through their songs.

CHAPTER 6

One day Debbie came back to the apartment on Thompson Street and announced that several men in the street, including a guy leaning out of a truck window, had shouted, "Hey, blondie!" at her and she thought that would be a good name for the band. Blondie played at CBGB's for the first time on October 12, 1974, and an ad for this show in the *SoHo Weekly News* seems to be the first instance of the band's name in print anywhere.

The Ramones gave the scene a boost and they fit in well with our friends in other bands like the Miamis and the Fast. The summer nights on the street in front of CB's were memorable, lots of time spent hanging out there. The Bowery was very rugged and the band kids would interact with the locals who were frequently around. Some of these guys were homeless and some lived in transient hotels in the area. The Palace Hotel was directly upstairs over CB's. In its heyday, around 1950, the Palace was the biggest flophouse in the city with 105 cubicles and 224 beds with one bathroom on each floor.

CBGB's would frequently be pretty full but never to the point of standing room and early on there was little or no dancing to the bands that were playing. It was a bit like the old beatnik coffee-shop days with people showing their low-key appreciation by snapping their fingers and applauding politely. Roberta Bayley had been dating Richard Hell, and Television's manager, Terry Ork, suggested that she sit at the door and charge two dollars for admission. When Roberta and Richard broke up, Hilly asked her to keep her position. (Roberta bought a camera in early 1975 and three months later shot the Ramones' first album cover. She's been shooting fantastic images ever since.)

A guy started showing up dressed in a neat suit with a Lucha Libre–style wrestling mask. It might have been only a short time before the reveal but it felt like a couple of weeks at least that the masked guy would come into CB's. This was Arturo Vega, a Mexican artist who appeared mysteriously and was living in a big loft right around the corner from CBGB's on Second Street. Artie had a great aesthetic. He was the first one I ever saw leave toys in their clear plastic packaging and then hang them like artworks. He had a way of narrowing focus on an everyday object until it became something bigger. A series of large paintings of supermarket-food-price ads were an homage to Andy but also something more stripped down and raw. He did a series of brightly colored swastikas that became a statement about the cheerful embrace of evil.

Arturo quickly befriended the Ramones and they all hit it off. They would rehearse and sometimes sleep at his loft. Artie made some attempts at styling the Ramones early on. Like many of us, he was a frequent shopper at Fourteenth Street's many cheap and weird surplus clothing stores. There was a Flagg Brothers shoe store that I used to go to. It sold slightly damaged but new platform shoes very cheap, like five bucks a pair.

I don't recall actually observing this, but Arturo got the Ramones four cheap suits at one point. It didn't take. He found these polyester T-shirts on Fourteenth Street with this red, white, and blue zigzag pattern. Dee Dee wore one at least once that I recall. Artie incorporated the zigzag design into a logo he made for the Ramones that was based on the eagle motif on a JFK fifty-cent coin. The zigzag pattern is on the eagle's shield. Arturo became embedded with the Ramones. He and Danny Fields, who started managing them the following year, became like extra band members; Artie was frequently referred to as "the fifth Ramone." By the end, Arturo had been to nearly every Ramones show, more than 2,200, missing only two, one because he was in jail.

Debbie quit working at the salon in New Jersey and got a job at a Wall Street bar called White's. This place was on the fringes of Wall Street and catered to the afternoon low-level execs and drunken worker drones as well as the occasional street person and gangster. The girls had stations—that is, set locations along a very long bar—and wore bikinis and bathing suits. The first week that Debbie was there, of course all the customers swarmed her; she got all the tips and the other girls wanted to murder her, but soon balance was restored. I would go and visit but they didn't want boyfriends hanging out, so I'd buy a drink and act like a customer, which was weird because I still looked like an outsider freak. We even played some shows there, setting up on the floor in front of the bar. Debbie developed some regular customers. One guy supposedly had such a huge cock that he'd start to pass out from low blood pressure if he got aroused. No one verified this, as far as I know. Another guy was some mobster and he would give Debbie tips on the horses. He gave her a tip on the daily double and I went to OTB and bet ten bucks. To our amazement we won over a hundred. I don't know if I would have bet more if I'd had it, but I didn't have it.

One afternoon I was in there and they had these big speakers and they were playing some music and there was a wineglass on one of the speakers and at some point, some specific note made the wineglass shatter, and this is the kind of stuff I remember forty-five years later.

Eli Siegel, the founder of Aesthetic Realism, said, "All beauty is a making one of opposites, and the making one of opposites is what we are going after in ourselves." There's some dumb stuff in Aesthetic Realism about sexuality but I always liked the opposites part.

The early band period was exciting and vital while at the same time it was occasionally dull and frustrating. We didn't make any money. The music scene was getting little attention from the outside world. Everybody I knew would say how awful, dirty, and dangerous it was in New York and how they were leaving, but nobody left. There's a great Lou Reed monologue where he says how miserable he is in New York but how much more miserable and uncomfortable he is everywhere else. The audience at Max's and CB's was largely composed of other bands and their entourages.

Maintaining the car in Manhattan was a major project. Debbie would wake up early and go sit in it and wait for the seemingly arbitrary alternate-side-of-the-street-parking times to shift in her favor. There were several instances when she was a few minutes late and her pleading and seeming nervous collapse convinced the towing guys to release the car. She said she did a lot of writing while sitting around in the car so I felt less guilty about sleeping, but also I couldn't drive. The battery got stolen twice and we chained the hood closed with a bicycle lock. One day while driving around we came upon a construction site on lower Greenwich Street that took up several blocks. The big, empty sandy lot looked like a small fenced-off desert. By some miracle there were no street signs on these blocks and we were able to leave the car for days at a time. This state of affairs lasted for months till the powers that be realized they were missing the income stream from towing, and signs went up next to these big empty expanses of holes and dirt.

Meanwhile Tony and MainMan were going strong. Tony directed a series of concerts for Wayne County at Westbeth in the West Village, called Wayne County at the Trucks. These were produced by MainMan and were very innovative, as they had the band offstage with just Wayne in front of the audience. Most consider this the model for Bowie's Diamond Dogs tour.

Tony was on a roll and MainMan produced a play for him. It was called *Fame* and was about Marilyn Monroe, whom Tony was enamored of and obsessed with. We saw it a few times in previews downtown. It used moving stage elements that were all white and it centered on a white telephone. The Marilyn character was visited by the father-figure ghost of Clark Gable, who wore a fancy white cowboy outfit. The play was well received for the months it ran downtown and then it opened on Broadway on November 18, 1974. We all waited for the reviews at Sardi's like you do after the show. I don't know how delusional everyone was that this eccentric fringe outsider was going to make his way into the Broadway establishment mainstream, but the reviews were toxic. They killed the play and Tony. One review suggested that no one should ever see anything this guy did ever again, and Clive Barnes, who was the god of critics then, called it "a limp dishrag." I suppose part of the objection was that the play suggested that Broadway favorite and sacred cow Arthur Miller considered

Marilyn a trophy, but Marilyn's wig slipping off in the middle of a scene didn't help the cause. *Fame* had only the one performance on Broadway.

We shared a rehearsal room on West Thirty-Seventh Street with a bunch of rich kids who we knew from somewhere or other. These guys had a set of brand-new Peavey amps and a matching small PA. We started off paying rent but ran out of money and though they got pissed off, the rich kids never threw us out. One evening we came into the building to find the elevator not working. We walked up the fourteen flights to the room. Looking down the stairwell, we saw that a bunch of guys were holding the elevator about five floors below. A lot of yelling of "Fuck you" back and forth ensued, with these guys finally challenging, "Why don't you come down here motherfuckers," et cetera. We just went into our room and rehearsed and it was just as well we didn't go down there, as it turned out they were robbing a furrier on that lower floor. Later on we came into the space only to find that all the Peavey amps had been sawed in half. In some misguided quest for smaller gear, the rich kids had opted to chop up their equipment. The half amps sitting there looked like they were embedded in the floor.

I took a trip out to Sheepshead Bay in Brooklyn with Eric and Barbara to see the Dictators at a club called Popeye's Spinach Factory. The place was packed and everyone was extremely drunk by the time the band went on. They played for a while and then announced, "Our roadie is gonna sing a song!" and this guy with a giant Afro came up and sang a really dirty rendition of "Wild Thing" while the crowd went crazy. This was Dick Manitoba's first appearance as lead singer of the Dictators, a job he kept through several band breakups. After the rich kids gave up on the rehearsal space, we began sharing it with the Dictators.

Tommy Ramone began subletting my First Avenue apartment. Tommy was pretty normal and things were stable till Dee Dee moved in. There started being more late-night events—some guy got locked in the hall in his underwear, somebody else pissed in the hall, et cetera. I had a life-size painted plaster statue of Mother Cabrini, the first American saint, that I'd bought at a junk store on Second Avenue for ten bucks on a really hot summer day. I dragged this massive thing back and up five flights to the apartment. When I got it home I noticed that the eyes had been painted over. I carefully scraped off the paint to reveal realistic glass eyes that made it even creepier than it already was. It really made Dee Dee nervous. I still have the statue today and it still has holes that Dee Dee stabbed in it with a kitchen knife.

We kept playing at CB's and Max's and various other little bars like Brandi's and Monty Python's and the Mushroom, most of which were around that strip below Fourteenth Street on Third Avenue where *Taxi Driver* would later be filmed. My West Village buddy Steve, whose car broke down on the Bay Bridge, reappeared on the scene, now calling himself Stepanji. We played some shows with him on congas. We were at one of these little bars playing to a handful of people when we were approached by a group of uptown-style folks who had been either slumming or at a downtown horse show or something, I don't know how they happened to be there. A girl who introduced herself as Maude Frank asked us if we were available to play at a party she was having. A few days later we arrived at a very opulent uptown town house and set up our crappy amps in a first-floor parlor room in front of the big picture windows. Stepanji was playing congas instead of a drummer. A bunch of guests arrived and we did our best to rock it. "Lady Marmalade" was a huge hit and we would bow to public demand and play "Lady Marmalade" a lot. I'm pretty sure we played it at least three or four times at this event. The party ground on and finally the cops came and the guys giving the party were thrilled! The police had, of course, never come to their door before and they couldn't give a fuck. They said they'd double our fee if we kept going past our agreed-upon cutoff time.

Billy was so conflicted about his drumming versus his alternative life in pharmaceuticals that it was stressing him out. We were doing a show at Max's and he had a panic attack and drank himself semi-unconscious and Jerry Nolan sat in. We still weren't getting paid very much; I can sympathize with his predicament. Billy gave it up and we put an ad in the *Village Voice*. The ad read:

Freak energy Musical Experienced drummer needed female fronted estab. working NYC rock band. Excell opty. money. Fun. Call NOW.

And it gave the phone number at Debbie's apartment. I don't know if we spent any time on the punctuation or capitalizations but that's exactly it. (Michelle Shinn of our crack research team unearthed the ad recently.) We got a lot of calls and held drum auditions at the rehearsal room. A lot of weirdos showed up mixed in with actual musicians. Some of them wouldn't leave. One guy in a fringed jacket hung around and watched other auditions. We started out being very organized and taking Polaroids of the candidates but gave it up after a while. I think we really saw forty-odd people. Then the very last guy was a kid from New Jersey who had a very "I got this" attitude. He actually knew who we were, had been to a Stillettos show at the 82 Club. He had great hair and a cool pair of boots on, so that was it, an easy decision. We started rehearsing with Clem Burke within a few days.

We went out to Bayonne to visit Clem, and his room was filled with copies of *Tiger Beat* magazine. He was living with his dad, his mother having recently died. He was nineteen or twenty when we met him. Clem was a student of popular music and culture. His father had played drums and Clem worshipped Keith Moon. We rehearsed with Fred and Clem. Ivan Kraal came around briefly before joining Patti's band. I think we played with Ivan at CB's at least once.

The rich kids had thrown us out of the rehearsal space for lack of funds but we had managed to find some hippie in a smaller room right down the hall who let us in. The rich kids' room was demolished and they were never there and we sold an old beat-up player piano that was in there. There were never any repercussions.

We eventually did a gig at CB's with Clem and sisters Tish and Snooky who were briefly our backup singers. The girls had jungle-themed costumes made out of animal prints and bits of tied-on fur. Two things happened that night. One was after the show we were approached by an older guy who said he could hire us to go to Alaska and live and do shows on some military base for two months. We'd get transportation and room and board. Since this seemed more like a kidnapping or human trafficking than a showbiz scenario, we declined and said thanks. The other thing was Fred told me after the show that Television had asked him to temporarily replace Richard Hell. Television with Richard had been really dynamic and I'm glad I got to see them during this period. I got the depressing impression that Fred's move wouldn't be temporary. Television was higher up on the food chain than we were, and Debbie and me spent a couple of weeks being paranoid and sulking. Debbie auditioned for a top-forty band to try and add to her bar-girl income.

We also supplemented our income by moving some weed. We met this guy who was a low-level Greek gangster named Pando. He was balding, around forty, with the eternally open shirt and hairy chest with a gold chain. Pando lived in a modern basement apartment on Twenty-Third Street. Said apartment was usually inhabited by a bunch of half-passed-out kids who he was selling weed and whatever else to. I don't know how the hell we met this guy; maybe from buying pot. At the same time one of the guys from the Magic Tramps who lived in the Ansonia was able to get his hands on pounds of high-end pot, in this case gold grass. It was actually light yellow in color, not something I ran into in later years much. So we would buy a pound or a half a pound and drive downtown and sell it to Pando for a profit of maybe fifty bucks. It was a meager profit, considering the level of paranoia. One time we delivered some normal-looking green weed and Pando dumped a bunch of red food coloring on it. This went on for a little while until we gave up the life of crime.

Eric and Barbara Winter had left the loft they were in. Before they moved, Eric had gone around punching holes in the walls and dismantling various improvements he had made. Oddly, they moved to a brand-new luxury building on Greenwich Street right where we had been parking the car due to the lack of street signs. These couple of big-tiered buildings had gone up in the ensuing months while the parking signs had returned, and Debbie was back at early-morning car sitting.

The big building Eric was in was very sparsely inhabited. Tribeca wasn't called Tribeca at that point; it was just a sort of no-man's-land with empty lots still all about. It reminded me of scenes from Truffaut's bleak but modern *Fahrenheit 451*. I'm not even sure there were any other people living on the same floor as Eric. These buildings were not very popular initially and in later years the city took them over and made them into public housing. They filled up, and by the nineties there was a ten-year waiting list for apartments. Of course, when the neighborhood blew up and became Tribeca, the city pulled the subsidizing and the buildings finally succeeded in becoming fancy and exclusive. Eric's apartment was very big with a great terrace that had a river view and we would sit out there and smoke weed. Eric also had a Teac four-track so I would visit and keep a couple of tapes of things I was working on there. I remember doing versions of the Doors' "Moonlight Drive" and Ike and Tina's "Sexy Ida" on that machine.

One day we were sitting on the terrace talking about Candy Darling dying. Eric had brought me with him to visit her in the hospital and she had looked scared and bored at the same time. Eric picked up his guitar and improvised a song about how he was feeling and the theme was about his feeling trapped by being fulfilled. It was sad. Eric was in great physical shape, he exercised a lot and was quite built up, but he was also doing a lot of heroin.

Debbie and I were there one night sitting around with Eric and Barbara smoking pot and watching him shoot up. He got super-high and tried to convince us to stay later for a foursome but we bowed out and said good night. As we left he was asleep on his feet. We went home and the next morning the phone rang and it was Barbara saying Eric had been hit by a truck and killed. I suppose it's possible that he went for a bike ride in that state but I'm inclined to think he overdosed.

Eric had been a link for a lot of things to me. I mightn't have met Debbie without the connection. I always think that if he'd hung on for another year, he would have had some success as a musician and actor. His energy suddenly vanishing was strange and tragic.

The night after he died I had a dream that I was berating him, telling him how dumb it was for him to have left like that. When I spoke to my mother, who had been close to Eric too, she told me she'd had a dream the same night where Eric had come to her and said that people were making fun of him.

Clem would call us and be encouraging, saying, "Let's get it going, you can do it" and such. It was daunting. Replacing the bass player, a quarter of the band, was like starting over but we went into rehearsals with Clem. Clem was a local hero in Bayonne and after a while he would show up with a group of kids from his hood. It reminded me of my friends from

Brooklyn. There was a guy named Prash or Crash and another kid named Ronnie Toast who had allegedly burned down his parents' house and then gone back when it was a boarded-up shell and written TOAST on it in spray paint.

Along with this motley bunch was a very bright, good-looking nineteen-year-old kid named Gary. Gary was starting out playing bass and guitar and was enthusiastic, so that was it. Gary was in trouble with the law back in New Jersey for having been with his underage girlfriend when he became adult age himself. Her parents had gotten him busted and he wasn't supposed to leave New Jersey. This was the impetus for Gary and Debbie writing "X Offender." "Heart of Glass" in an early incarnation as "The Disco Song" was floating around and we worked on a version of the Doors' "Moonlight Drive." The first gig we did with Gary and Clem was at Broadway Charlie's bar that I think was on Broadway and Eleventh Street. It was a very warm steamy night. We soon went on and did a few shows at CB's.

With the addition of Gary, the band felt more stable even though we were still struggling. Debbie continued at the Wall Street bar and they still let us play on the floor occasionally. At least another girl from the scene, Anya Phillips, started working there and she and Debbie became friendly. Gary, who'd been almost homeless, would frequently sleep at the Thompson Street apartment as he disconnected from his New Jersey base. Gary and I shared a love of comic books, mysticism, and smoking pot.

In February of '75 the Dolls started a series of shows at the Hippodrome, a club up on Fifty-Sixth Street, under the auspices of Malcolm McLaren, who was now managing them. I don't know any of the backstory of how the Dolls transitioned from longtime early manager Marty Thau to Malcolm, but several years earlier I'd gone with Eric to the Chelsea Hotel, where Malcolm had turned one of the rooms into a showroom for his clothing. This was during his Let It Rock period and some of the Dolls' members, including David, were there hanging out so they all were aware of each other already.

Malcolm quite successfully styled the band and the shows. The Dolls were all dressed in coordinated red leather and vinyl outfits and their backdrop was a big hammer-and-sickle motif. Maybe some statement about fashions overtaking revolution, the hedonism of rock dressed up as working-class struggle—I don't know, I never asked. But they sounded fantastic; the band was measured and specific and the sound design was great. I thought it was the best I'd heard them, and I'd heard them a lot at this point. They even started on time.

Ironically the first weekend they played, the opening act was some very pretentious Bowie-clone conceptual deal that included the protagonist singer hatching out of a giant egg. The band for this epic was the rich kids from our rehearsal room, the same guys who had sawed their amps in half. When they came out at the end and did a number as just a band, they got a better response than with the fake Jobriath-egg dude. The next weekend Television opened.

To quote Debbie: "Soon after that the Dolls went down to Florida with McLaren to start a tour, and about twenty minutes later we all heard that Johnny Thunders and Jerry Nolan had left the group, flown to Paris and that was that. Another twenty minutes later we all heard about the Sex Pistols." That's a little condensed but works as hyperbole.

Shortly after Gary joined we got involved with Alan Betrock, a journalist with the *SoHo Weekly News* who expressed interest in managing us and offered to help us make a demo. The thrust of this was that Alan had some tentative connection to songwriter and singer Ellie Greenwich and since we had been doing the Shangri-Las' "Out in the Streets" (which Ellie wrote with Jeff Barry) and were vaguely slotting into the girl-group formula, we would record that song and Alan would get it to her. I'm not sure exactly what the next step was supposed to be but we plowed ahead.

We went to some guy's basement recording studio in Queens. Nobody had a clue as to where we were. The guy's setup was a one-inch eight-track. If I'd known more about recording I would have been more curious about the setup. Out of everybody, I had the most recording experience, which was basically me screwing around with tape recorders. It was miserably hot in the basement but we managed to get five tracks done, including a version of what would later evolve into "Heart of Glass." I'd worked up the then untitled "Heart of Glass" demo on a Teac four-track inspired in part by the Hues Corporation's "Rock the Boat." The sessions were engineered by Kevin Kelly, the guy whose basement it was, and produced by Betrock.

The demo went nowhere except for a bit of a fuss over us trying to buy it from Alan later on and him not wanting to sell it. Alan went on to produce a good local music paper, the *New York Rocker*, and he did feature us in the first issue. But pretty soon he gave up on us and instead took up with a band called the Marbles.

On Thompson Street we would frequently see Tony, who, despite being brutalized by the corporate New York theater community, was still attempting to work. MainMan had closed up in New York, as Bowie and Defries fell out. Ingrassia recruited us to join him in a production of the first act of Jackie Curtis's play *Vain Victory: The Vicissitudes of the Damned*, which had originally been put on at La MaMa in 1971 and had starred Candy, Eric, and many others in the Warhol milieu. We learned a bunch of songs and jams for the soundtrack and Debbie had a part as a character named Juicy Lucy. The script made lots of references to old Hollywood films. I found these shiny blue three-piece sharkskin suits in a junk store on Broadway, and the boys wore those.

We were getting out of a cab for a *Vain Victory* rehearsal and Clem opened the door right in front of an oncoming car. Nobody was hurt but the door didn't make it. When the taxi driver asked Clem for his name, Clem said Joe Dallesandro.

The play was a success and we got a positive mention in Danny Fields's *SoHo Weekly News* column, which was a morale boost.

Debbie's parents had moved to Cooperstown, New York, and opened a gift shop near the National Baseball Hall of Fame and Museum. I went once but Debbie would visit more frequently.

I was waiting for her to come back from a trip to see her parents and was standing in front of the building on Thompson Street. The neighborhood then was as depicted in *Mean Streets*, complete with the old guys sitting on chairs in front of "social club" storefronts. A fracas broke out right across the street. A bunch of neighborhood dudes were pounding on a lone Black kid who was accused of purse-snatching but was probably the victim of a territorial dispute—he'd come into the area and had the wrong skin tone. There was a crowd casually observing these three or four guys stomping this lone kid. Suddenly somebody started yelling, "No! Stop! Call the police!" It was Debbie, who at that *exact moment* had just arrived back from her trip. Up to that point I guess the locals thought of us as just harmless eccentrics. I still had long hair and wore makeup and Debbie would wear miniskirts and platforms. The crowd turned on us; I had an image of the villagers with the pitchforks as I pushed Debbie into our hallway and up the stairs. We never found out what happened to the kid who was being pounded. After that, the apartment got broken into a couple of times. On one occasion somebody stole Debbie's fluffy winter coat, which was odd, and another time, pieces of the ceiling were pulled down, covering things with plaster dust. We'd been friends with the super of the building but when we appealed to him, it was like the scene in *The Godfather* where Tom Hagan tells Tessio he can't get him off the hook for "old times' sake."

On top of our continuing lowly band status and lack of funds, we had to leave and seek new lodging, which was depressing. Again fate intervened, as one day we ran into my old acquaintance Benton Quinn on the street. He told us he was living on the Bowery and we could join him. He wasn't really a regular at CB's but he was there often enough to know what was going on and who was who. Benton was staying in a massive crumbling three-story loft space that was located over a nameless liquor store at 266 Bowery. Anne Wehrer, who was a girlfriend of Iggy's and would later write "I Need More" with Iggy, had rented the place and when she left she turned it over to Benton.

Debbie's three cats had been living with us and they were happy to have more space. Daniel was the leader cat, with Sunday Man and Gray Girl as the troops. I called Gray Girl Gregor. Within days of us moving in, we returned from outside to find the three cats sitting calmly around the corpse of a huge rat that they had vanquished.

But the loft space was amazing. A long, steep, narrow staircase led up from the street. We got the first floor, which had the only somewhat working bathroom, giant closet, and kitchen in the building. In the back was our bedroom. It had two big windows that opened onto a densely overgrown courtyard that seethed with wildlife. The windows were covered with massive iron shutters that looked able to withstand a siege, and there was wire mesh embedded in the windows themselves, which were riddled with bullet holes. We found some posters and flyers indicating that this place had at one time been the headquarters of one Louie DeSalvio, who was a long-time New York assemblyman. I don't know if he was a gangster or Mob connected, but one of his various political insights was that the World Trade Center was totally stupid and was only suited to be used as a slingshot by NASA. We also got the impression that the place had been a doll factory that employed child labor. I don't know where we gleaned this information from but it became part of the narrative.

The front of the loft had enough space for us to rehearse in and we were able to borrow a small PA system from my buddy Robin in exchange for him being able to occasionally play there. Joey's partner Howie arrived one day saying that he had procured a piano somewhere and did we want it. We were literally three blocks away from CBGB's and we somehow recruited Hilly to help us with the piano. Hilly had a part-time moving company and was really a powerful guy, one of those dudes who weren't all muscled but were superstrong. Getting the piano up the stairs would have been impossible without Hilly. The move was accomplished with him on the bottom pushing and four of us pulling.

The loft was a weird environment. In the kitchen I found a can of seal meat. We opened it. It was maroon-colored and smelled fishy. No one ate any of it. The place was also decidedly haunted. It was my only experience with poltergeist manifestations. Gary stayed with us a lot and I thought they might be centered on his youthful angst, as is their wont. There were the standard knocks and taps in the walls. I was hanging a picture in the front, and as if in response to my hammer blows, something came crashing down in the back, far away, where no one was. The jerry-rigged pipes continually broke and spewed and there was a theory floated that the spirits considered us dirty.

There was a big fireplace near the kitchen area. One night a bunch of us attempted to light a fire but with no success. We eventually stopped and sat there, whereupon the bundle of old newspapers burst into flames seemingly by itself. All of this stuff is easily explained but I lean toward poltergeists.

One afternoon I was in the back when I heard a couple of odd grunts, and when I came out to investigate I saw Gary standing in front of the fireplace clutching a lamp and grimacing. He was getting shocked and was frozen. I knocked the lamp out of his hands and he collapsed. He was okay after a while.

Debbie had by then stopped working at the bar and had a piecework job soldering colored glass belt buckles for some local designer. This entailed creating a rounded ridge of solder around the edge of a small square of thick glass and attaching it to a brass frame. She did this up on the extremely derelict top floor. The top floor was a veritable shell—exposed beams and brick walls and a small hole in the roof. The belt-buckle creation was a tedious, painstaking operation, and Debbie insisted that invisible forces sometimes nudged her hand.

The veil was thinner on the Bowery. Everything was in flux around us. The proximity to CB's made for a constant stream of visitors. This was where we first met Nancy Spungen, who came to visit. One winter night a small group of people were sitting around when someone arrived from the street and announced, "There's a dead guy downstairs." We rushed down and, indeed, there was some poor dude laid out on the sidewalk in the snow almost in front of our door. He was on his back facing up with his hands extended as if in a gesture of greeting or supplication. His eyes were open and he had no shoes on. What had been a cheerful gathering became very sober and people drifted off as an ambulance arrived to collect this guy. Somebody said they had seen him walking barefoot in the snow earlier.

The homeless population was pretty big and some of these guys were very distressed. We were somewhat friendly with one fellow who we nicknamed Lon Chaney. He would wear odd clothing and was pretty upbeat about his situation. He would appear on the block wearing a top hat and long underwear that was spotted with dabs of paint that reminded me of Pollock or Larry Poons. We would donate to these guys when possible but we were broke most of the time. There was a wrecked empty storefront across the street that was lived in by some of the homeless locals. Some disagreement between the inhabitants of the abandoned storefront and their associates on the street led to a daylong siege that featured a couple of guys repeatedly hitting the front of the place with big wooden blue-painted police barriers. The resounding thuds went on for what seemed hours.

The liquor store was tragically bleak. The interior must have looked the same in 1930. The shelves were mostly empty and stocked with just a few varieties of booze. A brand of cheap wine, Night Train Express, had a really great label that depicted a silver-on-black mighty steam engine with its headlight blazing plunging through the darkness. The store did a brisk business; they sold a lot of Night Train, and the empty bottles were everywhere. The store was sometimes closed and on these occasions it would fall to us to deal with the building's heating system. We had a key to the liquor store and someone would have to descend into the creepy basement and let water into the huge, rusted steampunk boiler. I have no idea how this worked but there was a little glass tube that was a gauge that had to be filled to a line marked on its surface.

It was around Christmas and people had mostly fucked off out of town to visit relatives and such. The streets were empty. The only ones in the loft were Debbie, Gary, Howie, and myself. In the middle of night, the cats woke Gary and Howie and those guys woke us. The flame had gone out in the boiler and instead of heat, it was pumping whatever sooty oily substance fueled the thing into the building. I was quite dizzy and we all had black around our nostrils from breathing this stuff. We ran around opening windows and sat there freezing while the place aired out. The cats had without a doubt saved us.

I thought I glimpsed the ghost of a little kid watching me as I painted the wall around the doorway to the street stairs black. This could be attributed to intoxication, but as I've only ever had one more disembodied spirit experience, I like to think the kid was briefly there. As of this writing, considering the possible reality of ghosts is rather simplistic compared to the complex belief trends in the general population these days.

Benton was an extremely eccentric character. He possessed this sort of gentlemanly Southern charm combined with a radical anarchist worldview. He was dating a guy named Jonathan who worked on Wall Street. Benton and Jonathan both espoused a kind of biker chic. Jonathan would come back from work in a suit with his long hair tied back and change into leather-man gear—a vest, chaps, et cetera—and the two of them would smoke a bunch of angel dust. Angel dust was having a little renaissance on the scene. I smoked it a few times; on one occasion I watched as Sunday Man the cat manifested aspects of Chairman Mao. I have no idea what it was. The consensus was that it was some sort of animal tranquilizer but nobody really knew. People would be standing around in front of CB's smoking pot and some trickster would pass around a joint laced with angel dust and watch everyone get too high and stagger around like bugs. Benton and Jonathan smoked way too much of this shit. They got more and more nuts. Jonathan spent a whole evening screaming about seeing the ghost of Eric and how Tompkins Square was melting. He lost his voice for a few days. Benton became infatuated with a young Hells Angel.

One summer I stayed with some friends across the street from the Angels' headquarters on East Third Street. To me they didn't appear that menacing. They were more involved with personal projects; one week it seemed like all their bikes were converted to three-wheelers. I was walking down the block with a girlfriend and a big Angel who was standing in the middle of the sidewalk cracking a bullwhip actually stepped out of our way to let us pass. Still, we tried to dissuade Benton from making any contact with these guys, as we assumed they would frown on his advances. But he did go see them and they didn't really stomp him too much; he came back with a black eye and some bruising and might have been a little pleased with himself, though he did give up the idea of any further forays. The other issue with Benton was that he didn't always bother to come downstairs to the one functioning bathroom, resulting in his floor being cluttered with beer and malt-liquor bottles filled with piss.

The neighborhood wasn't evolving much; it was still a totally fringe community and very run-down. One of the local flophouses must have closed because Benton found a pile of doors on the street that had been used for the little cubicles that were rented by the day. He thought it would be a good home-improvement project to fence off the little roof in the back of the second floor with them. We spent hours hauling these gross old wooden doors up the stairs and out the back window. They did sort of enclose the space that was surrounded by a million windows that overlooked the big, overgrown feral-cat-filled courtyard. I don't know how much voyeurism went on there but there was plenty of opportunity.

Around the corner on Houston Street were a series of junk stores that we frequented a lot. In various pictures of Debbie from that period, she can be seen wearing a certain pair of what look like designer sunglasses, but actually they came from a big cardboard box in one of these stores that was filled with pairs of them. They came in black and tortoiseshell. They cost a dollar. A lot of people had them; Dee Dee wore some for a while. Another one of these stores was a fence, the guy selling small-time local stuff that was pillaged in the area. I was always borrowing guitars then. My favorite was an old Supro Ozark but I eventually had to return it. The fence dude, I guess, knew I was a musician and took me in the back to see a guitar he was selling. It was a Gibson ES-345 stereo model, a guitar that could easily be worth ten grand or more in today's predatory vintage-instrument market. I somehow scraped the two hundred bucks together and got it but I was paranoid that, since it obviously had been stolen out of a car or someone's house locally, if I played it I would get harassed. I didn't think it out much and took it to Forty-Eighth Street and traded it outright for a new and much worse Les Paul Junior that I didn't like and that I sold for a slight profit. So maybe I made fifty or a hundred bucks on the deal. The first in a long line of electric guitars that I sold but should have kept.

Everybody noticed these flyers on lampposts around CB's that said PUNK IS COMING. We assumed it was a band with the dumbest name possible, but it was John Holmstrom and Legs McNeil, two guys who were into cartoons and music who were attempting to start a magazine/newspaper with a much more hands-on personal approach that was closer to the musicians and local freaks than even the *Voice* or *SoHo Weekly News*. Everyone liked these two and were glad to contribute. *Punk* definitely provided us with a sense of empowerment. By the fourth issue, Debbie was the foldout. We did some sexy shots but John wanted something "more punk" so we did the images with her wearing the Vultures T-shirt and a black leather bikini bottom that Benton had made. (Benton was a good designer and cartoonist and he made us some life-size painted figures that Debbie would attack onstage.) The studded belt in the shots had been "borrowed" from the Dictators, who had left it in our mutual rehearsal space. The belt was an object of mild contention between the bands. The Vultures shirt was something I had that had been donated by Joey and Howie. They got it at an old-school sporting goods store in Brooklyn. We never found out what it was, exactly. It has since been framed.

I was walking on the street one day with a slightly drunken Legs, and just as we got in front of CB's he decided to jump over a parking meter. He succeeded only in bashing his head on the sidewalk, which created such a loud cracking sound that people in the club came running out. He was somehow okay, though.

John devised and directed two very involved *fumetti*, which are comic-style stories with photos instead of drawings. *The Legend of Nick Detroit* and *Mutant Monster Beach Party* were both collaborative affairs that involved many members of the scene. Roberta, Tom Hearn, and I shot a lot of the main images. Richard Hell was Nick Detroit, a private-detective type battling the Nazi Dykes, who were played by a whole bunch of the girls from the scene, including Terrence Sellers, Anya, Helen Wheels, and Debbie. A lot of the action was filmed on the Staten Island Ferry; the whole thing was very entertaining. Later the Mutant Monster found a tribe of surfers led by Joey Ramone battling Nazi Bikers. Another star-studded cast included cameos by Andy Warhol as a mad scientist and Edith Massey, John Waters's Egg Lady, who we'd all met at the First Annual Sleaze Convention in Wilmington, Delaware. Debbie was the female biker girl in this Romeo and Juliet tale. After much ado, Joey and Debbie finally hook up, whereupon Debbie turns into Edith, much to Joey's dismay.

Legs went on to describe various violent events and compile them into a book called *Please Kill Me*. I, of course, recommend the book, but all these things put together make the scene seem a bit more maniacal than it in fact was. I was party to two of the extreme events.

Jerry Nolan got into a fight with someone at Max's and in the course of wrestling around, his opponent stabbed him in the femoral artery with a broken bottle. I remember Jerry briefly sitting on the bottom of the stairs in the little foyer, which was covered in his blood, before Tommy Dean hustled him into a cab. If they'd waited for an ambulance, he mightn't have made it.

On a spring night Debbie and me were walking down the Bowery toward CB's when people came pouring out of the club. Apparently while Wayne County was onstage, Dick Manitoba had either heckled him or somehow provoked him, and Wayne, who was a tough customer, hit Dick with a mic stand, fracturing his collarbone. This led to the whole community splitting into Dick and Wayne factions that culminated in a big

to pot smoking, but I don't know how I could tell since I was stoned most of the time. We went back to smoking during rehearsals.

Then Clem took a trip to the UK to visit his girlfriend, Diane, who was studying at Oxford, no less. During the six weeks he was away, we all did more rehearsing and songwriting. There was a lot of concerted effort to develop things during this period, and we worked up a bunch of new songs. Clem had always been an Anglophile; he loved the Beatles and the Bay City Rollers, so he must have had a blissful vacation. We figured out a scheme whereby Clem would call the phone booth in CBGB's collect from a street callbox in London. We just would have a time figured out that fell within the club's primetime hours and various people would hang around asking Clem about his British adventures and going over the local gossip. A few months later, the phone company must have gotten onto Hilly because he said something to us but there wasn't anything for it and he seemed more amused than annoyed.

We were having a raving party in the loft on the day Clem returned. All the bands and friends of bands were there. Clem arrived straight from the airport. With him he had the new Dr. Feelgood *Malpractice* album, which was immediately put on the turntable and worshipped by everyone. The tight raw sound of these guys and the fact they were a three-piece wasn't lost on anyone, and comparisons were made to the Ramones. Dr. Feelgood influencing the New York music scene is a little-known footnote and by the time they played in Manhattan supported by the Ramones, their status for us was legendary.

During the aforementioned festival Hilly had a recording truck parked outside taping everything. By the time Hilly was attempting to put out a *Live at CBGB's* album, none of the A-list bands wanted to be on it. The record industry had descended and there was a lot of scrabbling for position. Bands wanted to stress their individuality and not be lumped into a whole scene, so the album missed recordings of us, the Ramones, Television, Patti, et cetera. The record that came out has tracks by the Tuff Darts, Mink DeVille, the Shirts, Sun Ra, and others. It's pretty great but there is a whole lost section that maybe still exists somewhere. The recording sessions were produced and engineered by Kim King, who'd played guitar with Lothar and the Hand People, and Craig Leon, who'd recently worked for Sire Records and was intrigued by what was happening in the New York scene. Marty Thau had always been a supporter. We knew him from the Stillettos days. Marty had a good sense for what was up and coming; his enthusiasm as manager of the Dolls was full-on, considering that they would never break in America. They were just too weird for the masses at the time. Marty had just formed a production company called Instant Records with Craig and Richard Gottehrer. Richard had been in the sixties group the Strangeloves, which had a big U.S. hit with "I Want Candy." The Strangeloves did a whole shtick that involved them being from Australia rather than the Bronx and Brooklyn. They have a long complicated backstory: Richard and his two partners, Bob Feldman and Jerry Goldstein, wrote the classic "My Boyfriend's Back" for the Angels in 1963 and "Sorrow" for the McCoys in 1965, a song that Bowie later recorded on his *Pin Ups* album. Richard came out of the Brill Building milieu in New York and I'm going to suggest you look that up if you're curious because I'm not getting into it here.

CHAPTER 7

Marty was really the one who pushed a Blondie agenda and after coming to some of our rehearsals, Richard liked us and agreed to do some recording with us. The consensus with the Instant Record crew was that our musical ideas outdistanced our abilities. We did a bunch of prep rehearsing and preliminary recording at the old Bell Studios where the Shangri-Las had recorded and then moved to Plaza Sound.

Craig had produced the first Ramones album with Tommy Ramone at Plaza Sound studios. They did it in a week for six grand. Plaza Sound is an amazing cavernous space up on the eighth floor of Radio City Music Hall. It was either constructed or modified for Italian conductor Arturo Toscanini. (Toscanini was an interesting character. Italian dictator Mussolini said he was the greatest conductor in the world. He started out as a Fascist but ended up declaring his hatred for Mussolini and getting beaten up by Blackshirts.) The whole floor is suspended on massive coil springs that prevent vibrations from orchestral rehearsals leaking out into the rest of the building. The Rockettes would rehearse up there too. The springs meant that equipment had to be dragged up a final set of stairs after arriving on the elevator. Radio City is famous for its huge Wurlitzer organ and there is another matching one in Plaza Sound that presumably was built for practice. The workings of the organ take up an entire room and blew our minds. Much of it is built of clean pale wood and is visually beautiful although only a handful of people have seen it. It has percussion modules!

It's got tuned snare and bass drums, shakers, bells, everything, and they're all physical, mechanical. It's got a MIDI interface now.

We had a lot of songs. We all decided on "X Offender" and "In the Sun" as a B side if this ever saw the light of day as a single. I played bass on "X Offender" and Gary played guitar. "In the Sun" was directly inspired by a song I was enamored of at the time: "Summer Means Fun," by Bruce and Terry, later covered by Jan and Dean. Richard pushed for the spoken-word intro to "X Offender" that was like the intro of "My Boyfriend's Back." Debbie wasn't that crazy about it but went along. Craig at the time was in love with compression. Compression is an audio process whereby top and bottom, high and low frequencies, are shoved into the middle. It makes loud softer and quiet louder and produces a punchy overall effect. I've seen comparisons drawn between "X Offender" and "Born to Run," but I didn't hear the Springsteen track till quite a while after we had recorded.

Craig and Richard shopped the tracks around and got nowhere. It seems incredible that there was resistance because we had a girl singer and a raw sound, but there we were. The whole downtown scene was in part a backlash against the trends in middle-of-the-road rock that had taken hold, all these guys who were lauded as master musicians and who didn't put their pictures on their album covers. The gatekeepers had established this boys' club that didn't want a bunch of do-it-yourself maniacs as members.

Marty and Richard both had connections to Larry Uttal, who had a label called Private Stock. Larry was another old-timer who had moved on from Bell Records to start his own label. Larry was also another Marty Scorsese character who wore leisure suits, polyester shirts, and gold chains. Private Stock was an odd choice; that year, Larry had a big disco hit with Walter Murphy's "A Fifth of Beethoven." They also had Frankie Valli and this guy from New Jersey, Peter Lemongello, who was super-middle-of-the-road but still was selling tons of records. Larry agreed to put out the single with an option for an album. The only thing he requested was that we rename the song, as "Sex Offender" was objectionable somehow. Aside from the being-told-what-to-do aspect, nobody minded changing the title to "X Offender"; we all thought the X was cool and presented a little double entendre.

Larry's daughter Jody was Private Stock's director of publicity and she had a pretty decent handle on the Blondie situation. The single started getting a little buzz. Reviewers asked for more copies. We would visit the stockroom at the company and take boxes of singles ourselves. I still have a bunch. Clem famously was very excited by hearing "X Offender" played on the CBGB's jukebox. Private Stock picked up the option to do an album.

The next time we played CBGB's, lo and behold, there was a larger-than-usual crowd that was paying attention. We played Max's with the Fast. Up until this show, older brothers Mandy and Miki shared the lead singing, with Mandy doing most of it. Younger brother Paul wasn't in the band but he was so popular that people were always lobbying to have him join. One day Jimmy arrived and said, "Mandy has abdicated!" This show was Paul's first; he'd just turned eighteen. Debbie and I are still close to Paul forty-five years later.

We did three shows in Cambridge, Massachusetts, that were amongst our first out-of-town endeavors. This involved a rented station wagon, since we needed a vehicle that could haul our gear and also have enough room for all of us. The shows, with local act the Boize, were well received and we drove back to Manhattan, arriving at the car-rental place, which was all the hell uptown, at seven in the morning. The car was returned and Debbie, Gary, and myself got on a bus going downtown. It happened to be July 4, 1976, which was a huge deal, being as it was the Bicentennial, the two-hundredth anniversary of the thing that is America. In New York it was designated the day of the tall ships, and the Hudson River was clogged with boats of all sizes. In later years it came out that this event had been the perfect cover for a couple of dudes to smuggle eight tons of Colombian weed into New York on sailboats.

We were quite burned out from having gotten little sleep and the three days of shows, and here we were on a bus that was packed with early-riser cheerful tourists wearing red, white, and blue outfits. The ride was long and we finally arrived at the Bowery at the very moment some extremely heavyweight large guy was, and there's no way to put this delicately, shitting on our doorstep. This actually happened and I will leave it to the reader to consider what the metaphor might be.

Gary was the first to get a haircut, with Clem and me following shortly after. Jimmy's hair was only a little long. At this time the stuff still available in thrift and junk stores was, by modern standards, amazing. We found a store right on the main street in Hoboken, New Jersey, that was a treasure trove of sixties men's fashions. What's called new old stock—unsold items still with labels and in packaging. Tab-collared shirts, pegged pants, pointy shoes, narrow ties, the whole nine yards. (We knew some people with clothing stores in the East Village and told them about the place in New Jersey, showed them samples, but nobody cared.) This went a long way toward shaping the band's design aesthetic as we attempted to embrace the Mod Rat Pack look and back away from the bell-bottomed excess of the seventies. Steve Sprouse had already given Debbie a pair of thigh-high black boots and designed some minidresses for her.

We had signed an album deal with Private Stock and, being idiots, didn't have a lawyer go over the contracts. I'm not sure how we would have actually paid for legal advice anyway. I think the prevailing attitude of everyone in the band then was "What the fuck." There wasn't much thought about legacy or how our current actions might affect the future and we all just wanted things to move forward.

In my collection of ephemera, I've got a little red Winsor &: Winsor & Newton (per company site) Newton notebook. In it are some weirdly overworked pencil drawings of people wrestling, drawn by Eric, and several pages in Debbie's handwriting of lists of band fund disbursements. One of the pages goes as follows:

$800 dollar advance from record company for equipment
Gary advanced $70.00
DH & Chris rent $200.00
Jim $50.00
Gary $10.00
Jim $10.00
Marshall amp head $240.00
Volume pedal Jimmy $40.00
Gas and toll Boston Larry $10.00
Sticks Clem $20.00

Strings-couch-cord-pot $50.00
Broom keys T.P. D.H. $10.00
Party pre Max's date $20.00
To Pay C.P. expenses $40.00
Parking lot $5.00
Jimmy $25.00

There's some mysterious stuff here like the couch and some of the initials, and I suspect we'll never know who Larry was. We did have a guy with a truck for a while but his name was Monty. He looked like he came from another century, as did the truck. He might have been a pirate; always wore a very stained seaman's cap and a very stained pair of overalls. His whole demeanor shouted pirate. I don't remember if we got more than eight hundred bucks for signing our first record contract, but probably not.

We were just about to start working on the album when things declined past the point of no return with Benton. His friend Jonathan and him had procured two gigantic Irish setters and moved to the demolished third floor after Sprouse had fled. Benton would wander into Debbie's and my room in the middle of the night, leading these dogs, and after waking us up, he'd rant for a while. We thought that his extreme sugar intake combined with whatever substances he was taking was contributing to his instability. He consumed tons of sugar. Maybe he just wanted to move closer to the bathroom or maybe he was just sick of us; we had gotten all serious of late with all the business and self-management stuff, and he threw us all out. We tried appealing since we had a lot going on, but we had to leave. We found a small floor-through loft on the top floor of a brownstone-type building on West Seventeenth Street and moved in. It had a big skylight in the low kitchen ceiling and I set up a darkroom in the bathroom area. One of our first guests was Marty Thau and we sat around playing the single repeatedly.

The recording process commenced. Gottehrer and Craig were enthusiastic and fun to deal with. Somewhere we found this giant advertising banner that we added to with spray paint. We hung it in the studio: BLONDIE SAYS SUPPORT MENTAL HEALTH.

These two guys, who were sort of stalker superfans, lent us a Marshall amp that, according to them, had belonged to Hendrix. Nobody believed them but we used the amp. These two guys, Gino and Mike, would take out odd Blondie ads in the *Voice* that would have strange catchphrases that I don't remember.

Most impressive, Richard knew and delivered Ellie Greenwich. Look her up if you don't know; there's just too much to get into. As I said, by this time I had come to rapturously adore the Shangri-Las, which Ellie had helped establish. She cowrote "River Deep—Mountain High" for Ike and Tina Turner with her longtime partner Jeff Barry and Phil Spector. She wrote scores of early and midsixties hits.

Ellie sang on this ballad we had called "In the Flesh" and on a sort of Latin-influenced track called "Man Overboard." She was a pro. It gave the project credibility as well as the great sound she delivered with the two girl singers she brought, Micki and Hilda Harris.

Clem and Gary's friend Ronnie Toast would give me these lyrics he wrote on little notebook pages, envelopes, napkins, et cetera. His poems were great in a surreal, deconstructionist way and Gary and me did four songs with him: "Starbeast," "A Slip of the Razor," "Cautious Lip," and "Rifle Range." "Rifle Range" made it onto the record.

The songs were done with a semi-live feel; we were dealing with things we had been playing for close to a year. We did a few overdubs and Debbie overdubbed the vocals. There wasn't that much refining in the studio; we all just tried to do our parts as best we could.

One of the last songs to be recorded was this odd one I had called "Attack of the Giant Ants," basically a sort of calypso conga line homage to the B-movie horror genre and an expression of my affection for giant monsters and things apocalyptic. We decided to create a sound-effects section, a sort of Orson Welles *War of the Worlds* reference. Gottehrer knew how to get this done and sent us to a sound-effects specialty company. It was in a huge loft in midtown filled with racks of records. These records all had the same label and were categorized into sections. This was what we'd now call samples, but you'd buy the record (for more than what a regular record cost, maybe twenty or thirty bucks, which was a lot) and with it the rights to the material. I looked at a lot of titles; one that stuck in my head was *Children of Evil*. There were lots of musical cues for sale but we just got sounds: people walking, crowds, screams, traffic, explosions, and animal noises. We used a slowed-down elephant as the voice of the monster. It came out great and the very last thing on the record is Marty Thau playing some cocktail piano in the fade, a few bars of "Laura," which he said was the only thing he knew how to play.

Gottehrer knew this guy, Peter Leeds, who had managed Debbie's folk-rock band the Wind in the Willows in the late sixties. Richard played the record for him and Peter liked it. We saw him at a party and he expressed interest in managing us. He told us that if things didn't work out, we could just walk away from the deal. You know that meme GIF of Justin Timberlake in a suit staring blankly into the camera that has as one of its captions *You can't possibly believe that?* That should go here.

I was still dealing with my old apartment, collecting welfare checks once a month, and paying the rent as it changed hands; various friends were always coming and going. The weird advantage that I gained at this period was the guy I was assigned as a caseworker at the Fourteenth Street welfare office was a CBGB's attendee who knew who I was and was very sympathetic. It was a bit like *Fight Club* where the conspiratorial club members came from all walks of life. It drastically reduced the amount of time I had to devote to dealing with New York City welfare red tape.

We kept at it, doing lots of shows and in late October, we signed on for this sort of mini-festival thing with the Dictators, Mink DeVille, and the Demons at this large venue that was right on Second Avenue and First Street. This was an ancient crumbling gym/hall called the Quando Gym. Our old buddy Tim Jackson, Thoth, made a spray-paint poster that misspelled the name as *Cuando*. An odd bit of synchronicity about the poster is that it lists places where tickets were available and one of these was Harnik's Happy House at 1403 Avenue J in Brooklyn, a little greeting-card shop right near where I'd grown up. Harnik's was where I'd bought my first records in the days before full-on record stores were everywhere. It had a rack of bins for singles that somebody carefully labeled with the song titles.

The gig at the gym, of course, ran way later than expected and Debbie, me, and a few others found ourselves sitting inside a small martial arts studio/dojo storefront that was next to the entrance to the gym on First Street close to the junk store where I'd bought the plaster saint. I don't remember exactly who knew the owner dude or if he'd just invited us in to be sociable but he was a nice guy. After we sat around bullshitting for a while the door opened and this large guy who was obviously pretty drunk came in and joined the conversation. Things started out okay but this guy gradually got more belligerent and rude, to the point that the dojo owner asked him to leave. This, of course, made the drunken guy more pissed off and he finally grabbed the owner by the shoulders. I guess this person was too dumb or stoned to realize where he was, and in an instant, just blurringly fast, the martial arts guy zapped his hand onto the guy's face and pressed on his eyes with two fingers, and the guy collapsed into a heap on the floor. It took maybe two seconds. The martial arts guy looked at him lying there and said, "Gee, I hope I didn't do that too hard." He then grabbed him by the heels and dragged him out to the street in front of the place, where he lay for about ten minutes before getting up and staggering off toward Houston Street. We went on at two thirty in the morning and opened with "I'll Be a Big Man in Town," by the Four Seasons. It is really an awesome song and summed up our finally rising out of the downtown scene. The crowd had stayed to see us.

That album, *Blondie,* was released about six weeks later. Leeds, who'd slipped into a default management position, got a photographer he was familiar with from advertising, Shig Ikeda, to do the cover and associated promo shots. The cover image is one of the strongest of all the album covers; everyone did their neo-mod look very successfully. But when they were doing some solo shots of Debbie, she was urged to wear a see-through black mesh shirt that was part of the small wardrobe brought by whatever stylist was there. When she expressed hesitation about having her tits out in these shots, she was told that the frame was "from the shoulders up." I witnessed this exchange. Of course Private Stock then proceeded to print a ton of posters of the whole image, boobs and all. I don't think it was the semi-nudity thing that bothered Debbie so much as having been bullshit-ted. The posters were all over Times Square and we heard that people had thought they were ads for a massage parlor called Blondie. We yelled at Larry but he just gave us this pleading "I just want to break you!" line and we gave up. The posters are valuable now, I suppose.

The album was well received and a theme of various reviews was

"These guys sucked but the record is good," with most mentioning our sixties and girl-group references. I'd always suspected the power of recording was tangible, that the process could produce something greater than the sum of its parts, as it were. The apartment on Seventeenth Street was the first place I heard one of the songs, "X Offender," on the radio.

The apartment was a little suspect. There were three other tenants who each had a floor. Below us was a girl Jimmy had briefly dated, a model, Maria. Then a photographer guy who I knew very vaguely from the art-school scene, then, on the first floor, this Bobby Short–like pianist who was also some kind of crisis counselor. He was really nice but some of his clients would occasionally lurk around and we found a bloodstained mattress on the roof. Also at this time everyone in the Greater New York area was favored with the attentions of one Son of Sam, a serial killer who was stalking the outer boroughs and shooting people. Sam had a predilection for girls with long hair, so walking home at night was spooky at times. It eventually turned out that Son of Sam lived next to and was connected to Untermyer Park in Yonkers, where, after he got busted, he claimed to have gone to satanic cult rituals, et cetera. Mr. Untermyer, whose first name was also Sam, was a rich guy who took over this big estate and made it into a park filled with all kinds of imported columns, fake man-made concrete grottoes, and waterfalls. He wanted to leave it to the city as a public park but after he died nobody wanted it and it just sat there rotting. Earlier, the buddy of mine from Brooklyn who had a car would drive a bunch of us there to hang around the fake nature and get high. We did see some weird things. We came upon a fake cave that had a Virgin Mary statue in it, the walls all around painted with pentacles and the usual awkward devil stuff. We were walking away with the statue when these younger kids approached us and asked us to please give it back to them, saying, "We need that!" As far as I know Untermyer's is still there, deteriorating and providing sanctuary to satanic stoners.

The year 1976 was nearing its end and somebody from the Parks Department got in touch and asked if we would play a New Year's Eve show for the city. The show took place at Bethesda Terrace in Central Park. The stage was set up in the fountain! It was a cold night and there was snow about. A couple of those heat-blower things in the fountain with us helped a little. Debbie was wearing some silver lamé winter coat that might have been borrowed because I don't remember it later on. The Bread and Puppet Theater was a radical theater group active around New York since the early sixties, and at midnight these giant puppet hands came marching down the stairs to the fountain; it was a great surreal moment. We played Booker T.'s "Time Is Tight" to go with the hands-of-time theme. We got paid five hundred bucks about two months later.

We played a bunch in January and then Leeds booked a series of gigs in California and flew us out there. I think it was Gary's first plane ride. This was the first time I'd gone from a cold climate (New York in February) to a warm, sunny one (Los Angeles), and after the flight we all stood around the hotel lobby in a shell-shocked blur with too-heavy clothes on in the balmy weather.

The motel we were at was the Bel Air Sands, a kind of Spahn Movie Ranch deal without the cowboy/horse vibe; it was all the way at the end of Sunset where it crosses the 405. This place had a half-finished atmosphere, lots of raw dusty spaces between the rows of rooms. Leeds had cut a deal with the hotel guy for us to do a big blowout show on Catalina in exchange for some reduced rates. Of course, bringing a bunch of raving punks out to this pastoral little island didn't fly with the town council or whoever; they were worried about bodies being pitched off the ferry even before anyone got there, and the gig never happened. By this time our biggest West Coast supporter, Rodney Bingenheimer, the mayor of Sunset Strip, was pumping the record on KROQ radio out of LA and the scene there was primed. We had a big party that ended up with a mild fight with some other guests and we got kicked up the hill to worse rooms.

Before the first show at the Whisky a Go Go, which had Tom Petty opening for us, we were summoned by Leeds to his room at the Sunset Marquis to finalize the management deal. On the way up in the elevator, Gary expressed his grave concerns. He didn't like Leeds at all and of course we should have listened to him, but we didn't, just pressured him to go along. Leeds told us that if we didn't sign his management deal, he'd go back to New York and leave us in California. We had had some jokingly sparse legal advice back in New York—we met with a Private Stock attorney for half an hour, and his whole assessment was "If you trust the guy, then do it." I often wonder if smoking so much pot made me a business idiot. I'll never really know.

We were in the Whisky the night before the first show at an album-release party for a Kim Fowley–designed band, the Hollywood Stars. These guys were sort of the end of an era. They were all dressed in bell-bottoms and long scarves. Maybe these guys were a glimpse into the hair-band future but at the moment they were behind the crush of coming events.

Gary's girlfriend, Lisa Persky, knew a guy who was working on a science fiction movie, and Gary, Lisa, Debbie, and myself were invited to a soundstage where they were doing miniature photography. The movie was called *Star Wars* and we saw a bunch of little spaceships with funny wings on stands and a lot of gray-painted wooden pieces that they said was from a trench on a space station. I thought about stealing a piece of the gray-painted wood, since they said it had been already filmed, but I didn't do it, something about which I am eternally regretful. In an office area there were big, very detailed blueprints of some of the ships that I later realized were just made to entertain the people working on the project; they were that deep into it.

We played at the Whisky for ten days with Tom Petty and the Ramones. Debbie had a wedding dress she'd found in a junk store and one night before going on, Petty spray-painted his initials on it. She would pull off this massive dress and reveal whatever outfit she was wearing. This caused much of the fake-news music media to gleefully report: "She pulls her clothes off onstage!" We noticed that as the days wore on, the kids in the crowd were starting to emulate our mod aesthetic. Just a few shows in, people in the crowd were wearing a lot of suit jackets with narrow ties, miniskirts, et cetera.

After one of the shows with the Ramones, we were all in the dressing-room area upstairs with a lot of people. Malcolm McLaren was there with a small entourage. He said something snarky to one of his friends and Johnny Ramone overheard whatever it was and took issue. He picked up his blue Mosrite guitar and came at Malcolm swinging it at his head but narrowly missed and Malcolm fled the room. This was another of my favorite rock and roll moments.

We traveled up to San Francisco for a couple of shows at the Mabuhay

Gardens, which was a weird old Filipino-themed nightclub that was on the Broadway main drag in the middle of all the strip joints. The local punk scene was thriving and we did shows with the band Crime.

When we got to the Mabuhay, there was no graffiti on the dressing room or the backstage area walls, nothing whatsoever. We did the first graffiti, writing stuff about Ronnie Toast and whatever else. Local musician and great photographer Jonathan Postal documented this. There are pictures he took of us in front of the stuff we wrote on the otherwise bare white walls. By the time we returned, the walls were not only covered in writing, they were obliterated. In places, the walls had seemingly dissolved under the layers of graffiti.

While in LA we got word that Iggy, who was mounting a sort of comeback—it had been four years between the Stooges' *Fun House* and his first solo album, *The Idiot*—wanted Blondie to open his U.S. tour. Amazingly his band would include David Bowie playing keyboards. Our minds were blown. We came back to New York, had a couple of days off, and did two nights at Max's. The second night we did two shows to make sure we were good and fucking wasted. The second show was at two a.m. and right after that we got into our very crappy RV and headed to Montreal. Let me interject here that touring in 1977 was nothing like the modern Live Nation type of industrial artifact that it is today. Our shitty RV was a good example of the primitivism of the era. I think we had a kind of day off that was spent traveling. What I do remember is staggering out of the crappy RV and climbing the stairs to our dressing room in Le Plateau Theater, and Iggy and Bowie just standing there in the hall waiting for us.

They were great. There wasn't any class warfare. The tour was more than twenty shows and we got a sound check on all but one. Iggy and Bowie were about having the whole show go smoothly and being as entertaining as possible. It was amazing as an introduction to what we'd keep doing for the next forty-five years.

The Iggy band was Soupy Sales's two sons Hunt and Tony on drums and bass, respectively; guitar was Ricky Gardiner, who remains a bit obscure but is brilliant. Ricky wrote "The Passenger" with Iggy and provided that most amazing guitar pattern. He wore overalls at every show I recall. And Bowie was on keyboards. Bowie would position himself off to the side on stage right. He was being quite generous in this situation, acting as a sideman because he loved Iggy. Everybody knew he was there but he wanted Iggy to be the star. It was pretty inspirational.

David's keyboard rig was simple but effective. He had a large Hammond-style organ with a synth on it. I don't know what brands or models they were but I'm sure they were very specific and borderline exotic. Part of Bowie's feed went through a large Leslie cabinet (basically an amp with a physically rotating speaker) that was possibly modified to produce huge sound levels. This thing was kept in the wings, far away from the stage, and miked.

Bowie was in this period where he wouldn't fly. I don't know why but he wouldn't do it. He took ships to and from Europe. He traveled in a limo with his driver/bodyguard Tony Mascia. Tony fittingly plays Bowie the alien's driver in *The Man Who Fell to Earth*. Tony was a super-nice unassuming guy, and Debbie and me got to know him some over the following years. So David would take these long trips in the back of this limousine, stretched on the seat. There were a lot of dates, though, so the drives weren't too horrendous, but almost everyone else flew.

I saw Iggy's show a lot as the tour progressed. We all hung around a bit, though Iggy spent a lot of time in his various hotels with his girl-friend, and David spent a lot of time driving. We had some weird conver-sations with Bowie about Tom Verlaine's hairdo. The punk or new wave emerging scene fascinated Bowie and I got the impression he would have liked to have been around more during the early CBGB's period. I think it was backstage at the Chicago show that I managed to get some photos of Debbie with Iggy and Bowie. Bowie was a little cautious and I got only a couple with him, but Iggy was down and I took a nice series of him and Debbie interacting.

One day Debbie told me that David had been alone with her and asked, "Can I fuck you?" to which she replied, "I don't know, can you?" That really happened; I guess he figured it couldn't hurt to ask. It didn't affect Debbie's opinion of him; she, of course, still thought highly of him and she also told me that he'd given her tips on working the stage. He'd told her to think of it in three parts, to consider the different sections and keep her movements and attentions evenly distributed between the corresponding audience sections. Iggy hit on her too but she was gracious about it; she gave them both rainchecks, as it were.

When we got to the Masonic Auditorium in Detroit, the Iggy home-town crowd went crazy. Girls in the front row threw underwear at him and the crowd tossed leather jackets, cameras, money, and assorted offerings up on the stage.

In Seattle we stayed at the Edgewater Inn, a big building that sits out on the water of Elliott Bay. In 1964 the Beatles stayed there and the place is filled with press shots of them hanging out a window holding fishing poles. After the show some kids approached us and invited us to a party at their local punk house, an old beat-up Victorian-style small mansion that these guys had somehow taken over. Clem, Gary, and Jimmy went. The place was an Iggy shrine. The walls were covered in Iggy graffiti. I showed up an hour later with Iggy. The place was buzzing. Iggy sat around and talked to people for a while and then we went upstairs to where a bunch of kids were jamming furiously in a little room. The stage was a big board on a mattress. Iggy jumped up and grabbed a mic, followed by Gary, Clem, and me, and we commandeered the kids' instruments. We did "Backdoor Man" and "Gimmie Shelter" and improvised some other stuff. We proba-bly went at it for over a half an hour on the bouncing stage. The room was full of kids with more standing in the hall. On several later trips to Seattle, I'd be approached by somebody who said they or someone they knew had been at this legendary event. I don't think any of us had thought about contributing to Seattle's underground-music history.

The tour wound down in California. We'd been on tour for three months and things were fragmented. We were invited to a party for the Tubes in San Francisco. Jimmy, Gary, and Clem got there late and were denied access due to overcrowding. Bowie was inside this storefront al-ready and naturally a fight broke out with the bouncer and in the ensuing melee, Jimmy managed to smash one of the big plate glass windows of the place. The owner wanted to take out a contract on Jimmy but Bowie paid for the window. In later years I found out the guy throwing the party who'd wanted to smash Jimmy was in fact someone I knew from my 1969 insan-ity period: Super Joel. Super Joel had briefly lived in an apartment next to my mom's on Ocean Avenue and we'd gotten pretty close. I wonder if it all could have been avoided if I'd gone. During the fight Penelope Houston of the band the Avengers, who was with the Blondie guys, jumped on the bouncer and allegedly bit him. Word reached us months later that at an Avengers gig at the Mabuhay, someone jumped onstage and bit Penelope in retribution. I can't attest to the reality of any of this.

The final show was in Santa Monica. For a first big tour, it was an amazing introduction. We went on to do tours with bands that were competitive and weird, and maybe this setup spoiled us somewhat.

We went to LA for another week at the Whisky. One of the nights included a big jam with Joan Jett, and Hunt and Tony Sales, and a version of "I Want to Be Your Dog" that included Debbie on a leash and Rodney playing a single note on the keyboards.

Marty Thau had started his own record label back in New York. Red Star records would release albums of Suicide, the Real Kids, the Fleshtones, and others. Marty was always ahead of it and he asked me if I would help him land and produce the *Eraserhead* soundtrack for the label. He set up a meeting between David Lynch and me at our Hollywood hotel. Somebody had erroneously told me that *Eraserhead*'s director was also the star of the movie, so when Lynch showed up at the room, I wasn't sure who he was, and he didn't know what I looked like, and in what was a very David Lynch sequence, we both sat there without speaking for about five minutes before either one of us thought to introduce themselves. I saw Lynch a few years ago and asked him if he remembered this, but he said he didn't. Marty never got the soundtrack.

The West Coast Blondie buzz was full-on and Phil Spector appeared backstage at the Whisky in a long black cape. He kept everyone stuck in the dressing-room area while he held forth and was totally weird and belligerent. He invited Debbie and me to visit him and left with his bodyguards. Later that night Debbie was walking on Sunset when a limo pulled up and the door opened. It was Phil and he creepily told her to get in, but she thanked him and beat a retreat. The next day we went up to his mansion/castle in Alhambra.

Phil came to the door with a bottle of Manischewitz wine in one hand and a presumably loaded model 1911 .45 automatic in the other. He was acting performatively drunk and doing a W. C. Fields voice for almost the whole visit. We were with a couple of other company guys and he herded everyone into a big living room, which was absolutely freezing. He indicated that we had to remain seated and proceeded to talk about nothing I can remember. There was a big grand piano in the room and he played a while and then asked Debbie to join him sitting at the piano bench for a duet of some Ronettes song that I also can't remember. Debbie was wearing tall, tan, thigh-high boots and after they finished the song Phil stuck the .45 into the top of her right boot and said "Bang, bang!" in the W. C. Fields voice, which he obviously thought was hysterically funny. I remember that.

Finally he asked us if we wanted to hear what he was working on and he took us into a music room and played us a Leonard Cohen track. But he played it back so loud on these little overdriven speakers that it just sounded like a distorted mess. Industrial moaning. We stood there politely pretending to listen and one of the record-company guys poked me and whispered sarcastically, "If you play your cards right, you can sound like this too." In later years I found out he'd pulled a gun on Leonard Cohen too. I don't have any doubt that he killed that girl, although whether by accident or deliberately, we'll never know.

CHAPTER 8

We'd made some inroads on both U.S. coasts, and presumably people in other parts of the country saw Debbie in her zebra outfit in *Creem* magazine, even though they probably hadn't heard the music. Back in New York we did two nights at the *Punk* magazine benefit at CBGB's. *Punk* was saved and we immediately headed to the UK with Television on a hastily thrown-together tour that would be presented as a "New York experience."

I love Television; we would frequently cover Verlaine's "Venus" and in later years "See No Evil," but the pairing of us and them was a little disparate. Besides that, everybody then, myself included, was pretty egomaniacal, and seeking fame or success under these difficult conditions made for, shall we say, a lack of harmony. "Marquee Moon" had gotten to number thirty on the UK charts and there was a lot of anticipation for Television; for us, maybe a little.

We were set up in a completely wrecked formerly grand hotel in Kensington. This place was under construction but it was hard to tell if it was being renovated or torn down. One of the main issues was the phone system not working, and we went elsewhere to make calls. Our room was a literal garret near the top, picturesque but really little. Debbie said the spirit of Coleridge, presumably Samuel Taylor, the English poet, entered her. I don't know if he had ever stayed there but if he did at least he wouldn't have had to deal with the shitty phones.

We spent a few days acclimatizing and doing press, including a visit to the offices of *Sniffin' Glue* magazine, which was a couple of guys in a pretty empty few rooms that had graffiti all over the walls. *Sniffin' Glue* had started out as a Xeroxed-type fanzine but wound up with a circulation of fifteen thousand and some influence. King's Road had been central to rock lifestyle since the sixties and we found it entertaining. Malcolm and Vivienne Westwood's store at World's End was in its Seditionaries phase. The original Boy shop looked like it had been decorated by a flamethrower; the back wall had a giant charred burn that circled out from a central point. They had some singed shirts in the window. The road was also home to an endless parade, a children's crusade of fantastic punk fashion, by then a well-established aesthetic that was do-it-yourself and radical. Over the years I've seen many portrayals of this period in films and on TV, and most present the punks as a bunch of grizzled mid-fortyish killer types rather than the young, somewhat innocent, and beautiful kids that were everywhere.

On top of all this, the whole country was in the throes of the Queen's Jubilee, which marked the twenty-fifth anniversary of Elizabeth II getting elected queen. The Sex Pistols were happily in the midst of it all with their anthemic "God Save the Queen," which was number two on the UK charts. Posters for the song that portrayed the officially sanctioned royal portrait pierced by a safety pin were everywhere. It was an exciting moment.

One of our earliest, if not our first, encounter with the BBC was very Britishly eccentric. The Brits have a wonderful connection to language, speaking, and storytelling that I appreciate more as time goes on. We were reached out to by an older gentleman who asked Debbie and myself to appear on his radio show. So one evening we went to the great old Broadcasting House that's between Oxford Street and Regent's Park, across from the very beautiful All Souls Church. At this point there were still old-timers in the building wearing tuxedos, a throwback to the Blitz years when people would dress up in their finest during those dark times to maintain the stiff-upper-lip sensibility in the face of the Nazi onslaught. We went on the show, which was in a little old-fashioned studio with charming antiquated gear. And here's the thing: The host probably didn't have too much of an idea about Blondie but he knew we were punks and his other guest was an

older gent who had written and self-published a book about punts. *Punts,*
we learned, are these odd rectangular boats that are pushed with long poles
about the waterways of Cambridge University. I think these things are exclusive to Cambridge; I don't know. Anyway, the whole point of the episode
of this dude's show was this semi-elaborate pun that contrasted the punks
and punts. I can't remember exactly what we talked about, but the punts
guy didn't have a clue about punk music.

The first show we did in the UK was a kind of warm-up in a place
called the Village Bowl in Bournemouth, a town about five and a half
hours southwest of London. This band called Squeeze opened for us. I
don't know exactly what we were expecting. We knew things would be
different over there. Again, in New York, there really wasn't very much
rock dancing; the audiences were still in the beatnik-coffee-shop mode of
sitting and paying attention. The LA crowd was a bit more demonstrative
but they also would stand around and watch. So we were very pleasantly
surprised when we got onto the very low stage and the surrounding crowd
went absolutely fuck-nuts, thrashing around and pogoing madly. It was
extreme; I was sucked into another unknown alternate life. I think I'd seen
representations of this but I'd never been in the middle of it.

The gig, being a sort of preview, wasn't open to the press but one of
the papers made a big deal out of having snuck in a female journalist in
a boilersuit. I had to have *boilersuit* explained by our new British press
agent, Alan Edwards, who was thrilled by the whole situation. Alan is still
with us—hi, Alan!

The next day we were in Glasgow for the first time. By some quirk of
fate, the Ramones and Talking Heads were playing at Strathclyde University. The local media was all about "CBGB's in Glasgow," with the
four bands playing on two nights. We went to see them and it was a nice
reunion with all these guys, even though we'd seen each other only a
short time before. The show was in some kind of big gym room and when
the bands came on, the old wooden floor bounced along with the crowd
jumping around.

When we showed up for the sound check the next day, we were perturbed to see all our gear set up in front of Television's. Nowadays I'm
spoiled from what's called the changeover, where one set of gear is moved

offstage and replaced by the next. We had only two roadies in 1977 and this wasn't gonna happen. The other thing was that the Glasgow Apollo theater was this cavernous space with a fifteen-foot-high stage that I guess was made to discourage an interactive audience/band concert experience. In other words, the fans couldn't rush the stage without siege ladders. Successfully playing in big echoey places is a learned skill. Another reminder that the room you're in is a part of your equipment. It takes a while to get this.

There was a lot of scuttlebutt about Verlaine needing all that room onstage to just stand there somberly while Debbie, who was pretty active, was allotted less real estate. It was two sets and we weren't happy. We had Television's soundman onstage complaining; sound issues, of course; and general discouragement. The press probably mentioned that we sucked; I don't remember. There was a lot of up and down in the media. Again, it was an odd pairing of bands. Television had this kind of serious persona and was dubbed "the Ice Kings," while Blondie was pushing this "fun" manifesto that Ronnie Toast had written for the liner notes on the album.

The tour wound around the country and we took in as much as we could. There was no show in Liverpool, but on a day off in Manchester we took a train there to see the legendary landscape. Lime Street station was beautiful; wildflowers were growing in cracks. The remains of the Cavern Club was a rubble-strewn empty lot. I took some pictures.

I have this theory that the farther east one travels, the more people group together in mass clumps of humanity. In Los Angeles, extreme pedestrian distance is maintained, but in London, crowds on the street all squeeze together. People see you coming toward them and walk into you anyway, not out of discourtesy; more out of not being so avaricious about personal space. The crowds at the shows had a tribal affinity for each other that I loved. We were getting great reactions, always got encores, but the press was still up and down in its appreciation.

Finally we got to London for two nights at the Hammersmith Odeon. The Hammersmith, nowadays called the Apollo, is a great room that we went on to play many times. I think by then we were a little more comfortable with playing on these bigger stages. On the night that the media was in attendance, right before we went onstage, somebody gave all the band members a hit of cocaine. This was a help in providing a more frenetic display and the crowd seemed to love the show. We did encores of Ronnie and the Daytonas' "Little GTO" that was probably much faster than the original and we did the Dolls' "Jet Boy." We must have been a hard act to follow at that moment. In a lull in between songs in Television's set, an audience member yelled out, "Prove it, Tommy boy!" which was a reference to a Television song title as well as a demand they live up to their hype—meta heckling. The press turned in our favor. One influential journalist devoted his over-the-top review to discussing his love of Debbie and how amazing we were.

We pledged to return to the UK and moved on to Europe. We played at the Paradiso in Amsterdam for the first of many shows over the years. Amsterdam was then and still is this magical, hedonistic safe-house city. The huge stained-glass windows at the central American Hotel have a decidedly pagan vibe, with depictions of what appear to be witches or Saint Lucy celebrants wearing crowns of lit candles. Clem and me bought some hashish from a guy on the street that turned out to be a piece of a candy bar.

I had this little cheapo radio with a built-in cassette recorder and was frequently making radio tapes as we traveled. Still today I will get very obsessed about some piece of music, some song fragment that I'll play repeatedly. We were in Belgium and I was out somewhere in a park or such listening to the local radio. I was switching stations when I came upon this neoclassical piece playing. I'd missed the beginning and any title but recorded about two-thirds of it. After it played, the DJ just said, "*Quelle musique!*" and that was it. During the final section of the piece the Belgian radio played three hourly signal beeps—*beep, beep, beep*—that just showed up and weirdly became part of the track for me. The song itself is achingly beautiful; it's become one of my favorite pieces of music. I played this song fragment for years. It would always bring me back to this wild period of my youth, running around with Debbie and the band, Europe, love, loss, the envelope of time that consumes. But I couldn't find out what the hell the track was. I played it for people—nothing. I listened to the tape for thirty years or more. Finally, around 2003 or so, I saw Pedro Almodovar's film about sketchy nuns, *Dark Habits*. This piece of music was the opening title! I knew it predated the movie and was from elsewhere, but you know what? Pedro didn't credit it! I studied the end titles and listened to the four tracks listed *and it wasn't there*! I couldn't believe that Pedro used this thing for opening his movie and left it anonymous. Another few years went by and by some quirk of accidental research I found an IMDB message board for *Dark Habits* where people were asking about the same track! Then finally, after checking this message board for another year or so, somebody who I'll always be grateful to posted the solution and it took me a minute to find the track on YouTube. It's "Valse Crépusculaire" from a Dirk Bogarde movie called *Providence* and it's by legendary film composer Miklós Rózsa, who scored *Lost Weekend, The Killers, Ben-Hur*. I don't know if holding my phone to the speaker and finding out what song it was immediately might have taken some of the romance from the project but I probably would have still listened to it for forty years anyway.

We came back to New York and intended to start another record. As I mentioned, everyone was somewhat of an egomaniac, and rifts appeared in the band fabric. Maybe there are some bands that have all harmonious relations, maybe the B-52s always get along, but conflicts seem to be part of humans working together in any situation. A band should be a monarchal democracy, where everyone has a voice but there's one shot-caller. Maybe this is what makes cults successful. I always identified with Debbie and we were very closely together, so I just never felt threatened by her getting more attention than me. Debbie was frequently pulled aside to have her picture taken alone and it made for some tension. I can't pretend to know, however, what being outside the Chris and Debbie bubble was actually like for the other guys.

Before we left, Debbie's Camaro got stuck in reverse and she'd backed it downtown from Thirty-Fourth Street and put it in a garage. One of Clem's buddies from New Jersey, Vinnie, picked it up and said he would try and fix it. As we were recovering from our overseas jaunt, Vinnie called and told us of the car's ultimate fate. He couldn't get it going, it was dead, and he couldn't take it to a salvage yard to be squashed into a cube without a bill of sale, so he'd pushed it off a cliff. Maybe bits of it still exist on this plane. Debbie wrote a song called "I'm on E" that references these events.

We did a few shows at the Village Gate on Bleecker Street. Gary wanted to play guitar and sing more. He was dissatisfied. We were assembling songs to go on the next record. I'd come upon some K-Tel golden oldies–type collection and I immediately got stuck on this one track called "Denise" by Randy and the Rainbows. An old doo-wop song that I must have heard over the years but hadn't previously focused on. Debbie and me started playing it on repeat. We both thought it was a great song with a terrific hooky melody. I thought that a familiar old song might make inroads with American radio. Gary and maybe other members thought it was a bad idea when we discussed doing a version of "Denise." There were rivalries forming. There was some focus on Gary's stage movement; Leeds especially was worried that he would knock Debbie in the head with his bass. We liked Gary's song "I'm Always Touched by Your Presence, Dear" but were less enthusiastic about another one called "Scenery." We did a demo of it and Gary thought that Debbie was holding back while I felt that she just couldn't deliver it that well. Clem and Gary remained close but the conflicts were too apparent. Finally, Leeds called us and told us he had fired Gary. Gary was on record saying he quit. Leeds said that we never would have done it. It was scary to have our familiar situation altered like this and I still liked Gary, but we didn't object.

We went back into Plaza Sound with Gottehrer. Marty and Craig had gone their various ways and weren't involved directly. There were still tensions. Clem was pissed and missed Gary. There was too much material and a lot of competition about songs. We thought about doing a double album but were discouraged by Private Stock. We needed a bass player, and Clem brought his friend from New Jersey Frank Inafante, or Frank the Freak. Frankie was a local guitar hero with his band World War III and had a neighborhood following. Frank was more of a sideman on the record. I played bass on a few things too. I'm fairly certain that this is the first record to ever have an EBow (guitar-string sustainer) credit on it.

The record is darker than the first, maybe reflecting some of our internal turmoil. Gottehrer took a lot of vacations, but we persevered. Then when we were in the middle of the recording, Leeds showed up to tell us that he was sick of Private Stock and that we should move to another label. This was his biggest move; he probably already had Chrysalis on the hook but he made it seem like he was going to go hunting. Debbie describing our reaction to Peter presenting this news: "He's up. He's Mr. Energetic

College Boy, like Kennedy in his sneakers and preppy shirts. Great! Go for it! Kill them!" Unfortunately, although he knew how to strategize, Leeds didn't have any people skills. I began to think that he was an impatient cranky guy who might have been better suited to be some corporate boss rather than a personal manager.

On Labor Day weekend we found ourselves in a lawyer's office on Columbus Circle at midnight. We were housed in this guy's office while representatives of Chrysalis and Blondie attempted to hash out a contract before we'd finalized a separation with Private Stock. We were stuck there so we could sign off whenever these guys actually finished arguing and running up their bills. We were there for hours and around nine in the morning we went to Central Park, got some weed, came back, and got as wasted as possible. We trashed the guy's office. We threw his papers around, moved furniture, made phone calls to Hawaii, then hung the phones out the window by the cords. We started fires in ashtrays. When the crew of attorneys eventually came to get us, they were just completely fucking horrified. At least we had maintained our punk aesthetic. Naturally we once again didn't have any actual legal representation. Clem was distraught through the whole process, saying that we were getting conned, which we were, but we didn't listen to him and we all signed off.

The next time we played CBGB's we broke whatever flaky attendance record had been established. A couple of shows were filmed by Plasmatics manager Rod Swenson. During a particularly crowded sweaty set, the fire department showed up in full gear carrying axes. I always suspected that Rod had called them for the sake of the movie.

Instead of having us rehearse and try to tighten things up with Frankie, Leeds booked us for more West Coast dates, another week at the Whisky. A lot went on during that particular excursion. We shot a really great set of potential album-cover images with photographer Philip Dixon in and around the Tropicana Motel, which was central to the LA rock scene. Debbie wore a white pillowcase that we took out of one of the rooms. She was wrapped in red duct tape. One of my favorite aspects of the shoot is that in some of the images, printing on the pillowcase is visible and it's the name of another motel, like the Tropicana had stolen or bought a bunch of used pillowcases somewhere.

One of the reasons we were out there was for Chrysalis Records owner Terry Ellis to check out what he'd paid for. Chrysalis's big act up to that point was Jethro Tull, who Terry used to manage. Chrysalis was the two guys, Chris Wright and Ellis, hence the name Chrysalis—Chris-Ellis; get it?

Prior to owning a record company Terry was known for having been cringingly abused by Bob Dylan while Terry was a young student journalist trying to interview Bob in D. A. Pennebaker's film *Don't Look Back*.

One of the Chrysalis staff people was Russ Shaw. Russ was the nephew of Hollywood OG photographer Sam Shaw, and Terry hired Sam to do a film about Debbie and the band. Sam is legendary. That series of pictures of Marilyn Monroe with her dress blowing around her legs from *Seven Year Itch* was shot by Sam. He was in the middle of golden-age Hollywood, shooting the great stars of the fifties and sixties. Sam shot footage of Debbie running around on a beach and jumping in the Pacific for the first time. He introduced us to a buddy of his, screenwriter Ted Allan, who had an Oscar nomination and a Golden Globe win. Ted collected some interview material for the film. The thing was, these old Hollywood guys loved Debbie. They saw it early on. Sam was also close friends with John Cassavetes and he recruited John to shoot some footage of us playing at the Whisky. We sat around with Cassavetes one afternoon during our sound-check time. He was so enthusiastic about the modernity of it all. He invited us to several screenings of *Opening Night* that he used to gauge audience reaction to different cuts. I probably didn't appreciate all this as much as I do now.

Staying at the Tropicana was also a great bit of cultural absorption and we met a bunch of local kids and musicians. I remember a girl who kept a snake in her hat. We met this trio of Pleasant, Randy, and a kid named Jeffrey Lee Pierce, who said he was running our fan club. Joan Jett had an apartment down the block from the Whisky that was another meeting place. We met Kim Fowley, who for years thereafter, every time he would hear we were recording, would send me weird demo tapes. And Rodney, of course, was always about and the king of the scene.

Then we found out we had a hit in Australia. "In the Flesh" got to number two on the charts there. It had been the B side of the Private Stock

"X Offender" single and the story is that it got played on TV by mistake. I've always been skeptical of the veracity of this accidental-playing tale, mainly because the guy who played it on his very popular music show *Countdown*, Molly Meldrum, is supersmart and knew exactly what to present to his market. It's a good story, though.

Meanwhile Leeds's cohort press agent Famous Toby Mamis steered us toward Nigel Harrison and we went to see him play bass with Ray Manzarek's post-Doors band Nite City. The next night he came and played with us at our sound check. Nigel had actually been out in the music-biz world for a while at that point. He'd been in a band called Silverhead with actor/singer Michael Des Barres. Nigel is a charming guy and he had taped one of our shows and learned the songs, and everybody liked him so it was pretty much a done deal.

I was always in touch with my mother and she was a big supporter. We were in San Francisco and I got a call from her. She said, "Don't get upset, but your apartment burned down." We got the landlord on the phone and he was very apologetic and said he'd get the place in shape for us to occupy by the time we got back. We got back to New York and the apartment was demolished with a big pile of rubble in the charred kitchen where most of the actual burning had taken place. Luckily, the cats had escaped by hiding in a closet. The girl downstairs, Maria, who had been watching the cats, had lent us what was allegedly a dress of Marilyn's from *The Seven Year Itch*. The dress was badly singed in the fire and we did that photo series of Debbie wearing it while holding a flaming pan in the burned-out kitchen. We lost a lot of stuff. Debbie had a few pieces of jewelry that went missing and I lost my collection of Archie Comics' *The Adventures of the Fly*. The Fly is in thirty issues before he becomes the less desirable Fly Man, and I'd had almost the whole set that I'd put together over years. I was missing two issues of the thirty.

When I was a kid, one could take a tour of DC Comics in New York. My parents took me and we joined a bunch of other kids for a tour of the DC offices. At the end of the tour, *they gave us original Superman art panels!* Black-and-white on boards; they were from a daily strip in some newspapers. I had traded the two panels I had for key issues of *Fly* comics!

The other thing I lost was a sacred notebook that I had started around

1966 that had drawings and notes from my sixties California adventures as well as clippings and assorted memorabilia from my past life pasted in it.

We weren't sure if the fire was the result of an overloaded electrical circuit or perhaps related to someone lurking around the building, maybe connected to the bloody mattress we had found on the roof.

Terry Ellis didn't like the pictures we'd shot for the second album, thought they were "too punk," and Philip Dixon was quickly flown to New York to do another hastily arranged shoot. Whoever was art directing rented a police car from the NYPD. It was a special little one that they hired out, a promotional cop car. Debbie wore a dress she'd made based on Anya's designs. In the background of the shot was a store sign that said PLASTIC LETTERS. Terry said, "Let's go with that as the title," and we all thought that was an okay approach.

Debbie and Leeds went to Australia on a promo tour. My mom had moved to Manhattan to the then very sketchy Camelot Apartments on West Forty-Fifth Street and I would visit her and try to call Debbie in Australia. Debbie reported that Leeds was disrespectful and that all the journalists kept asking her if she'd continue tearing her clothes off during shows. Two of the cats had gone to Debbie's sister Martha and I was staying at the Edison Hotel on Forty-Seventh Street right off Times Square with Sunday Man, the most soulful of the cats. The Edison has a million rooms and was the most noir place imaginable. Every room had a neon sign out the window. A maid who had a deep facial scar wouldn't come into my small room because she was afraid of cats. Sunday Man was a very sweet, docile creature who had only ever attacked that rat on the Bowery but she couldn't be persuaded and left the clean towels in the hall.

Nigel came to New York and did some rehearsing with us. We had a little room in the Music Building on Thirty-Eighth Street. It's still functioning as a rehearsal rental space. We made the mistake of putting a sign on our door that said MONSTER ISLAND MUSIC, which was the name of our new publishing company. Somebody smashed the door down and stole all the guitars.

The record was gaining in Europe and the UK. The band flew to London, where we would meet Debbie, who was returning from Australia. She and

I had a passed-out reunion for a day or so before press and shows began again.

At our first visit to Chrysalis's offices we were struck by posters all over the place for something called Blonde on Blonde that was two gorgeous model-type blond girls, Nina Carter and Jilly Johnson, in what was an early iteration of the girl group. Debbie was appalled. "What the fuck is this?" she asked Terry. I think he was embarrassed; it looked like Chrysalis was trying out a Blondie clone before arriving at the real thing. We didn't see the posters around after that, but Blonde on Blonde had a Japanese following and kept going till the eighties.

We were playing in small halls and large clubs, which is where we should have been on the first tour. This time we were turning away large numbers of people who couldn't get into the overflowing venues. Leeds was flipping out that we would be playing to two hundred people and turning away another hundred. Famously, some members of Led Zeppelin couldn't get into one of the shows.

There were degrees of audience interaction at the shows. This was the period of "gobbing," whereby fans would show their affection for bands by spitting on them. Debbie shut this down by stopping a song and saying, "Thank you, but it doesn't match my dress." Debbie would get pulled into the audience and I would have to yank her back onto the stage. I felt like a Secret Service agent looking for potential threats during the shows.

I got into a fracas at one of the gigs with a kid who had been taunting me from his standing position in the front row. There was a little back-and-forth (n.) and he grabbed my ankle. I swatted at him with my guitar and he managed to grab the guitar and pull it into the audience. Mike Sticca, a crew guy who had been with us since CBGB's, and I dove into the simmering crowd. Miraculously the guitar was still plugged in so we just followed the cord and retrieved it. As this was going on, the lights went off and plunged the whole scene into darkness. Mike and I reversed and followed the cord back. The lights came back on. I jumped up on the stage with my shirt all torn up; the crowd went nuts, very dramatic; we played the next song.

We were subject to the slings and arrows of the UK music press. We discovered that the up-and-down effect we had previously suspected was in fact a tactic perhaps to keep up paper sales with conflict. If Debbie jumped around a lot, there would be comments about her being too sexy. If she just stood there someone would write, "She just stood there!"

The flights to neighborhood Australia from London were arduous. Recently, in 2012, I timed a trip from my house to the hotel in Auckland: thirty-five hours. The plane made stops in Bahrain and Singapore and I got a little sense of non-Western culture, even if it was just an airport. I wore the Singapore Lion City T-shirt I got at an airport gift stand a lot. We were, of course, in coach with the babies spitting on us and all the old people going to retire or go back home to the desert after visiting England's green and pleasant land. The tour had been grinding along for months with just a week or so between legs, and the endless plane rides were a perfect metaphor for the limbo of road life.

We arrived in Perth in the evening and border-patrol dudes actually came on the plane and sprayed clouds of bug killer around while everyone was still in their seats. We got to the hotel, went to sleep, sort of, and had a show *the next night*. We had had the number two song in the country, so the pressure was on. The mayor of Perth was coming. Right away I noticed that we were in a kind of time warp, that things were akin to the fifties. Australia now is very modern and almost futuristic. In 1977, not so much. A lot of the women were dressed in floor-length flowered-print skirts that were something like Mennonite or Mormon fashion. The gig was in a very new hall. We did the show and everybody was completely jet-lagged and uncoordinated. Debbie collapsed into the drums, and Frankie, I guess attempting a rock and roll move, tossed his beloved Les Paul in the air but then was too spaced out to catch it and watched it smash on the stage, its peghead breaking completely off. On top of all that we sounded nothing like what the audience anticipated based on "In the Flesh." I don't know what these guys expected—maybe some kind of Olivia Newton-John thing—and the aggressive rock stylings were probably alarming. There was a contingent of enthusiastic fans but the mayor never came backstage. We did get flowers from him.

As everyone left the stage grumbling and fighting, we were met by our new Aussie tour manager, Ray Maguire, who defused the tension by crushing a few beer cans on his head. Ray had a stutter that he said was the result of PTSD. He'd been driving on his motorcycle in the outback when he crashed into a herd of wild horses. He woke up embedded in a dead horse with several broken limbs and he'd had the stutter ever since.

We were taken to the local fancy disco, Beethoven's, and stood around outside for a while until they agreed to let us in in our T-shirts and sneakers. The place looked like a Holiday Inn and we got drunk and left. Then, in a very crowded pizza place, Clem and Jimmy got into a food fight and chased each other around overturning chairs and wreaking havoc. Some of the guys who were working there leaped over the counter and held down Clem and Jimmy while the Australian record and press people looked on, aghast. Back at the hotel we hung out with our opening act, the Ferrets. They had had a number one with a Marc Bolanish track called "Don't Fall in Love." They had a sort of innocent-hippie-grunge look but were a bit dark under the surface.

For the non-flying parts, our tour bus was a bus. With seats. A regular, somewhat elderly bus that both bands sat in while driving these vast distances between towns and cities.

The kids that came to the shows were very young and enthusiastic; they would swarm around after the shows and keep us from leaving. But there was a lot of pushback from the press and the adults in the room. Our somewhat manic approach to music and Debbie's antics drew some condemnation from conservative factions and media. We did a lot of press and many still were fixated on Debbie potentially tearing her clothes off, and there were frequent inquiries about nudity.

In Melbourne we were invited to a screening of Peter Weir's *The Last Wave* and met great Australian actor David Gulpilil. It's a great film that deals with issues of Aboriginal magic and marginalization. We didn't see much of the Indigenous people; their presence was kind of invisible then. In later years it feels like there's at least an attempt to embrace the Aboriginal culture as part of the country's history. Australia and America have both lifted so damn many Indigenous names for places, it's almost as if the natives weren't murdered en masse.

At that time Australian cities were overwhelmed by flies. There was frequent reference to the Australian Salute, which was waving your hand in front of your face. I realized that those hats that the guys in Monty Python wore when doing their Aussie sketches, the ones that had wine corks dangling on strings around the brim, were actually intended as fly-defense tools.

Walking on a city street, one would inevitably observe flies on the back of the person walking ahead. We saw this phenomenon addressed with meta-irony: the occasional T-shirt that had small life-size fly images printed on the back shoulders that emulated the walking-down-the-street-flies-on-back reality.

I don't know how they got rid of the flies; probably nothing as dramatic as the countrywide massive anti-fly, -rat, -sparrow, and -mosquito campaigns that went on in China. Maybe the flies left on their own, but in later years, fly encounters were similar to anywhere else in the world.

John Denver was down there at the same time on a similar tour circuit and he was being worshipped as a god. We would show up at a city and discover it had been declared John Denver Month there. This had a direct effect on us, since our amps and such were rented and every time we would ask for a replacement or new bit of gear, the answer would be: "John has it." John Denver had rented every amp in Australia. Also on the same route was Uri Geller. We got to a couple of places that had backstage graffiti that said *Uri Geller levitated this building* with a date. People would say he did it. I was sitting in an airport cafeteria reading a local paper that had a big brooding picture of Uri staring out from the front page. Inside there was a reference to the front page that said one should stare back at the picture and something would happen—your broken watch would be repaired, whatever. I concentrated and stared at the picture and immediately a nearby cafeteria worker dropped a big tray filled with utensils. Everyone in the place turned to look at the crashing spoons and forks. It was a sign from Uri, no doubt.

I think the only Blondie shows to ever have been canceled have been because of natural phenomena—floods, plagues, and such; force majeure. Debbie got sick and we had no choice but to cancel our Brisbane show. After an hour's wait the crowd got word that we weren't going to play.

Clem went onstage to apologize and got stuff thrown at him. A bunch of the people who pulled themselves onstage got arrested. The headline of the *Brisbane Telegraph* screamed "Wild Rock Scenes" with a big picture of a slightly scuffed stage door. Now we had *starting a riot* on our list of crimes against humanity. Debbie said she'd gotten ill from food poisoning. She did an interview with a journalist, who, seeing a bunch of cherries in her hotel room, decided to write that they were the cause, and when this got reinforced by a quote in the *Telegraph* from tour manager Ray about Debbie's unfamiliarity with fruit, she got hammered for being somehow too soft or even just making the whole thing up.

Weed was hard to come by but we were able to dig some hash out of the landscape. At the same time, there was a lot of heroin around. I had only done it once, back in Brooklyn. A buddy of mine transitioned from selling pot when he realized he could make a lot more dough selling dope. He bought a massive home stereo, a BMW motorcycle, and a waterbed from the proceeds but he also got hooked on the dope. Debbie had told me that she had developed a slight habit back in the sixties. We got stoned on it a couple of times during the tour but back then it wasn't something I was interested in pursuing. I later found out it requires some work to get yourself really messed up.

Everybody was pretty burned out and pissed off when we landed in Melbourne a second time. We were walking through the airport, punching each other's arms, and being generally stupid and grouchy, when our handlers herded us all into a room filled with journalists for a press conference. Being in front of the fourth estate didn't do anything to reduce band tensions, and the arm punching and verbal abuse continued—if anything, slightly heightened now that there was an appreciative audience. The press people thought this display was terrible and the next day one of the papers ran a picture of Debbie wearing shades and looking sinister with a skull and crossbones on her jacket. The text accompanying the image read:

New York's five man one woman punk rock group Blondie hit Melbourne yesterday . . . and it took less than a minute for the swearing, belching and rude antagonism to begin. Even the group's promoters Evans Gudinski and Associates walked out of a press interview. Deborah Harry said she wasn't sure Australia was "ready for us yet." Her use of four letter words belied her press release description which said she was "actress, personality, a human being with depth, sensitivity." I didn't recall any belching and I'm sure Debbie never would have signed off on this gruesome description being in a press release about her. A day or so later we were walking in the street when a passerby yelled at us, "Why don't you go back to America where you are somebody!" This guy had no sense of humor, or irony, for that matter. As usual, the masses had had their minds massaged by the medium.

At the end, during Christmas, we were to have a vacation-ish week on Great Keppel Island. A beautiful little place off the coast of Queensland; we were happy to get there and relax. We were going to do three nights of shows for other guests. We were in these little bungalow buildings on a nice beach and I set up an amp, rhythm machine, and effects and made weird jam tapes during the balmy afternoons. We hung out on the sands and rode Jet Skis. I had some hash that I was smoking and the whole deal was very idyllic.

On Christmas Day, Clem, Frankie, and I commandeered a little motorboat to drive around and look at some of the smaller uninhabited islands. We got too close to one and, not knowing what we were doing, beached the boat on the sharp coral. The engine fell off and we were stranded with cut feet. After a few hours Debbie got worried that we'd been swept away or eaten by sharks and she asked one of the old pirate-type guys who worked there to go find us. As he was towing us back, he kept saying there was nothing worse than "cunts at sea." We had to pay for boat and motor repairs.

The shows were us jamming and doing whatever weird cover songs we had in the repertoire. I was always looking for the ultimate rock song, and this might have been the period when I was sure it was "Louie Louie" by the Kingsmen. While we were playing for the twenty-five or so drunken patrons who were there, thieves went into all the rooms and stole things. They took an old Baume & Mercier watch that my mom's boyfriend had given me. I realize now that it probably was actually valuable, but I'll never know. Worse, they stole my carefully protected hash. When the cops showed up we gave them descriptions of some guys that we'd seen lurking around, and amazingly they caught them and brought them back to the island in handcuffs before sending them off to do forty years' hard labor in the mines. The watch and the hash were history, though.

Before heading to Japan we were booked for four shows in Bangkok. We've been back to Bangkok a couple of times and the contrast to 1977 is extreme. Where there were a lot of parks and trees and evidence of nature, now it's pretty industrialized and cemented over. There were a lot of grim aspects then; right outside our fancy hotel were streams of sewage. Lepers would come at you begging. These guys were in rough shape. The whole place smelled of a mix of decay and jasmine. Jasmine was everywhere, people selling bouquets and garlands.

In 1976 left-wing student unrest led to a military coup that outlawed all political parties and political gatherings of over five people and instituted a curfew in Bangkok whereby nobody was allowed on the Bangkok streets from midnight to five in the morning. Anybody found on the street would be put in jail till the next day or possibly chopped up and thrown in a canal.

We arrived at six in the morning and were greeted at the airport by Mr. Idibah, who was our promoter and also the chief of police. He was an OG dude who had a great entourage in tow that included gorgeous girls and guys in black suits wearing mirrored shades and smoking cigarettes. Mr. Idibah owned a bunch of radio stations that were all pumping our record. I found the local radio situation very intriguing. There were absolutely no FCC-type regulations in place, so whoever wanted to throw up an antenna and become a radio station just did exactly that. As a result, there were hundreds of stations. Every increment of the radio dial was another channel; there was no space in between, and whichever station had the most broadcast power was the one that you'd hear. It was every frequency for itself, a radio battle royale that appealed to my fondness for chaos.

The hotel was modern and styled in an exotic motif. It was populated by a lot of international types, everyone smoking cigarettes. It took us a day or so to realize that we could ask for regular Western-style pillows to replace the rock-hard opium-den ones that came with the room.

We ran around the city, discovered we could have custom clothing made at absurdly low prices, went to clubs in Patpong and saw the girls wearing numbers, visited the Old City with all the amazing temples, and went on the river. The river had its own human ecosystem surrounding it. People lived in shacks that had walls made of blankets and right next door would be some modern mansion that was built by a guy who'd made it and come back to the hood to live. The long narrow boats that ferried us around were powered by V-8 car engines attached to long poles with propellers on them where the driveshaft would be.

At a bar we met an expat guy who said he'd been a member of Sounds Incorporated, the band that opened for the Beatles on their first American tour. He invited us to his house. Debbie was wiped out and stayed in the hotel. After the relative weed shortage in Australia, everyone was smoking their brains out in Thailand. At that time in the U.S., people were just barely starting to get the idea of sinsemilla and cultivated pot, and Thai weed was deep. The guy's house was really nice with round doorways. He had an old Thai housekeeper who, as we watched, took fifty Thai sticks out of a giant plastic bag of them this guy had. Thai sticks, which were occasionally available in the U.S., were just high-end sensi weed buds tied to little sticks. She chopped them up and put them into a banana cake she was making for us; she was laughing the whole time. Everyone staggered back to the hotel leading each other. I think it was that night that Debbie and I had some unspoken psychic communication on the astral plane, me being in a semi-trance state and thinking, *Where are we? In the hotel?* and her answering verbally in her sleep, "I think so. In bed."

The two nights of concerts were sponsored by something called Green Spot, which was a kind of orange soda that came from the U.S. but was popular in Thailand. There were big BLONDIE GREEN SPOT banners hung around the hall. The stage was decorated with big floral arrangements, more jasmine and big bouquets that spelled *Blondie*. It seemed like a lot of guys who had never previously dealt with an audio system were setting up the PA. I watched them for a while as they struggled with piles of cables that hadn't been marked, so a misplacement meant a total redo and they had to unplug everything and start over again. I thought I saw one dude praying to the cables.

I was talking to a maybe ten-year-old kid at the sound check and he went to shake my hand and slipped off a silver bracelet that Eric had given me that I'd been wearing since he'd died. The kid was a real pro; it didn't even register at first. I chased him and gave him a harmonica in exchange for the bracelet.

The shows were fun; there were whole families with toddlers at them, people who had possibly never been to a concert or seen a rock band anywhere. Somebody told us that the city "wasn't grounded"—that is, there was no way for excess electricity to escape from the circuits. I have no idea if this is the case, but at times during the show there would be a surge of volume and everything onstage would vibrate.

But the big deal was that on New Year's Eve, the curfew was lifted and you could stay out all night. Bangkok is a real party town and the masses went crazy, a lot of people in the backs of trucks yelling and blowing horns, the whole thing with a background of fireworks and more jasmine, a lovely moment.

I'd heard that Japan was very strict about weed so I left a whole bunch of Thai sticks in an ashtray in our hotel room, and of course the Japanese customs guys barely looked at us. We flew on my twenty-eighth birthday. Leeds had joined us because he wanted to check out Japan and we were in a fancy hotel in Tokyo. On the first or second night, Frankie and roadie Mike Sticca were running around in a hyper state possibly caused by the sudden pot withdrawal that was certainly affecting me; it was difficult to sleep. They managed to demolish one of the decorative pictures, a bridge or a flower garden or something that was on a wall. They hid the wreckage under Frankie's bed and when the maid found it, we all got thrown out of the hotel and went to a lesser one. Leeds was mortified, but we thought it was funny. Shortly after we arrived at the new hotel there was what felt like a big-ass earthquake and all the mirrors and pictures on the walls bounced around but the staff girls were standing around giggling, so my earthquake anxiety decreased.

If we had gone to Japan six months later we might have had more interest and gig attendance. After we had overflow club gigs in the UK, Leeds booked us into Japanese halls that we weren't filling. If we'd played clubs, we would have done better.

We discovered that the Japanese never said "No"; they only said "Yes, but . . ." We were to do a TV show that involved a chroma-key blue-screen effect. They were too polite to tell Debbie not to wear blue and she wore a whole turquoise outfit and did the show covered in towels so as not to have the galactic background projected onto her.

Some of the press were fascinated by our punkness and would ask us to curse or be offensive, which they found amusing. They asked Debbie weird personal questions about how sexy she felt onstage.

We got to see some things. We went to a shouting restaurant where the staff all yelled everything and the clientele was encouraged to do the same. We went to a club that was filled with guys who all had the same greased-back rockabilly hairdo and were all wearing the same black leather motorcycle jackets. Our promoter, Mr. Udo, was pretty gangster image-wise and he took us to his buddy Mr. Gun's club. Mr. Gun was more gangster-adjacent and his club had an area with guys lifting weights. He gave Jimmy one of those tourist-level samurai swords. The gangster ethos was pretty entrenched and we were intrigued by the guys on the street who would be dressed in flawlessly neat suits and pure white over-coats. We went to a party and when someone pulled out the tiniest third of a joint, the whole place crowded around. We weren't sure what the gangsters actually did, crime-wise.

We went on the bullet train and it broke down and we sat there for an hour while everyone apologized profusely, this being supposedly the first time it had ever broken down. We were doing a show at a big modern hall that was only half full and before the encore I couldn't make it to the bathroom so I pissed in a cup. The reaction might have been the same had I shot or stabbed some of the audience members. We had to do a lot of apologizing and send flowers to the injured parties.

The endless flight back to the UK stopped in Moscow. It was January; the whole place was frozen. The runways, the buildings, parked planes were all covered in ice. In our leather jackets and sunglasses at night we must have looked extremely alien but nobody reacted; it was too dodgy in the airport and people just stared straight ahead so as not to make eye contact with the wrong person. Debbie and me had been regularly writing to my mother and we thought we'd send her a postcard from Moscow. We bought some Lenin stamps that had really terrible glue—they kept falling off—then we sought out where to mail them. The mailbox for the whole of the Moscow airport was a sad little white-painted wooden box with a really half-assed cheapo padlock that was barely attached. It felt like it was about to fall off the wall when we put things in it. Everyone got very nice copies of *The Communist Manifesto* that were free on a rack. They were very determined and had it in twenty languages. We bought some Lenin pins and got back on the plane.

The plane was very sparsely populated and the crew didn't mind that we were lying on the floor in the aisles trying to sleep. It was also on this flight that Leeds decided it was a good idea to tell all the band members that they could be replaced. Needless to say, this didn't go down well with anyone. Sometime later he told Debbie she could be replaced too. Again, the guy's people skills were severely lacking.

In London I got whatever had afflicted Debbie earlier, fever and flu mixed with battle fatigue. We had a show that would be laden with press that night and I was flat on my back; I think I missed the sound check. We had a doctor come to the hotel and he gave me a shot of what he said was B_{12} and nicotinic acid. I've never been able to get another doctor to do the same, and I've asked. Whatever the hell it was, I got a metallic taste in my mouth and immediately felt way better but it didn't last and by the time I got to the gig, I was staggering around again. Dingwalls is a big club in Camden that has stone walls and was pretty echoey. Luckily there was a pillar on the stage that I could lean against. As the set progressed I couldn't get my bearings too well. Jimmy was producing massive waves of volume with his Polymoog, and Clem, who was in a keyed-up state, kept plunging ahead and starting songs without letting the guitar players tune in. I tried yelling at Clem a few times to slow down, but either he was too buzzed or he didn't hear. Finally, near the end of the show, I cracked up and threw myself on Clem and the drums. An exit door was very close to the stage, and the whole band, locked in a death struggle, spilled out into the alley, where we were separated by crew members and bouncers. Everybody was fine the next day and we flew to Leiden in South Holland.

We got to Marseilles, which was super–*French Connection*–dodgy. To my delight I discovered that they sold cheap out-the-front switchblades on the street at newspaper kiosks. I bought one and the cute older lady at the kiosk said. "Ah! Le Flash!" The switchblade had a name! It didn't last too long and soon fell apart but it looked great.

At the gig there was a gaggle of bratty guys in the front row who spent the whole show taunting me and Jimmy and being obnoxious; one kid threw a wine bottle at me and I managed to catch it and underhand it back at him, getting him in the stomach. Backstage Jimmy and me filled paper cups with honey and when we came out for the encore we dumped them on our antagonists. That night after the show Debbie and me were asleep in our hotel room when two guys came in, turned on the light, then said, "Oh, excusez moi," and left when we jumped up screaming. The people at the front desk said it was a mistake. It was all very casual with these guys. In Bordeaux the local Fascist and Communist groups got word to the promoter that they were all going to kill each other at our gig that night, so it was canceled.

We got to Berlin and one night we went to Checkpoint Charlie. I had a camera and took some flash pictures and someone on the eastern side started popping off flashes as if they were taking pictures of us in response. Was this standard intimidation procedure? The wall guards just hanging out with their cameras waiting for the enemy?

Our schedule was insane and we were getting really fed up with Leeds. Everybody in the band was exhausted and I remember eating a big dinner and still feeling fatigued afterward. A doctor came and checked us out and said most of us were suffering from very low blood pressure, probably as a result of our itinerary.

In February "Denise" was released and that, as they say, was that. It went top ten all over Europe, number two in the UK. We had already been doing lots of European TV and back in London we got booked to do it on *Top of the Pops*, which was a big deal. Back then the BBC had this really strange ritual that we were compelled to take part in. They expected the *Top of the Pops* guest band to go record a new version of the song that they would then lip-synch to on the show. In order to facilitate this, they would send some overseer dude around to observe the recording in progress. The reasoning behind this was something to do with some union red tape, that you had to produce a new track, licensing, publishing, whatever. What happened, and we were told this was standard procedure, was that the band would bring a copy of the actual recording to a recording studio, put the tape on, and pretend to be recording while the guy from the BBC watched. The BBC guy would watch for a bit while the band was in effect lip-synching to their own track (while pretending to record it) for the up- coming lip-synched TV spot, and then somebody would take the BBC guy out for drinks, and Bob's your uncle. That's what happened. Maybe somebody was getting something out of this weirdness beyond free beer. We went on *Top of the Pops* with a slightly different mix of the original "Denise" track and Blondie momentum built up even more.

(We did a radio show in France that required us to lip-synch in front of a small studio audience. The irony of lip-synching on the radio wasn't lost on any of us and when it came time to do it, nobody took it very seriously. Clem pushed his drums over and the rest of us wandered around the stage taking guitars out of guitar cases and then putting them back in. It was all very performance art as the track played. Naturally we had horribly offended the people at the radio station and there was a lot of record com- pany intervening and flower sending.)

The press subjected us to increased scrutiny and were more savage than when we were less successful. Debbie and I had an interview with the same influential British journalist who had championed us after our Hammersmith debut show. We sat down with this guy in our hotel room and he was completely charming and effusive. We had a nice chat that delved into drug use, with him admitting to an affinity for speed and us being open about all of our nonsense. After the interview he took us to his paper's offices and introduced us around; his similarly influential girl- friend who worked there was equally welcoming. When the piece came out we were amazed to see that he'd done his best to actually try and murder us in print. The gist of the article was that we were dumb lying capitalist sellout drug addicts who were prepared to destroy everything in our paths for personal gain and that Lene Lovich was far superior anyway. At the time we were upset about this shitty approach; I would much rather have been challenged directly. Later on that same tour, in Amsterdam, I did an interview with what I took to be a hostile journalist who asked me if Blondie was a "Jewish band." At that point I just said thanks and left but when his article came out, it was very positive and complimentary. I've said lots of stupid crap in the press, not least of all presenting myself as some media strategist when I was just making shit up as I went along with very little forethought. I do like the modern climate and the immediacy of social media where one can act like a public asshole and make idiotic comments on one's own without being guided in that direction by a journalist or outsider.

We went to a Sid Vicious gig at the Electric Ballroom. Sid and his girlfriend, our old pal Nancy, had put together a sort of punk supergroup that was called the Vicious White Kids. Members included ex-Pistols Glen Matlock and Stella Nova. They didn't have that much material and wound up doing "I Wanna Be Your Dog" three times. Rat Scabies of the Damned kept it all afloat with his great drumming. That apparently was the only gig they ever did. We met a bunch of friends and left with Joan Jett, Sandy West, our pal Eddie "The Ant" Duggan, and a few others. Eddie was a young kid who we had found on the first tour who had dragged himself along with us till we gave him a sort of intern job. On a later tour we had a goofy ant costume for "Attack of the Giant Ants" and Eddie would come out during the encore and do some hand-to-hand combat with Debbie while his antennae wiggled. Eddie was a great sport and didn't even mind that much when the crew pulled his clothes off and gaffer-taped him to a mic stand, which they left in the middle of an empty stage. Eddie is married with five adult and semi-adult children now. That night as we were leaving the Sid and Nancy gig, some guy offered us a ride in a moving van. Everyone was pretty drunk and got into the back of this giant metal box and closed the door. It was like riding in a tank and soon everyone was going nuts, pounding on the walls and yelling, Joan and Eddie getting really crazy and collapsing all over. A week later Clem showed us a paragraph in one of the papers saying that we'd left the Sid Vicious show in a limousine.

One of the last UK shows was at Queensway Hall in Dunstable. About two-thirds of the way through the set, a large group of skinheads and fans crowded up onto the stage and stood around doing this sort of *Dawn of the Dead* type of stumbling dance. I didn't know what their intentions were and I grabbed Debbie, who was still attempting to sing, and half carried her back to the dressing room. I can't remember if we finished the show.

We flew to Germany to do yet one more TV show on the way back to New York. We waited in a German airport for ten hours while the waves of dullness and fatigue washed over us. We'd been out for about six months straight.

CHAPTER 9

Back in Manhattan Debbie and I checked into the Gramercy Park Hotel. Humphrey Bogart got married there and as a kid, JFK stayed with his parents at the Gramercy for a while. It was funky and run-down then. We were staying in the residential section that we shared with a lot of old people who dressed in tweed suits and looked like retired writers. Later, in the modern era, it evolved into a fancy boutique hotel before closing altogether. We were burned out and as soon as we got settled, Debbie's sister called and said that Sunday Man had run off. This resulted in several days of extreme mourning. The next bit was Terry Ellis calling to say that if Debbie didn't do a U.S. promo tour we were toast in America. Leeds had taken to giving us a hundred and twenty-five dollars a week allowance and we were talking to a lawyer we had met about getting away from him. Debbie agreed to do the tour only if I went with her. The press junket was relatively painless and involved a lot of hotel-room interviews and visits to local radio. It seemed like every radio station we visited had an Elvis promotional gold record on the wall. Colonel Parker knew how to extend the hustle. In Detroit we hooked up with Billy Bass, who was the main U.S. marketing and promotion guy for Chrysalis. He was extremely helpful and always lightened the mood.

One night we were at the Fontainebleau Hotel in Miami Beach, which was a monument to kitschy chintz replete with painted plaster tableaus

and columns all over the place. We got to our room and it was freezing
from the excessive air-conditioning. The TV was on. I opened these big
French doors onto the balcony and it was so hot and humid outside that
all the surfaces in the room became instantly covered with condensation,
including the inside of the TV, which belched out some smoke and sparks
and dramatically died a fiery death.

When we got back, the Gramercy raised our rates and we moved to a
weird situation called the Southgate Towers that was across the street from
Madison Square Garden. This place was rented out by various corporate
entities for businesspeople who were away from wherever they came from
for long periods. It was a grimly furnished space that quite resembled
the room that Choi Min-sik's character is locked up in in *Oldboy*. Those
pinup-style shots of Debbie against a blue background in her white dress
were taken at the Southgate Towers. I was dedicated to photography and
would always carry a camera around, but again, I wish I'd taken more pictures than I did. Having the music job was fairly all-consuming and the
picture-taking was frequently not a priority.

Besides getting the call about our old apartment burning when we
were out in San Francisco, I also got a call saying that my welfare had
been terminated. I'd sort of forgotten about it and there were probably only
a few months that overlapped with my earning money, so the criminal
activity is questionable. I made one final trip to the apartment on First
and First. There was a huge pile of rubble in the front room and in it I
found Dee Dee Ramone's draft card, which I think I still have in my junk
somewhere. I have no idea where I stored the Mother Cabrini statue in the
period when we were drifting around; probably with my mother.

Steve Sprouse found a big apartment on the second floor of a building
uptown, and Debbie, who had been regularly interrogating the super of
the same building, eventually found out that there was a vacancy on the
top floor. Steve's space was a couple of apartments put together so it was
basically a very big loft. The building, 200 West Fifty-Eighth, was very
close to where I went to high school, just a few blocks away, so I was quite
at home in the neighborhood. We had to get my cheapish uncle who'd
covered my first year at art school to cosign the lease, since we didn't have
any anything—no credit cards, no bank accounts, et cetera. But it was a

great apartment. It was a small four-room terraced penthouse that cost five hundred bucks a month. People in the building told us that Lillian Roth, the singer and actor, had lived in this same apartment. I'd shipped a Teac four-track back from Tokyo, the first one I owned, and I set up in the living room using a kitchen appliance rack for gear. Our neighbor across the hall who'd been there a long time had knocked his walls down and extended his apartment onto his terraces. His place looked like a mountain cabin. Great photographer Kate Simon lived one floor down. Kate shot the Clash's first album cover, Bob Marley's *Kaya*, and lots of other things you probably have seen. We put Astroturf on the main terrace and had an awning installed like the ones that are on the front of small stores; you cranked the handle to open and close it.

All this time we were still running around doing shows but the impetus was on making the next album. I made demos on the four-track. I wrote (*wrote* for me being the recording process whereby I would get things from head to tape, as it were) "Sunday Girl," which was a lyrical reference to the Seekers' "Georgy Girl" and about our missing Sunday Man the cat. I've always been into world or roots music and at the time I was listening to a lot of the Mighty Sparrow's calypso. "Sunday Girl" was in part inspired by the Afro-Caribe melodies I was hearing.

I started hanging out more with a guy I'd known peripherally, Glenn O'Brien. I knew him a little from his band, which was named after the American Cold War early-warning system but with a *K*: Konelrad. Glenn was very bright and, like me, a massive pothead. He was a literary dude and found jobs as an editor or columnist. Around then he was the editor of the absurdly ahead of its time *High Times* magazine and one day he said we could go watch them shoot the centerfold. We went to an apartment in the West Village and sure enough, they were taking pictures of some attractive large buds. I don't know how we swung it but we bought the model for the centerfold and smoked it. I grew a really great marijuana plant on the terrace—it got really big—but we went out on the road and though I tried to explain to the neighbor girl who was watching the place how to identify and remove the male plants, she didn't get it done, and the plant just yielded an ounce or so of pretty average seeded stuff. I kept the big central stick for ages.

After a big Blondie show at the Palladium, Robert Fripp approached us and offered us his services. Everyone liked and admired Robert and we did a couple of shows with him; the first was a benefit for Dead Boy member Johnny Blitz, who had gotten stabbed, and the next was a full show at the Palladium. He had suggested that we work up a few songs that we could do together when we were all in the same place. We did a version he came up with of Iggy's "Sister Midnight," Donna Summer's "I Feel Love," "Louie Louie," and a couple of others.

Another guy I began hanging out with more was Walter Steding. Walter would do these one-man-band shows at CBGB's where he would allegedly have his violin plugged into his brain, the whole thing accompanied by strings of lights and light-up glasses that he would wear. Walter also worked for Andy, helped around the Factory. When I met him he was living in a rented utility closet in an office building near Union Square. It only had a sink in it and one small high window. He called it "the Little Room."

In the penthouse apartment we had cable TV because now we were privileged and living above Fourteenth Street. Joey Freeman and me had been too early in 1972 with our videos but in 1978 the airwaves of public access were at a weird high point. Some amazing strange shows found their way into people's homes. Ugly George was this guy who ran around midtown in a silver lamé romper attempting to coerce women into undressing for his huge portable camera. I would see George around the streets but he would never engage with guys; he always gave me the cold shoulder if I said hi. He did succeed in getting enough girls in some state of undress to fill up his time slot and later sell VHS copies of his exploits. George walked so *Girls Gone Wild* could run.

Robin Byrd was a former adult film star whose show was mainly focused on whichever male or female stripper she had on that week. Now that I think about it, Robin was really at the fore of the sexual/cultural revolution. Debbie and me later on had a little interaction with Al Goldstein and went on his show *Midnight Blue*, which was an extension of *Screw* magazine. There were non-prurient cable shows as well. There was a guy who just played cocktail music on a piano while wearing a tuxedo, and there was radical feminist Coca Crystal whose show was titled *If I*

Can't Dance You Can Keep Your Revolution, after the Emma Goldman quote. Glenn was on Coca's show one night and the next day when he was recognized on the subway he had the brainstorm to do his own show. Glenn O'Brien's *TV Party* aired shortly thereafter and went on weekly for four years. We did around eighty shows. I was the cohost and Walter was Doc Steding, the bandleader. There were no drums, so Lenny Ferrari, who played drums with Walter's band, played a close-miked magazine on a music stand. Our friend Amos Poe was the director. We'd known Amos for a while as he attempted to instill French new-wave cinema ideals in the downtown crowd. Amos's directorial style was experimental and included a lot of dissolves between the two cameras and occasional shots of feet. This is probably the first time I encountered Basquiat, who would sometimes operate a camera and would sometimes stay in the control room writing things on screen with the character generator. Fab 5 Freddy Brathwaite was also a regular guest and camera operator.

The show was broadcast around the city from ETC Studios, the Experimental Television Center, at 110 East Twenty-Third Street, which were wired to Manhattan Cable TV next door at number 120. The guy who ran it was this very smart Mr. Rogers–type, Jim Chladek, who had the patience of a saint when it came to putting up with our antics. A lot of consideration went into deciding what day of the week was the best, and we arrived at Tuesday since we figured more people would be home. I never saw much of the first seasons of *Saturday Night Live* because I was never home on Saturday night, for example.

I really liked taking the on-air phone calls from whoever was crazy enough to watch the show and call in. A fan base developed and the same weirdos would call frequently. There was a guy with a gravelly Brooklyn accent who would repeatedly say, "Ben is dry!" and "I'm gonna come down there and break your legs." As far as I know he never appeared. An anonymous caller: "You have poles up your asses!" Me: "No! We have Russians and Czechs up our asses!" The show had theme nights: On Halloween Night, Freddy dressed up as a nickel bag. Primitive Night was people in a bunch of loincloths, and Medieval Night brought out capes and cardboard armor. On Heavy Metal Night Jean-Michel graffitied *Mock Penis Envy* on the freshly painted back wall and we had to pay the pissed-off studio. The shows cost around ninety bucks to produce and the audience of around twenty to thirty people would chip in, like paying cover at a club. In fact, the one night a week was very club-like with everyone meeting across the street at the Blarney Stone bar and then proceeding to the studio. Everybody was on the damn show. Klaus Nomi was on several times; David Byrne; Nile Rodgers; Fripp; the B-52s; the Clash. Maybe most remarkably, the great George Clinton, who appeared on television only a handful of times, was on *TV Party* with the Brides of Funkenstein. Iggy was on one of the very last shows, of which no copy survives that we know of.

Near the end of *TV Party*, when it had transitioned to color, we sent tapes to a public-access channel in Los Angeles, and the Black Flag song is allegedly referencing the show. Also when I started dragging a portable VHS recorder around, we sent a couple of tapes to Glenn from the road. (The recorder was a huge unwieldy device that was fraught with problems. The battery, which lasted less than an hour, was huge. I had the fifteen-pin cable break in Florida and despite it being a Panasonic product, it took days to locate another; we found it at a little specialty tech store that was hidden in a strip mall on the outskirts of somewhere.) If *TV Party* had gone a few more years it might have found its way onto normal TV, but it ran its course and everyone moved on.

Also Debbie and I went on Al Goldstein's cable show *Midnight Blue*. Al of course liked Debbie and we got a cover story/interview for *Screw* magazine. Al was a singular character. He had a segment on his show called "Fuck You," which was him complaining about things. But the things he was annoyed about were sometimes really questionable. He would do ten minutes raving in anger about something he bought for two bucks that broke, like one of those cheapo portable fans that look like flashlights or just a crappy plastic pen that didn't work for him. We went to his town house once and it was relatively normal except for the numerous pairs of objects all over the place. It seemed that Al would compulsively buy two of things he liked in case one died or got lost or whatever. He had two ashtrays next to each other, two toothbrushes, two copies of books, two of the same knickknacks, et cetera. One of the last times I saw him was when he invited us to lunch in SoHo. Also at the lunch was Bernard Goetz, who had gained notoriety as a result of shooting four guys on the subway. Bernard's date was a lady cop.

Terry Ellis and Leeds did their best to encourage producer Mike Chapman to check us out and consider working with us. Leeds had already convinced him to see us at the Whisky in LA and Mike seemed to think we were amusing. He came to New York, where we had a mutually suspicious meeting, but after we played him some things he warmed to the idea. Chapman is connected to something like seventy hit singles and although he wrote a lot of them, he assured us early on that he only wanted to deal with our material.

In June we started up with Mike at the Record Plant on West Forty-Fourth Street. Mike must have thought we were a bunch of maniacs, with all the fussing and attitude that was thrown around, but his bedside manner was awesome and he quickly grabbed control of the situation.

Gottehrer had a very different approach than Mike. Gottehrer would do four or five takes of the full band and pick the best one. For this record, Mike wanted only one take of anything. Nobody in the band was quite ready for the repetition. Mike was going for a combination of feeling, "emotional content," and precision. Being able to do something a million times and still keep it fresh is a very specific skill that's an advantage in many art forms. We adapted to this but it made for some resistance and squabbles; somebody flung a synthesizer at Mike. I enjoyed the techniques and I don't know how much bitching I did but probably some.

Mike would sometimes "conduct" the band; he'd play rhythm guitar and sing along with us to keep the timing up to his standards. The whole band would record knowing that we were just going for a good bass and drums take, intending to overdub the guitars and keyboards.

Famously, Debbie and me were in a taxicab in Tokyo and I was playing a mixtape that Jeffrey Lee Pierce had given me. On it was a track I really liked, "Hanging on the Telephone" by Nerves guitarist Jack Lee. The cabdriver, who was an older Japanese dude, started tapping his fingers on the steering wheel and we knew that the song had that transcendent something. I remember us trying to find a British phone number to call so we could record the opening ring; I don't recall whose number it was but it was someone we knew. The phone ringing seems to have been Chapman's idea but I've seen everybody involved—Mike, the band, engineers, and crew—taking credit for everything that worked on the record, so it's tricky. Then Jack Lee, the guy who wrote the song, arrived at the studio and he was so charming and such a good salesman that we did a second one of his songs, "Will Anything Happen." He did a very heartfelt performance of it with just a guitar that convinced everyone.

The other cover song on the record was a version of Buddy Holly's "I'm Gonna Love You Too." I knew this song from weird sixties UK band the Hullaballoos more than from Buddy. The Hullaballoos were just an odd Beatles counterpoint. The four of them would wear white buttoned-up dress shirts and they had long blond hair; they always reminded me of the Morlocks from the 1960 version of *The Time Machine* if the Morlocks had been in a band.

"Heart of Glass" was built around the Roland rhythm machine and synth, the drums pieced together with the kick recorded alone. Frankie's repetitive riff is brilliant. My rhythm guitar single repeating sixteenth notes were done with a Roland Space Echo tape delay and took a couple of hours to get every one in sync. I will take credit for the title, which I remember arriving at after the vocal sessions had already started, coming in and presenting the phrase that fit in with the rest of the lyric. At the time I had no idea about the great Werner Herzog film of the same name, *Heart of Glass (Herz aus Glas)*, about a glassblower. Supposedly the whole cast of the movie was hypnotized during filming; this might have worked great for Blondie.

I had this ballad, "Fade Away and Radiate," which was about Debbie always falling asleep with the TV on, and we asked Fripp to come in on it. He was as professional and fast as usual; just a few takes and he had it. His sound was just one fuzz tone and his Les Paul—less is more.

The recording took six weeks. The final session found everyone half asleep on the Record Plant floor at six a.m. as Mike and engineer Pete Coleman staggered out carrying the seven reels of two-inch tape, took a taxi to the airport, and went on to LA to mix.

Debbie had a poem and album title idea, *Parallel Lines*, that everyone was good with and it had the same initials as the previous record.

We did an extensive photo shoot with our buddy from the downtown scene, Edo Bertoglio, who's a great photographer. Leeds came up with the idea for bold black-and-white stripes being the main graphic motif. In retrospect the cover is great, but of course Peter did a terrible job of both selling and explaining the concept to us. During the session Leeds asked us all to take one image smiling. Everyone was looking all serious for the majority of the shots, doing their rock-star sucked-in-cheeks faces. I feel like Leeds could have at the very least put in the effort to try and sell his idea of Debbie frowning and the boys smiling but he didn't try at all. We all went over the images and picked out our favorite ones. When we saw a mockup of the finished cover, naturally everyone was pissed and Leeds was like, "Nope, that's it!" Plus we thought the logo of the name looked like the old Blimpie logo. It was another disconnect. Chrysalis execs listened to the record and told us to redo it. They didn't like it. Chapman convinced them it was okay. It's too bad that, like a lot more that was happening to us, the good things were balanced by the problematic.

We went out on tour in America with the Kinks. Like Iggy and Bowie, they were friendly and encouraging.

In Austin we had a day off and Bob Marley and the Wailers were playing and it was an amazing show and we waited with the crowd at the stage door to see them leave and I patted Bob on the back.

Fripp told us that he had it on good authority that Jimmy Carter, who was the president, was anti–new wave, presumably because he was a Southern rock fan and that Carter told all the top record and media people, "We don't want it, boys." I have no idea if this happened, but hey, we weren't getting any airplay in the States.

The emphasis on Debbie's looks was now a full-on characteristic of everything the band did. She was a poster. Leeds came up with the Blondie Is a Group campaign and might have been surprised when we didn't like it. It felt like an overstatement and a self-contradiction, but like the cover, it resonated with fans, and we let it slide after initial tantrums.

Our lawyer Marty Silfen was a major blessing; I don't know how we found him but he did his best to extricate us from a lot of what were potentially much crappier situations. Marty went on to write textbooks on entertainment law that are still in print. Leeds hooked us up with one Bert Padell, a high-profile showbiz accountant and business manager who almost immediately turned on Leeds and started advising us not to listen to him. We found out that we weren't contractually obligated to pay Leeds's travel expenses so when we went to the UK and Europe immediately after the Kinks tour, we went without a manager as such.

The band stayed at rental flats right off King's Road near World's End for what felt much longer than the week or two that we were there. The Runaways were staying on a houseboat nearby and we would see Joan frequently. We did a festival type of concert in Bilzen, Belgium, that was probably our biggest show at that point and included a lot of equipment malfunctions. Back in London we attended a big publicity-based photo event titled Blondie in Camera during which Debbie and me and some of the other guys and friends got whacked on heroin and shut ourselves into a small, very hot office for a while. The photo show was a media frenzy and we were mobbed by fans as we were leaving. I'm surprised I didn't become a junkie sooner, but there was still a way to go.

Canet Rock Festival in Barcelona was a full-on huge multi-act festival. When we arrived after dark the singer of another band was shooting up in our trailer and we waited politely till they left. Nico played to this huge crowd with her little pump organ and a mic. We went on at three in the morning to a vast sea of half-asleep Spaniards. Ultravox came on with the sunrise.

We continued around Europe and the UK and the record was finally released. The first single that Chrysalis released from *Parallel Lines* was "I'm Gonna Love You Too." The Buddy Holly movie with Gary Busey had come out and maybe they were hoping for a tie-in, for some American vibe. I also heard some stuff about a possible payout to Paul McCartney, who owns Holly's publishing. Whatever; the single did nothing anywhere. "Picture This" was released next and did better, getting to number twelve in the UK but nowhere in the U.S.

Touring never stopped. A common occurrence was us appearing onstage to a seated crowd and realizing that security was forcing everyone to sit. Debbie would ask everyone to please get up. The crowd would rush the stage and the whole event would elevate. At one UK show the audience tore up several rows of bolted-down theater seats and left them in a pile at the side of the stage.

We did a Hammersmith gig in September two days after Keith Moon died. Clem loved Moon and at the end of the show, he flung his snare drum into the audience while yelling "Keith Mooooon!" We were backstage and one of the crew guys breathlessly appeared with the drum after somehow retrieving it. Clem yelled at him: *"That was a sacrifice!"* We did one matinee at Hammersmith wherein when the curtain was raised we were all seated around a small folding table in the middle of the stage having tea, since it was teatime. We pushed over the tea set and table and ran to our places and I don't think anyone in the audience got the joke.

I think it might have been at one of these Hammersmith gigs that I had the bright idea of using Wagner's "Ride of the Valkyries" as walk-on music for us. *Apocalypse Now* had recently arrived and "the Ride" was in the zeitgeist. We played the track at full volume as we came out. It was a learning moment, as we sounded like Micky Mouse in comparison.

I was on the phone with Leeds complaining about some scheduling changes that we weren't aware of and in the course of the same conversation he told me that he'd been too busy to tell us and then, a few minutes later, that he'd told us but I was too dumb to remember being told. Debbie and I thought it was time to break up with him. The tour finished and there was a long flight back from Switzerland that involved the usual extended periods of sitting around in an airport. When we got back we met with Marty Silfen and Padell, who advised us to try and renegotiate our contract with Leeds. Naturally Peter wouldn't go for it since he had the upper hand, and we had to bite the bullet and go for a divorce. The legal wrangling was obviously going to continue on for the next several centuries and we went out on tour in America.

The New York show at the Palladium was particularly great, with Mitch Ryder and the Detroit Wheels and the Heartbreakers on the bill. Fripp did the encore with us. Mitch Ryder told us that after touring with Leslie West's Wild West Show, he lost his voice for six months.

Our friend Victor Bockris had earlier introduced us to William

Burroughs, and Debbie and I did a couple of odd concerts related to the 1978 Nova Convention; one, very late at night, was at Irving Plaza with Fripp, Walter Steding, and Debbie playing drums.

The year wound down with us in San Francisco opening for REO Speedwagon at Winterland. At our sound check after some dispute, Bill Graham strangled our tour manager Bruce Patron a little as everybody watched. Later Clem did a radio interview on KSAN during which he suggested that the audience "all leave after we play." Supposedly some of the Speedwagon members heard this and there was some tension, us wondering if Clem would be assassinated prior to the show. As it happened, we had a great show, even though we were denied an encore in spite of the cheering throngs. The Winterland people gave us a black-and-white in-house video of our set that didn't have audio.

After the show we went to a party at the Jefferson Airplane black mansion, where we met John Belushi. Maybe that same night we were invited to a very exclusive drugstore that was the top floor of one of those San Francisco town houses. We went up the stairs and on the second-floor landing were confronted by a couple of huge biker-type guys who checked us out and okayed our further ascent. In a big room on the top floor was the man: a guy who looked like John Denver dressed in a tan leather fringed jacket sitting amongst bowls of everything. All around the floor were wooden bowls, with little signs and prices, that contained various strains of weed, blotter acid, and some pills. They didn't have any coke or hard stuff for sale.

Also during the same trip we went to see the Avengers at the Mabuhay. A huge fight broke out. I have no idea what precipitated it but very suddenly the whole group of several hundred people there started rushing around madly like a bird murmuration. It pretty quickly gathered some focus; it became apparent that almost everyone in the room was in pursuit of a couple of people, who, after some more struggle, made a break for the doors and got away. Debbie and me were standing near the edge of all this. I turned my head and right next to us was a pretty big biker-styled guy who was wearing a black Debbie T-shirt with a white picture of her face. Blood was dramatically dripping from this guy's head onto her picture, another dumb metaphor for the period.

Finally, after the New Year, "Heart of Glass" was released. *Parallel Lines* had been on the charts for six months. Disco was still weirdly contentious and polarizing in America. This was the same year all the burning-disco-records nonsense became a thing, "death to disco," et cetera. There were some pretty hideous disco songs but my general rule of thumb when discussing trends in popular music is that fifty percent is and has always been crap and people only remember the good stuff. I'm not sure if we tried to hold back the track for fear of being labeled; I think we just didn't realize it would strike a chord with people. I don't know that it needs pointing out that today most modern pop music is closer to disco than to other genres. At the time I had no problem with disco; I saw it as an extension, a subset, of R&B. I like the Bee Gees' disco period best of their output.

The video for "Heart of Glass" was directed by Stanley Dorfman, who was the original producer/director of *Top of the Pops* in the UK. Steve Sprouse made Debbie a dress and made the boys shirts that were printed with his TV-scan-line designs. It wasn't shot at Studio 54 even though there's a shot of the club's exterior in the intro. It was some generic midtown disco.

Negotiations to break with Leeds were under way and the success of the song was bittersweet since he kept upping his price as it went up the charts. In a normal situation, as soon as we had a big hit, management would have been negotiating to get us a better deal with the record company—that was pretty much standard procedure. As it was, we were contracted to Chrysalis for three records a year, so we were always in breach and there were no inroads on our behalf.

We opened for Rush at the Spectrum in Philadelphia. The Rush fans hated us and we only did a few songs while being barraged with trash before Clem kicked his drums over and we left. According to reports, I exacerbated the whole deal by flipping off the crowd but I don't remember.

We even did a couple of shows for full-on disco crowds at disco clubs and they didn't react to anything except "Heart of Glass." "Heart of Glass" was getting more play at the rock clubs than at actual discos and only made it to number fifty-eight on the U.S. disco charts.

We did a bunch of U.S. TV: *Midnight Special, Merv Griffin, Mike Douglas,* and *American Bandstand.* In April we flew to Amsterdam for

Dutch TV, then to Italy for more TV. We were in Milan in our hotel when we all got phone calls from Chapman, who surprised us by asking us to meet him downstairs in the hotel bar right away. Debbie tells me she remembers that we didn't want to go to the bar because we were fried. We went and we were all sitting around a big round table in the midst of this Fellini-esque environment with women in black cocktail dresses and veils and Mike told us that "Heart of Glass" had gone to number one in America. He'd flown to Italy to tell us in person. A lot of toasting ensued.

In New York we began recording our second record with Mike, *Eat to the Beat*, at the Power Station and Electric Lady Studios on Eighth Street. It was then I discovered that there is an ancient stream running below Eighth Street that's called the Devil's Water. In the rearmost lowest room of Electric Lady is a little metal trapdoor that opens onto the stream. Jimmy and me tied a string to a plastic cup and pulled up some of the water that was horribly gross and had what looked like human hair floating in it.

While we were rehearsing for the record, we got a *Rolling Stone* cover story. The journalist, Jamie James, walked into the Blondie stress machine and was immediately called out. The first thing Debbie said to him was "You suck." I don't exactly remember what she thought he'd done but I knew it was a poor start. When the piece came out, the cover image by Annie Leibovitz was amazing and we all hated the accompanying article. I gave the writer a hard time and complained about the story in other press I did. Now I feel bad about my dumb response. It's actually a great piece, it's just dark, and James had captured what he witnessed, the tensions that were all over us at the time. Jamie James lives in Indonesia now; at least I think it's the same guy. Anyway, I'm sorry I was rude and egotistical. I frequently recommend the story to people these days.

The recording was a lot looser than *Parallel Lines*. Maybe we'd improved and Mike did less of the strenuous repetitive technique. The approach was more of a live augmented attack. More Robert Altman as opposed to Stanley Kubrick. Also I think we had a better handle on music production. Jimmy and me had both produced other bands by then; I know I tried to apply some of the techniques I'd picked up while working with Mike.

During the recording I was producing French duo Casino Music for

Michael Zilkha's Ze Records and Walter Steding for Warhol. With Walter we recorded a particularly great and insane version of "Hound Dog" that featured Fripp and became an obscure cult hit. I was also doing *TV Party* and dealing with the management-split situation. Also the Power Station was near Studio 54 and there was a lot of coke in the mix; everyone was on edge and stressed with the pressure of competing with our own current successes. Our booked time at Power Station ran out when the recording ran behind schedule and we went to Electric Lady.

Bert Padell coerced us into this show of very publicly looking for a new manager by interviewing candidates. Really, it was a publicity stunt. "Blondie is interviewing managers—unheard of!" was a thing. I think we listened to around forty different people. I don't know if any one band member saw all of them. The process got some showbiz buzz going, as intended, but it was a ludicrous exercise in futility as we all knew we were going to wind up with Shep Gordon, who Bert had been steering us toward the whole time. We saw a lot of actually great people but in the end Shep came in and, unlike many of the others who'd given us a sales pitch, just said, "Okay, I'll do it," and that was that.

Shep was well established as a heavyweight. He'd started out with and still managed Alice Cooper and when we knew him he was doing Teddy Pendergrass and Luther Vandross, among others. He had a great connection to old Hollywood. He was Groucho Marx's manager too. Also Shep didn't want a contract, and considering that we had to pay Leeds our children's DNA and a piece of Blondie forever everywhere in the universe, we were good with that aspect.

Next was a U.S. tour with Rockpile, which was a sort of British supergroup that featured Nick Lowe and Dave Edmunds and was managed by Jake Riviera. Jake was a major player in the UK music scene. He founded Stiff Records, amongst many other endeavors. This started out amicably enough but soon descended into weird competition and tension. At some mid-country show after Rockpile finished, one of their crew members led a blond girl who was dressed flashily in a leopard miniskirt ensemble right across the middle of the stage, and the audience went crazy and started cheering. I don't know if this was innocent or shady but Debbie had to be restrained from going and beheading Jake.

In New York we had a date at Wollman Rink in Central Park, the skating rink near the carousel that was used for open-air concerts during the summer. Walter opened up the whole show doing his weird electric psychic head violin for this big crowd as they filed in. After the show the scene turned into a *World War Z* scenario with a frantic crowd surrounding the fence. We were stuck there for an extra hour or so and finally left in a rush as flying bottles smashed on the roof of the car.

The tour was long, and at the end Shep sent one of his crew, Denny Vosburgh, to contend with us. Denny was great; he was a big guy with a kind of Wild West sheriff vibe. He'd been to Vietnam and had PTSD that wasn't quite recognized as a condition yet. If a war movie was on the TV he would leave the room, but if he had to fight drunks or act as bodyguard he wasn't fazed.

At the end of the tour we did *Saturday Night Live*, and *Eat to the Beat* was released. Right away we shot a video album with David Mallet, who'd directed the "Hanging on the Telephone" video as well as videos for every other musician in the world at the time. I've heard that it was perhaps the first long-form video album made—that is, every song on the record. Certainly one thing we did first was the little squares. Someone who worked on the album art utilized little squares, like graph paper, as a design motif. Little squares were on all of the *Eat to the Beat* ads and soon became ubiquitous; I would see them in graphics all over the place. Also Jimmy Destri, who had good drawing skills, designed the Blondie logo for the album.

The video album was done quickly with a lot of it filmed in the wilds of New Jersey. The video included a lot of our friends from downtown, among them Glenn, Freddy, and Jean-Michel. In the "Atomic" video, which was one of the more elaborate shoots, Basquiat, who had originally been relegated to join the dancers with everyone else, bugged me for a bigger cameo, so we let him meet the guy who rides up to the post-apocalyptic disco and take his horse as he dismounts. We did the shot and afterward Jean pulled me aside and said, "You gave me the Black man's job." He laughed when he saw how uncomfortable I got. In his scene, Jean is standing next to a Blondie Green Spot banner that I'd dragged back from Bangkok. (When I met him, Jean had been painting on cardboard. I asked him to do a piece on canvas for me and he did a monochromatic scene with a military theme, stick-figure soldiers and cannons on a piece of heavy burlap-like canvas. I suspect it was his first canvas but I don't really know. I gave him two hundred bucks and later heard from a couple of people that he'd told them he'd ripped me off.) Also in the "Atomic" video I'm playing a weird old Wandre Italian guitar that I had.

"The Hardest Part" video was another big production that included a white set that was grandly graffitied by Fab 5, Lee Quinones, and Basquiat. In later years I've thought it ironic that their painting was covered over in white probably within a day or so.

Then the "Union City Blue" video had a helicopter shot, so that was a big deal for us. It was shot on an old pier in Weehawken, New Jersey. While we were filming, Jimmy, Clem, and me wandered off and were smoking a joint in some nearby tall swampy weeds when we spotted a guy pulling up and parking a big Cadillac. As we watched he very suspiciously looked around for observers without seeing us, as we'd ducked and were observing. He took a white plastic bag out of his car, tossed it in the weeds, then quickly drove off. We hustled over and got the bag. It was either a small loaf of French bread or a big baguette. That was it, a boring mystery and yet another metaphor. The guy was just very nervous about littering, perhaps.

From the video shoot we went to Austin to be in a movie Shep was producing called *Roadie*. Shep went on to produce more films but this was his first endeavor. It was directed by Alan Rudolph, who's made a lot of cool films and was assistant director on Altman's *Long Goodbye* and *Nashville*. Meatloaf was the lead and Shep's Hollywood connection got Art Carney in the cast. Blondie was itself—we had a concert scene where we played "Ring of Fire"—and Debbie had a couple of scenes with Meatloaf. Central to our part was a big fight scene with a rival band of little people called Snow White during a tire convention at a Holiday Inn. (Sounds better than it actually is.) A lot of footage of this didn't make it into the movie. In the midst of this pretend mayhem, one of the rival-band guys shot me in the left ear with a fire extinguisher and ever since I've had a top-end loss. It was a perfect Zen-like shot that took place while everyone was charging around this hotel ballroom overturning tables and throwing tires. I can't hear the hiss of my fingers rubbing together in my left ear.

Our "performance" of the Johnny Cash song was filmed in pieces. An audience of extras was dragged in to stand around and act enthusiastic in the high afternoon heat. I think they got water but no beer. We would play the last few bars of the song and the audience was expected to cheer wildly, the full takes having been filmed prior to their arrival. Finally we did play a few Blondie songs for these guys.

I was still dragging around what might have been the first portable VHS video recorder, this massive Panasonic thing. The battery was bigger and heavier than fifteen iPhones. I actually shot one short scene that's in the final cut of *Roadie* but it wasn't enough to keep the movie from doing terribly. It's free on YouTube if you want to check it out.

CHAPTER 10

We were really big stars now and it was very weird. I'm a very optimistic person and through this all, I always perhaps egomaniacally assumed that everything we did would be successful. At the same time the pressures were immense and, for me, getting stoned definitely buffered me from a lot of tensions and helped me tunnel-vision more of it.

Debbie met Jane Fonda, and one afternoon, Jane and Kris Kristofferson, who were filming *Rollover*, came to our apartment and we sat around smoking weed and watching *The Tin Drum*. I would just keep smoking indefinitely, and by then I always had really great pot. I generally leaned toward indica if I could get it. Jane and Debbie dropped out after four joints or so but Kristofferson kept pace with me.

Bowie came over a couple of times and signed our David Bowie records. We had a party he was at that I don't remember much of. We didn't throw a lot of parties but we would frequently have people at our place.

We got back to the UK as the Soviets were getting ready to invade Afghanistan on Christmas Eve. Right at the onset we did an in-store appearance at Our Price Records on Kensington High Street. We'd been there previously and a lot of people, hundreds, had shown up to get autographs. This time there were a few thousand. The cops closed off the street. We went up to an office on the second floor and when Debbie stuck her head out the window and waved, the crowd cheered like they'd seen a goal at a football

AUTOGRAPHS AFTER A SHOW.
(PHOTO BY CHRIS STEIN)

DEBBIE AND THE BOYS IN THE BAND
ON A GERMAN TRAIN, CIRCA 1978.
(PHOTOS BY CHRIS STEIN)

**BACKSTAGE AT THE GARDEN WITH THE GRAND WIZARD
AND GREG "THE HAMMER" VALENTINE.**
(PHOTO BY GEORGE NAPOLITANO)

WITH BUNNY WAILER IN 2019.
(PHOTO BY TOMMY MANZI)

**GERALD GARDNER AND ROOTY
THE ROOT DEMON ON THE ISLE OF MAN.**
(PHOTO BY GREYSON DAVIES)

ROOTY TODAY.
(PHOTO BY CHRIS STEIN)

HAROLD IN HIS OFFICE, SIMPLER TIMES.
(PHOTO BY CHRIS STEIN)

THE DODGERS SHOULD HAVE
STAYED IN BROOKLYN!
(STEIN FAMILY ARCHIVE)

**BEN AND ME AT CONEY ISLAND,
CIRCA 1959.**

(STEIN FAMILY ARCHIVE)

STEL EARLY ON.
(STEIN FAMILY ARCHIVE)

THE FOLKS AROUND WHEN THEY MET,
I GUESS, IN 1949.
(STEIN FAMILY ARCHIVE)

Sex *Male*   Date *1 - 5 - 50*

BABY *Stein*

Room or Ward No. *16 - 20*

Doctor

Grammes *2705*   Color *White*

Lbs *5*   oz *15*   S398

January 7, 1969   *Laser Schondorf*

Mrs. Estelle Stein, Apt 4-A
1249 Ocean Avenue
Brooklyn, N. Y. 11230

Dear Mrs. Stein:

      This is our last and final warning
to you, and your son. The activities in your
apartment are extremely disturbing to your co-tenants
and unless you cooperate with our management and
curtail loud parties, loud noises, loud guitar playing,
into the early hours of the morning we will be forced
to commence legal action toward your eviction.

      This apartment was not rented to you
to use as a meeting hall for transient visitors at
all hours of the day and night.

      Truly yours,

      A. & J. MANAGING CO.

ls/lsk   BY:
                Managing Agent

603 EMPIRE BLVD. • BROOKLYN, N. Y. 11213 • INgersoll 7-5554

(STEIN FAMILY ARCHIVE)

Syracuse News Letter

Issued by: Communist Political Association of Onondaga County

333 S. Warren St. • Room 113 • Phone 3-2760 • Syracuse, N. Y.

NOTES AND FIGURES ON THE ELECTION CAMPAIGN IN ONONDAGA COUNTY

Non-Partisanship

The re-election of Franklin D. Roosevelt is not a partisan question. It is a national necessity dictated by the very needs of our national life. Franklin D. Roosevelt is no more the candidate of the Democratic Party in 1944 than Abraham Lincoln was a candidate of the Republican Party in 1864. The 1944 elections are a crusade of the people without consideration for party labels. A crusade on issues of life and death consequence for each of us; the speediest and least costly victory over Fascism, the surest and most lasting peace, the securest and most prosperous post-war America.

Nor is this non-partisan character of the campaign for President Roosevelt something new. Even in the less critical elections of 1936 and 1940, Franklin D. Roosevelt's candidacy was so understood by labor and the people. A glance at the 1940 figures for the City of Syracuse will clearly show this:

The Figures	Syracuse, Presidential Election 1940		
Registration	115,759		
Enrollment	102,748	Republican	76,595
		Democrat	25,676
		ALP	477
Unenrolled	13,011		
Total Vote	110,208	Republican	60,136
		Democrat	47,116
		ALP	2,956
		Roosevelt Vote:	50,072

The Conclusion:

It follows therefore, that even in 1940, Franklin D. Roosevelt was not a partisan candidate and that the campaign for his re-election was a non-partisan campaign. While only 25,676 enrolled Democrats could possibly have voted for him, at least 24,396 non-Democratic Party enrollees or slightly less than one-half of President Roosevelt's 50,072 votes, came from the 10,908 to 16,459 enrolled Republicans who voted for him, the 13,011 politically independent voters unenrolled in any party, and some 477 American Labor Party voters.

BORING COMMUNIST PARTY LITERATURE THAT I FOUND IN MY MOM'S STUFF.

(STEIN FAMILY ARCHIVE)

**SELF-PORTRAIT AT THE ABANDONED
NAVAL BASE IN BROOKLYN.**

(PHOTO BY CHRIS STEIN)

We did two shows at the Glasgow Apollo on the fifteen-foot-high stage. The second night was New Year's Eve and the show was broadcast later that night on BBC Two. The show featured a guest appearance by the Strathclyde Police Department bagpipers, who did a rendition of "Sunday Girl." Everybody in the UK watched this and we actually did a great show. The show was broadcast after the concert took place and we all watched in a hotel room while going crazy and breaking wine bottles. In later years someone told me that they'd been in a cottage out on the moors somewhere in the middle of nowhere watching.

We had two nights at the Odeon in Edinburgh. Part of our un-lavish special effects were flash pots, those things that produce showers of sparks and are beloved of metal bands. Right before our show, our lighting guy, Ed Gile, was onstage tinkering with one of these things when it blew up in his face in front of the whole audience. Ed lost his eyebrows and had to be sent back to the U.S. Luckily he wasn't badly hurt but it was a hard act to follow and when we did our show, the audience just sat there in shock for the first few songs. Also the lights sucked.

An ABC crew who were shooting a segment on us for 20/20 met us in Paris. We were interviewed by Pierre Salinger. Salinger had been a U.S. senator from California but was known mostly as press secretary and adviser to JFK. He was with Robert Kennedy when he was killed and Pierre then moved to Paris, where he worked as a journalist. When we shot with him I noticed he was wearing a really great PT-109 gold tie clip that JFK had given him. I asked him about the assassination but he stuck to the single-shooter story and he probably wouldn't have told me anything more anyway.

In London 20/20 shot us at one of a series of Hammersmith shows. Fripp did "Heroes" with us and a few others. By coincidence Iggy was there and I asked him to come out with us; he said he would see. The band knew "Funtime" and some more of his songs and maybe when he saw the crowd going nuts, whatever hesitancy he had dissolved. We did "Funtime" with Iggy as the last song. The 20/20 crew shot twenty hours of footage over several days. All that footage was cut down to a half hour or less. Luckily I have the encore sequence and the whole show was recorded on twenty-four tracks. For a couple of years now a filmmaker we know, Andrew Chinnici, has been trying to track down the tapes. He's been going at it in full-on detective wall-with-red-string mode, getting in touch with living relatives and ABC former staffers who might have a connection to the show. I don't know if the tapes will ever surface but I have to thank Andrew for his efforts.

When we were in Indianapolis we came upon this very old, funky, and large kind of pawnshop guitar store. This place was a guitar enthusiast's ultimate ridiculous wet dream. It was beyond. There was a huge upstairs area filled with shelves that were packed with guitars. The most they charged for a high-end old Gibson, Martin, or Fender was five hundred bucks. They must have had what's easily twenty, thirty million dollars' worth of guitars in today's overblown market jammed into this place. I called up my buddy Richie from We Buy Guitars on Forty-Eighth Street in New York, where I bought and sold a lot of stuff, and told him if he had any brains he'd get a truck and a bunch of money and come out here. Debbie and me bought a bunch of guitars, including a Gibson Trini Lopez custom, a brand-new in the case with the tags '64 Strat, and a Burns Split Sound Jazz. I might have bought the Burns mainly because besides looking cool, it had a tone setting called Wild Dog.

As we were doing the UK Blondie thing I saw ads in the music papers for new Burns models. One, called the Scorpion, particularly intrigued me; it looked a little bit like a Telecaster I had carved up in the early seventies and was just very severe-looking with a big kind of claw shape at the bottom. I reached out to Jim Burns and he came to one of the Hammersmith shows and before we went back to the U.S. we got to go out to his new company HQ in Cambridgeshire. Jim was a charming guy and I was able to get a couple of the new Scorpions, a prototype and one with a custom peghead. Jim said the Scorpion was "the devil's guitar." He'd been messed around with by the corporate guitar world. The deal he'd done with Baldwin kept him from using his own name for years after the deal was finished. I identified with his story.

We flew back to New York on Concorde. We managed to fly on it several times. It was great. If it had been an American-made plane, it would never have been discontinued after a single crash. On a trip to London, I had two suits stolen *off Concorde!* At least, the suits never arrived at baggage. On another flight to New York this guy was asked to put out his gigantic cigar and he played the "Do you know who I am?" card heavily. He was Lord something or other, and they made him put it out anyway.

Giorgio Moroder asked us to work on a track from an upcoming film. I don't know if he knew that we were playing "I Feel Love" at our shows or Stevie Nicks couldn't do it or that we were on the short list but he sent us a very fancy high-end cassette with his demo on it. The song was pretty great but the lyrics were very literal. It was called "Man Machine." The movie, *American Gigolo*, was about a male sex worker, and Debbie wanted to go for a more poetic approach. In LA we met director Paul Schrader and Richard Gere and saw a cut of the movie that inspired her lyrics. I was aware of Schrader from his having written the screenplay for *Taxi Driver*. Schrader has directed two of my favorite movies, *The Comfort of Strangers* and *Mishima: A Life in Four Chapters*.

Giorgio came to New York with a very tight basic track that we were supposed to overdub on. The band did a very fast session. Giorgio has a very no-nonsense get-it-done-as-easily-as-possible approach. There was no way he was going to handhold us through a lot of repetition. I think that the funky parts we laid down might have inspired some of the parts on the final track, but Giorgio went back to LA and finished the track with his own guys. It was briefly suggested that Giorgio produce a Blondie record but after he had dealt with the band members struggling with each other, I don't think he considered it much.

Debbie's vocal parts are a big improvement over the demo; the chorus particularly is a departure from the more monotone one that Giorgio presented. "Call Me" was a hit all over, six weeks at number one and biggest single of the year in the U.S. and also the biggest-selling Blondie single.

Right before *American Gigolo* came out, Richard Gere asked me to help him buy a guitar. I took him to We Buy Guitars on Forty-Eighth Street. I told Richie Friedman and the guys at the store that Gere was going to be a huge movie star. They didn't care and sold him a Strat.

The next year, 1980, was Blondie's least active year. Everybody was a little fragmented, drifting into different areas. Shep got Debbie a Gloria Vanderbilt jeans commercial. In 1980 designer jeans were a similar cultural phenomenon to today's NFTs; everyone was going to get rich from pants. Various designers did, in fact, get rich from jeans. We had free rein on the commercial, which we shot in the alley next to the Mudd Club. I did the music and got John Lurie to play sax. I'd done a bunch of recording with Lurie's group the Lounge Lizards. John is a very great eccentric cat and having him on this mainstream TV spot was a nice touch.

A friend of mine, British journalist Vivien Goldman, sent me a reggae compilation album, *Reggae's Hottest Hits.* I was drawn to this one song, "The Tide Is High," by the Paragons from 1967. The song just got to me and I played it incessantly. It really is a magical recording and the first reggae song that I'd heard that featured a violin. I recorded a demo of it and Debbie and me did a live version at the Mudd Club with Walter doing an odd version of the violin part.

Then Freddy took us to a rap event at a Police Athletic League in the Bronx. This was my first exposure to rap other than hearing the couple of rap tracks that were already out in the world. The rap event was up a flight of stairs in an old gym near the subway. Debbie, Glenn, Patti Astor, and me were the only downtowners in the crowd, which had people calling us Kool and the Gang, and the kids gave Freddy a humorous hard time for his outfit, which included a porkpie hat instead of the jacked-up stocking cap that everyone else was wearing. I found out that some of the guys even put a rolled-up piece of cardboard in their hats to make them stick straight up. The show itself was a nonstop kind of revue where the principals would change but the groove kept going. We saw Cold Crush, the Funky Four Plus One, Grandmaster Caz, and Flash as DJ behind a lot of them. The energy was fantastic and I left very buzzed about the hip-hop scene. How could I have not known about this? It was going on almost simultaneously with the downtown scene. I felt like this whole community of kids uptown had literally and symbolically found a collective voice.

We were setting up for the next record. There was lots of talk about potential other producers, like ABBA and Spector, but everyone was very comfortable with Mike and it was ultimately a no-brainer. I'm pretty sure any other producer at that moment would have been disastrous. You know that scene from *No Country for Old Men* where Carson Wells, about to be blown away, says to Anton Chigurh, "Do you have any idea how crazy you are?" Nobody in Blondie had any idea how crazy they were. Also, I realize now that we were working with Mike when he had reached a career peak, his years of successes arriving at this moment we shared. (We also were working at the height of analog-recording technology.)

I for one was all about pushing our boundaries. I felt that, like many other musical genres, the so-called new-wave scene had limited itself with a parochial set of rules and parameters. Debbie and me had gone to see a production of Lerner and Loewe's *Camelot* at Lincoln Center that starred Richard Burton. (When Burton says he's the king, you believe him.) I fell in love with a beautiful lyrical song that appears at an early critical moment in the story. Merlin, who lives outside of time in both the past and the future, knows that Arthur is going to get into trouble but also that he, Merlin, is about to be led away by a water nymph to sleep eternally in her cave. His vision of the future fades, and as Nimue, the spirit, leads him away she sings this song, "Follow Me." I thought this was a great metaphor for what happened to JFK (whose presidency was frequently referred to as Camelot) and the country as a result of his leaving too soon. I thought about making the record about American culture. When I suggested recording "Follow Me," all the band members decided I was completely insane and I was just trying to torture them. Telling them that Frank Sinatra had covered it didn't help.

The first stab at a record title was to call it *Coca-Cola*, because I thought that was super-American. The cover would be the white-on-red logo, Blondie Coca-Cola. We ran this by Coca-Cola and they didn't want to go near it so the second idea I had was to call it *Autoamerican*, which was about cars and auto erotica and the road and all that. I also knew for sure that if we recorded "Tide Is High," it would be a hit. It was the only song we recorded that I felt this certain about in advance.

I talked to Chapman about a couple of orchestral and big-band pieces and Mike brought in Jimmie Haskell, who was a Hollywood composer and film scorer who had a ton of experience. I had this big-ass cinematic piece that referenced Bernard Herman a little. I played my eight-track synth recordings for Jimmie, who added some embellishments and wrote out charts. The horn section for "Tide Is High" was based on the violin lines on the original. I played the lines on guitar and sang some of them for Haskell and he charted them out.

Tom Scott, who played the sax lines on Bernard Herman's *Taxi Driver* score and has played with everyone from Joni to McCartney, did the horns on "Rapture." He blew us away by coming up with the multitracked parts on the spot and playing them in just a few hours. There were really guys who'd played on Maurice Jarre's *Lawrence of Arabia* soundtrack in the orchestra that Jimmie put together. I was totally knocked out by this, as the *Lawrence* soundtrack was one of my early musical obsessions.

I recently reconnected with an old piece I wrote for *Creem* magazine in June of 1981. It's pretty amusing; it adheres to the *Creem* gonzo-journo style a little. It's written close to the events and has the advantage of that proximity. For whatever reason, when it came out, it was titled "And Now for Something Different, or The Making of the President's Chauffeur." I'm still not sure what that headline refers to:

Los Angeles, the city of lost angels and angles. Dreamland. And of course Hollywood. LA's not really a tough town. It has a strange feeling of fragility. Earthquakes on the brain may be part of the reason why the surface always seems about to crack with delicate tension.

In the boiling-hot, dry summer season the low-rider gangs leave the barrios and prowl around. The weekend car crunch on Whittier Boulevard has been squelched by the cops, and the gangs range further out, leaving their fantastic alien graffiti on stucco walls all over town. *VGV, VGF,* et cetera—it looks like Martian writing. The fires burn the hills. The Strip still throbs; dull reds and pinks and the lights of the Valley still look beautiful in the hot dusty nights.

This, then, is where the Blondies grudgingly choose to record their fifth album. The main reason is so Mike Chapman will retain his sanity, thus enabling us to work for a longer period (little did they know). While musicians and singers get to wander freely in and out of the studio, Mike must sit through it all, often for twelve-hour stretches. It's exhausting work for him and we all figure it's better for the whole project if Mike is allowed to burn out at home in his own element instead of Granite Canyon National Cemetery.

So planes, limos, airfreight, are booked. Instant displacement. We arrive at our new home. "This is the Peaceful Valley rent-a-condo?" we gasp. (On the way out we passed what appears to be an upper-class sanitarium, the gates wide open and *Dawn of the Dead* types spilling out onto the highway. A few of the guests have wandered quite a ways down the road.) Our new home has an air of wheeling and dealing about it and the first impression is of a minimum-security prison. There are jokes about Timothy Leary and Steve Rubell playing tennis. Drab orange bunkers are divided into little square cubicles; there are mazes of wooden stairs and hallways and parking lots and cars everywhere. "This sucks man, we're not near anything."

It's about three miles to United Western studios on Sunset Strip. Every day we get up, stagger into the blinding sun, get into our car, drive past the living dead and a huge moon-mobile vehicle from some ancient sci-fi movie that lies rotting by the side of the road in a used-car lot, and into LA proper, the Strip. The sessions get under way.

Mike Chapman arrives in his brown and white Jeep Wagoneer. The license plate says MC HITS. He heads right for the Asteroids machine! Yes, friends, Asteroids, perhaps the greatest diversion conceived of by reasoning beings since the Chipmunks. Asteroids—when the tension mounts, just blow up a whole field of huge boulders with your laser cannon, blast a few of those miserable little UFOs as they charge at you, sit in the dark with your head swimming in the video-vapor trails, hypnotized. Hyperspace . . . Taped to the Asteroids machine is a cardboard plaque that attests to the fact that Little Ferdie J. scored 1,255,000 in one hour and forty-seven minutes on one quarter. It's dated and signed by three witnesses. It's hard enough to get to ten thousand. Chapman's goal is one hundred thousand. He easily hits fifty, sixty thousand; not much compared to little Ferdie, though. The average Blondie during the first weeks of competition can barely break ten thousand.

Basic tracks are a long haul and we attempt to adjust to slow studio routine. All that stands between the lounge of Studio A and one of the sleaziest pockets of Sunset Strip are two huge glass doors. As we sit watching TV, the Strip strips by, day turns to hot glowing night and the smog creeps in. Winos, hookers, and assorted flotsam file past. They all seem to stare in at us, and it starts to feel like goldfish time or babies behind glass. Asteroids scores go higher and the beep and booms of the machine mingle with the pulse of whichever track is being formed in the studio.

New Yorkers start to snap after about two weeks in LA and soon the symptoms of California crazy begin to appear. We drive around a lot. We have weekends off and we drive through the hills, up and down the Strip. The Sheikh's house, now burned inside, looks worse than ever. The statues with the painted pubes and the puke-green walls are now offset by big brown boards and black soot stains covering the windows.

Driving is a religion here and the airspace around one's car (psychic territory) extends further than anywhere else in the world. In other words, "Don't get too close to the car." Cars in LA are extensions of one's body like nowhere else, so to get into the swing of things, the Blondies start eating cars, and I mean *cars*. Long-suffering tour manager Bruce Patron spends his afternoons at Budget Rent-a-Bomb trading Chryslers for Trans Ams and back again. An ant-infested white Lincoln Mark V convertible is the winner. Someone dumped a gallon of coke in the back seat then parked in the weeds for three days. As we tool out to Alta Dena on Saturday afternoon, the ants do their work.

One Sunday evening it's Rodney Bingenheimer's fifth anniversary as DJ at radio station KROQ in Pasadena. One of the good things about LA is Rodney. On one wall of his studio is an area that says it all—pictures of Rodney with almost every major rock star—Hendrix, Elvis, the Stones, everyone! Over the years, many of the greats have gone on, forgetting Rod of Mod, but Rodney still remains in the eye of the hurricane. Rodney's radio show started five years ago playing hard punk music when nobody else was, then power pop, followed by a brief foray into Shaun Cassidy, Bay City Rollers, glitter rock. Now it's come full circle back to hard punk. Black Flag, the Circle Jerks, the Surf Punks represent the forefront of the new wave of teenage bands. Some of these groups are pretty intense. Cars are driven into clubs and one place was burned to the ground on opening night. But to me it's not gratuitous violence; these kids are genuinely bored with plastic California lifestyles and are finally reacting. It seems to be a little less drug-oriented than just a few years back and almost a return to the more purist gang mentality of the fifties. It should be interesting this summer if the British Flower Power pirate scene reaches America and gets absorbed by these guys.

So, to Pasadena for the show. The parking lot of KROQ is covered with a smattering of punks and fans. The show goes by fast; we're joined by Siouxsie Banshee and Michael Des Barres. At midnight Rod waxes sentimental and thanks numerous people. Spacin' Mason arrives for the late-night shift and we leave. More dark roads and twinkling lights.

Monday and the sessions grind on. By this time, LA is into the worst smog alert in twelve years and the populace begins to enter the twilight zone. The smog creeps under the windowsills and around the corners; only the capsule-like air-conditioned vacuum of the studio is safe. But still, it's easy to space out. People walking the hot streets start to resemble our living dead friends back at the Sunnydale dry-out facilities. Smog is like eating angel-dust burgers at the beach and getting sand in them that enters your brain and grits around. Very abrasive, but good for the complexion.

The smog brings out the worst and sleaziest elements, and soon rent-a-condo erupts with violence and general weirdness. One morning there's a note on the old ant-infested Mark V from someone wanting to know if the car is for sale. Faithful roadie Scottie is burgled and divested of cash and stash. *Uh-oh.* Finally we are awakened one balmy, smoggy night by, yes, friends, the snap-crackle-pop of gunfire followed by the soundtrack of *Apocalypse Now* played full blast. It's real helicopters. Swooping in low over the hills, two big dark whirlybirds zapping the grounds with super-powerful searchlights lighting up everything. After a few passes overhead, they depart loudly. The next day we are informed of what transpired. It seems one of the condo residents "spotted some guys fooling around with my car, so I took a couple of shots at 'em, big deal. I wasn't trying to hit 'em." Anyway, the authorities frown on this sort of behavior, hence the copters and the SWAT team that smashed into one band member's room looking for the sniper.

The decision to move is unanimous. That very afternoon caravans of Blondie luggage arrive at the Chateau Marmont on Sunset Strip. This place is a great, grand old Chaplin-vibes type hotel. Hollywood once threw wild parties in these very bungalows. We're also directly under a full-size NOW THERE IS MORE *Close Encounters* billboard, which is quite inspiring and magnificent in its scope. About a month has passed. Tension mounts.

The basic tracks take over a month. "Rapture" is recorded twice, once slower than the current release. The feel of the songs is closely examined. There are many differences of opinion. Lots of time is spent discussing, hashing it out, trying to satisfy everyone. "Do the Dark" is written late one night on a cassette machine. "T-Birds" is named after the LA girls' roller-derby team. The percussion on "Tide Is High" includes eight-tracks of drumsticks tapping on a piano bench. Chapman hunches over the console into the wee hours. People are pressed flat against the back wall of the studio by his playback volume. Gallons of Jose Cuervo Gold are consumed.

Mike is called home to Australia suddenly on family business and we are adrift for a week or so. I honestly don't remember much of anything of this week, but something must have happened. We drive around and around, and the *Close Encounters* billboard gets changed for Gena Rowlands's *Gloria*. We see people—Kim Fowley, what's up, Kim? "Well, Brian Epstein and James Dean are having a two-way in hell, which will have the best musicians 'cause heaven will only have the Osmonds and Pat Boone. Christopher Columbus was Jewish, and Bugs Bunny is a Communist front. Rodney was seen with a certain famous movie actress's daughter who wrecked her car last week and went to the Starwood to see a punk band instead of going to her father's funeral. We still have them here; we're behind. That's the biggest gossip."

We run into ex-Cramp Bryan Gregory living in total seclusion on the Strip. When Walter Steding arrives from New York to play, he bears sad tidings. "I heard that one of the Cramps died." Oh no. Who was it? "Bryan."

Chapman returns finally. Little did he know his house was used while he was gone for the remake of *Horror of Party Beach*. Underwear adorns crystal chandeliers; sofas look nice on the tennis court. Heads roll.

Sessions resume, the participants slightly jet-lagged and hunover. Finally the basic tracks wind down and we move a block down the Strip to Studio B. The move marks the home stretch: the vocals, overdubs, and, finally, the orchestra with the horns, et cetera. The Asteroids machine also moves down the block.

Here is Mike Chapman's little magic room. In days gone by, these brown burlap walls saw the likes of the Righteous Brothers, Jan and Dean, Johnny Rivers, and the Beach Boys come and go. Now the control room is filled with a gigantic blue console that's hooked up to computers, satellites, and submarines off the coast of Maine. Here the songs get the chrome put on. Tom Scott adds the final funk punch to "Rapture." Ray Brown carefully works out "Faces." Flo and Eddie go berserk and spread mayhem (they're off to Tuff Gong studios in Jamaica to record the Turtles' greatest-hits reggae). The vocals go very fast and a certain lead singer is wont to complain about "sitting around forever." The orchestral session is tumultuous. Thirty pieces, some of the greatest old players in Hollywood, are turned out for the session by maestro Jimmie Haskell. Some of these guys played with Tommy Dorsey; a couple even played on the soundtrack of *Lawrence of Arabia*! Things get more and more cataclysmic every day as the smog builds up. Lights in the sky.

One day Orson Welles is in another room recording his voice for a wine commercial. Debbie got Orson's autograph in a gun-shaped notebook. She said he liked the notebook. Perry Como is recording his *Christmas in Israel* special with what sounds like the Mormon Tabernacle Choir when some kid backs up about two hundred feet into the parking lot across the way from the building and then floors it, driving right smack into the wall of the studio, making a big hole, a mess, and pretty much totaling what turns out to be his girlfriend's Audi. So the kid's name is Jeffrey; his girlfriend's name is Suzy. They had a fight on the way to get blood tests for their marriage license; Jeffrey got pissed and the rest is history. That's the official excuse, anyway. We wonder 'cause it happens Suzy and Jeffrey are in a black leather rock band called Deprogrammer and Jeff happens to have copies of his new single "Slammed in the Door" in the back seat of the no-longer-drivable Audi.

Luckily, no one is hurt and the police are merciful and don't drag Jeffrey off to the slammer. That's what the song is about.

That's pretty much it. This report covers some of the major events and a tiny percent of the lesser, more sporadic type of events that have occurred sort of constantly. For example, Carl's Flower Shop across the way from the studio wound up a pile of rubble by the time we left. One day we passed by what must have been a ten-year-old kid with his hat pulled down cruising along in a full-size brand-new station wagon. The police have strange priorities. All this junk is true. A few names have been changed to protect privacy and the console in Studio B isn't really hooked up to a submarine yet. I have to apologize to all you techies for not being too technical, but this is a real story. If you want to know who did what on the record, listen to it, 'cause, really, we all did it all or at least most of it, get it?

So in the end it came to the showdown. High noon, Mike against the Asteroids machine. Hundreds of dollars in quarters devoured by this insatiable electronic force. Still, Chapman (who can play Space Invaders indefinitely on one quarter) has yet to score one hundred thousand, his dream. So, late one night, the crowd is tense; the air is hot and smoky. Yes, Mike has ninety-nine thousand and one ship left. The Asteroids are all gone; it's between man and machine. Tension mounts. The little UFO makes its approach, beeping wildly and firing its lasers like crazy. If Mike hits it, it's one hundred thousand and a new ship; if it hits him, it's the end of a twenty-minute game. They close. Shots fly around; the crowd gasps. Mike explodes into little blue video dots trailing off into the darkness. Game over. But Mike is happy he's number one on the video readout score with ninety-nine thousand, the highest score of the season. The next day, technician Merwin unplugs the machine, erasing the highest score of the season. Man has triumphed.

I omitted a passage that attempts to explain to the audience that making the record wasn't a power struggle between the band members. I guess I was attempting to toe the party line and keep things sanitary in the eyes of the public. Everything was a power struggle between the band members. I was just higher up on the food chain with *Autoamerican* and managed to get a lot of my ideas embedded in this record. The struggles produced both some miserable anxieties and some great results. The very last thing on the record, during the fade of "Follow Me," is Clem saying, "Are you really going to put this on the record?"

Chapman was known for his absurdly loud playback levels. Some New York studio had made him a custom volume knob with an arrow on it that said CHAPMAN LEVEL, pointing to where eleven would be. One afternoon I was sitting in the control room trying to get some guitar feedback going with the studio monitors. The volume was ferocious and after a few minutes the left-hand speaker burst into flames. Some part of the coil or driver got so hot it caught fire. There's video of this and the studio guys replacing it. It was an apt metaphor for our relationship with Mike.

Lastly, the Sheikh's house was an amazing, somewhat obscure Los Angeles phenomenon. This billionaire member of the Saudi royal family bought an old conspicuous estate in the middle of Beverly Hills on Sunset and proceeded to decorate it in eccentric fashion. The best parts were when he painted it sickly green, covered the roof with orange mirrors, and installed a lot of life-size human statues that had their genital areas carefully and grotesquely painted. Supposedly the insides were equally bizarre, and the interiors were in fact used as sets for Steve Martin's mansion in *The Jerk*. Anyway, the neighbors were generally horrified and when it burned down no one seemed to mind.

We handed in the record and the Chrysalis execs told us that they didn't "hear any singles." Maybe it was revenge because Mike wouldn't let any of the A and R guys say anything during production. They were allowed into the sessions but they knew better than to comment or offer opinions.

Shep threw a Blondie party that we arrived at sitting on what I think was a Sherman tank. The tank wasn't allowed to drive around too much on the LA streets so it arrived a couple of blocks away on a flatbed truck. We all got on it and it pulled up to the club.

In New York I was approached by painter/photographer Martin Hoffman with a portfolio. One of his images was a model on a roof and I asked him if he could re-create the same illustration with the band. We did a photo shoot with him on the roof of his building, Georgetown Towers on Eighth Street and Broadway. Jimmy missed the photo session, which is why he's so small on the cover.

All this time I was collecting knives. Maybe it was in part a connection to my father and my past but it's still going on. As luck would have it, the midseventies and the eighties were a golden age of American custom knife-making and I was lucky enough to have met and bought knives from some legendary smiths. I think I first encountered some modern custom knives at Paragon Sports in Manhattan, which had a small knife department early on, and I was immediately inspired to check out this world. I knew and bought knives from Don Fogg, Jimmy Fikes, Jim Schmidt, Tom Maringer, Bill Bagwell, Gil Hibben, Pat Crawford, W. W. Cronk, and many others. Debbie and me would always go to the New York Custom Knife Show and in 1981 the guys from the American Bladesmith Society gave out their first Master Smith ratings, which meant that from then on you could put a little MS stamp on knives you made if you met some criteria. Bill Moran, the founder of the society, thought that if they had a celebrity make the presentations, it might garner a little attention. Moran is a legend in the field. He almost single-handedly started up custom knife-making and certainly kept pattern welding alive in America.

A lot of these guys knew that Debbie and I were at the shows, so, long story short, Debbie presented the first Master Smith ratings to Fikes, Schmidt, Fogg, Don Hastings, Bagwell, and Moran.

Over the years I sold off some great knives when I was broke but I've managed to hold on to most, and the collection is pretty awesome. I've got a Lloyd Hale out-the-front automatic that's the only one he ever made. He said it was too complicated to do again. I had Cronk's last knife, which I sold when I needed money. I have the dagger that Don Hastings used for his ads in *Blade* magazine and I have the Bowie that has his first Master Smith stamp on it. I still have all the Don Fogg knives I got, for which I'm grateful. When I got to some low points later on, Don would encourage me to pull myself together. I could go on dropping the names of knife makers. The few people who know about this world might appreciate this stuff.

Andy knew about my knife affinities and at one point asked me to bring some to the Factory for him to photograph. I brought some very fancy ones. He shot Polaroids of them but he wanted knives that looked seedy and dangerous, like prison shanks (of which I had several), so he never did any paintings of the ones I brought. He wound up doing some paintings of chef's knives and I have seen the Polaroids of mine in a book or two over the years.

We also made some forays into professional wrestling and would attend matches at the Garden in the WWF days. We met a lot of the greats. Vince McMahon was always very gracious and kept asking to "put Debbie in the ring," but we never took him up on it. On August 9, 1980, we saw Larry Zbyszko break Bruno Sammartino's arm in the steel cage match at Shea Stadium. We were into a lot of stuff.

We hung out with Andy more, went to dinner with him a few times, and would go visit the Factory; Andy eventually did Debbie's portrait. We did a few gigs with James Chance and the Contortions at Hurrah's. Bowie was on Broadway in *Elephant Man* and invited us. When he left the show every night, he would walk through a maze of tunnels and fire doors that connected the theaters in the basement level and emerge down the street to avoid the hundred or so fans that gathered daily at the stage door. Our friend Dennis Christopher was in a production of *The Little Foxes* that was Liz Taylor's Broadway debut. We met her briefly. They'd really painted her dressing room violet. She was gorgeous.

Guitarist John Fahey was always one of my personal heroes. I'd been listening to his recordings since I was a kid in the sixties and I'd even seen him play a couple of times, once at a West Village church to a very small group. Fahey was a musical historian as well and he seems to have loved records, the world of records. He's had a sort of unseen impact on the world of guitar. In 1979 Fahey sold a label he'd started, Takoma Records, to our company, Chrysalis. Jon Monday, who'd been the Takoma general manager since 1970, must have heard that I was a fan. He reached out to me about possibly producing John, and I actually had a somewhat surreal phone conversation with Fahey. My idea for producing him was to just play bass along with a drummer and do some simple rhythm tracks to support his guitar. I have a feeling that he thought I wanted to add strings and backup singers and create some extravagantly excessive John Fahey disco numbers. He told me that he couldn't do it because his wife had been run over. I got the impression that he knew I didn't believe him but didn't care. It was all pretty odd, but at least I got to talk to him.

CHAPTER 11

Behind everything was this lingering drug situation. Cocaine was everywhere all the time. We would meet some big celebrity and he would pull a bag of blow out of his pocket. But a lot of people were doing heroin as well. People we knew were functioning addicts. We began seeing a guy named Al who turned us onto the art of chasing dragons. A simple form that still requires a little technique—it's just inhaling the smoke of the dope while it is burned on tinfoil. We had screwed around with sniffing heroin already, but smoking it was pretty insidious. One night a neighbor of ours, the guy who built out his walls, got mugged in Central Park. He fought off his attacker but got banged up and came over to our apartment. He was all bruised, so we chased some dragons with him without mentioning what it was. I think he thought it was some form of weed. He definitely left feeling better. That was the problem; it made you feel better.

At one point in one of the eternal Blondie tours, everyone was about to travel from Switzerland to Paris. Somebody in Zurich had given Debbie and me a bunch of heroin. As we were boarding the plane, after Debbie, Clem, and I went through the metal detector, one of the crew guys right behind us had a metal container of hashish in his shirt pocket that set off the alarm and he got nabbed. Everyone in the band and crew from the culprit back was taken away. Two security guys came on the plane and told us they'd be removing our luggage to investigate and asked if we wanted to leave the flight and accompany our bags as they were searched. Clem left; Debbie and me said no, thanks, and stayed on the flight. We did have this fairly large quantity of drugs with us and we became concerned lest we get busted arriving in Paris. We dumped most of the dope in the plane toilet but put a small amount in a cuff of Debbie's pants. Of course nobody even looked at us when we landed, and we spent the afternoon stoned, wandering around the Champs-Élysées while everyone else sat around in an office at the Zurich airport in their underwear. We saw Klaus Kinski driving down the boulevard in a jeep.

On a European flight there was a guy in the last row who proceeded to get drunker and drunker, all the while shouting and raving in accented English. He was cheerful but creating enough weird volume that everyone on the plane noticed him. As we were getting off, I think in Germany somewhere, he pushed his way out of the cabin unimpeded and I noticed he was wearing a gun on his belt. He didn't have any luggage and I realized that he was the fucking sky marshal on the flight, there to protect and serve, presumably to thwart skyjackers or other criminal airborne elements. The guy getting completely tanked wasn't very reassuring.

Earlier, I guess in 1977 or 1978, I did get apprehended going into Toronto, Canada, with a small amount of weed. It was pretty pathetic. I had a hotel envelope in my bags that contained a third of a burned joint and some random ashes. The customs guy acted like he'd brought down Pablo Escobar. I was a bit burned out then and figured I'd just go to jail and do a lot of sit-ups but when I was turned over to the RCMP detective he was sympathetic. He told me that they'd recently had Keith Richards in the very same office and I was lucky I didn't have any "white powder" with me. He knew about Blondie and said that I just shouldn't tell my friends that I'd gotten off easy and we spent the remainder of my visit, about a half hour, talking about photography. When they eventually let me go, Debbie and others were anxiously waiting, on the verge of calling the lawyers.

In New York we had done a lot of recording at the Power Station where Nile Rodgers and Bernard Edwards pretty much lived full-time. They went home to sleep occasionally, I guess. I loved Chic. Nile came over to our apartment and we found out he was a rock fan, he loved Devo. We discussed a collaboration. Neither of us had worked with anyone outside our respective bands.

We wrote a bunch of songs separately and collaborated on two and recorded pretty quickly, as I was the only outside musician and the guys from Chic worked as a well-oiled machine. Nile got the whole album on two two-inch tape reels. One of the songs I had that was called "Chrome" on the project had originally been intended as theme music for the supposed remake of Jean-Luc Godard's 1965 film *Alphaville*. Amos Poe was going to direct, Glenn O'Brien wrote a screenplay, and Fripp was to be the male lead opposite Debbie. This didn't happen in part because we talked about it prematurely (which I learned not to do again. As soon as the story hit the media, at least one band and various other things, records, and clubs called Alphaville appeared). We did get to meet Godard, who questioned our sanity for wanting "to make this old movie" (French accent). We gave him a thousand bucks to option the rights and later found out he probably didn't have the rights himself but Amos got a contract with his signature, which we figured was worth a grand.

Right at the same time we noticed that Swiss artist H. R. Giger was having a show of his *Alien* illustrations at a gallery that was down the block from us on Fifty-Seventh Street. We went to the Hansen Gallery and by some quirk of fate Giger was there on his way back to Zurich after having won the Oscar. He knew who we were and he and his wife, Mia, came back to our apartment and sat around on the terrace. I'd known about Giger for quite a while from his graphics, and *Alien* was a cultural phenomenon. We had discussed doing something together and when we finished this record, we called him about possibly doing the cover. Brian Aris did a photo session that was the basis for the cover image. Giger had some input with the Koo Koo title as he sent us a sketch early on of Debbie's head being pierced by safety pins and suggested an acupuncture/punk reference. We traveled to Switzerland to work on videos with Giger.

Giger's place in Zurich was on a countrified neighborhood block in a section called Oerlikon. It was in a row of houses where he'd knocked several together to make a large studio space. As one might expect, his environment was very magical and magic-influenced. Like Rosaleen Norton, Austin Spare, and Alan Moore, Giger definitely identified as a magician. I don't know that he practiced directly but his work reminded me of the metaphysical diagrams of German philosopher and mystic Jakob Böhme, which were intended to affect the ether.

His Oscar lived on a shelf in his mural-decorated living room next to skulls, a shrunken head, and African fetish figures. The whole place was filled with *Alien* residue, including a life-size Xenomorph figure. Giger told us that while he was working on the film props, he would come upon the figure in the middle of the night and it would "scare the shit" out of him. His backyard was decorated with strange figurines and had what he called a ghost train that ran on miniature tracks.

Giger threw himself into the project and made a bunch of related props. He made a tiara that was based on the one on the cover image. The tiara had a round stone set into the front that was surrounded by radiating lines. The whole thing was a copy of an IBM chip, and, concerned that there might be some vague copyright issue, Giger had added a small rectangular element to the design so it wasn't exactly the chip. He was meticulous. I saw him working on a book while we were there and he sent back the test pages several times because of slight color variations. He was also working on a series of airbrush paintings of New York City. He said the city was like an inverted crucifix with the vertical buildings and the horizontal underground beneath the streets. The videos took a week or so and afterward Debbie and I went to La Prairie clinic on Lake Geneva and got treatments that involved embryonic-sheep-cell shots. After a week there I felt very relaxed and clear. We returned to Zurich and I remember considering getting stoned, smoking hash again, but I didn't consider too much. I knew I would cave and after getting high felt cloudy and depressed. We reentered the world.

One of the first things we did when we got copies of *Autoamerican* was bring one to the Dakota apartments and leave it for John and Yoko. The doorman knew who we were and we later heard that John had been playing it at home. More recently Sean Lennon has said that "Tide Is High" was one of the first songs he remembers from his childhood. It seemed like just a short time after that, John was killed. It was very disturbing and I flashed back to my father dying.

Autoamerican got mixed reviews but "Tide Is High" went to number one in the U.S. Then when "Rapture" was released, Frankie Crocker at WBLS, one of the most influential DJs in the country, got behind it and was a major part of its success. "Rapture" went to number one in the U.S. too. Blondie had the number one and number two records on WABC radio in New York, which, I was told, was a rare occurrence; only the Beatles and us.

Debbie was on *Saturday Night Live* and we played two songs, "Love TKO" by Teddy Pendergrass and "Come Back Jonee" by Devo. But we got to pick a musical guest, as Debbie was the host. We asked the Funky Four Plus One to do the show. Sha-Rock, the "Plus One" in the Funky Four, is considered the first female rapper, and the group was the first hip-hop act on national television in the U.S. I tried really hard to have their DJ actually scratch on *SNL* but they couldn't connect their turntables. The show even sent a couple of the kids from the group uptown in a limo to look for cables in somebody's apartment but it just couldn't get done and they wound up rapping to their tape at the end of the show as the credits rolled. Still it was a great moment.

Everyone in New York City wants to live in a town house. We finally had a bunch of money and started looking. We saw some different places and one thing I remember was going to see a building that this couple was selling and they had what seemed to be a Monet that they were also trying to unload. It was one of the Houses of Parliament, a predominantly violet work. They were asking two hundred and fifty grand, which seemed low even then. The ornately framed painting was resting on the floor; it was all pretty sketchy.

We bought a town house on East Seventy-Second Street. It was great, massive; five floors with an elevator, a beautiful elegant old building with an atrium area and even a small courtyard. Bert our accountant urged us to go ahead with getting it. I moved my mother into our old Fifty-Eighth Street penthouse.

We'd gotten the building from some wealthy family who were cashing out and no doubt fleeing to the suburbs. In one of the rooms was an antique little wall safe that had been left open; we never knew the combination. Inside the safe I found a scrap of gray cardboard on which had been crudely written *You will die* or some such cranky message, which I assumed was put there by a resentful kid who was reluctant to leave their childhood environs. I burned the note for the sake of bad juju.

I'd been in Canada working on the soundtrack for this cartoon that we were involved with. When I came back to New York, Debbie produced a big package of dope that someone had given her. I think that might have been the moment that we started developing more severe habits. I might have been better served here by returning to childhood fear states but caution wasn't a consideration. Heroin is like getting a loan consolidation: you trade a lot of problems and distractions for one overreaching one. We started getting into some trouble.

Chapman came and stayed with us while we worked on another record at the Hit Factory. *The Hunter* has a lot of okay material but lacks cohesion. Also, the cover is bad. The cover idea was to get Rick Baker or another great makeup artist to convert the band into half-animal hybrids; it never happened and we settled for Debbie's great wig and our mediocre makeup. While we were in the UK two guys had approached us with a very cool graphic of a woman from the waist down with a cheetah on a leash. We should have gone with that image but I went along with the consensus that Debbie's face needed to be on the front cover. I went along with some other stupid stuff. Debbie was offered the part in *Blade Runner* that eventually went to Daryl Hannah, and she remembers her being blocked by the record company. That might have been the case but I recall management telling her to hold out for the lead role and my going along with that.

Marty Thau came to our new house and said, "How does it feel to be able to buy anything you want?" I hadn't thought about it much. I bought a timpani, the kind with a pedal that tuned the head. I didn't play it too much but it was something I'd thought about over the years. I did also buy a whole twenty-four-track setup, an MCI tape machine, and an automated console.

Brion Gysin visited with a small entourage; it was the only time I met him. One night Debbie and I were home alone and the bell rang. It was Bowie and Mick Jagger with Ava Cherry and Jerry Hall. Bowie and the three girls toured the house and I got to sit on the couch smoking a joint with Jagger, which was a nice moment. I told him how much of an influence those guys had been on my musical life.

We kept working on various projects. We did *Making Tracks,* a book with Victor Bockris. At the same time we were working on our book, we got a call from Lester Bangs asking if we'd interview with him for a Blondie book he was working on. We declined and told him we were working on our own. I don't know if that pissed him off but his Blondie book is a weird rambling critique that suggests that Debbie flashing her underwear during shows horrifies him. I wished he'd lived into the modern era to see what the norms are now and I wonder if he actually thought Debbie's relatively innocent stage displays of sexuality were so intense and damaging to the male psyche.

I started up a record label called Animal Records with Chrysalis. I spent a lot of time at Blank Tapes studios on West Twentieth Street. Animal had some good releases that I produced, not least of which were Iggy's *Zombie Birdhouse,* the *Wild Style* soundtrack that I'd played on, and the Gun Club's *Miami.* The Gun Club was a particularly satisfying project because of our connection to Jeffrey Pierce. It was great to see him coming into his own. We were at the Paradiso in Amsterdam when Jeff arrived with a whole film crew that was following him around. He was very self-assured and was far away from the awkward kid that we'd met in Los Angeles. For whatever reason Iggy didn't have a bigger record deal and we did the record on my little label. The title, *Zombie Birdhouse,* was part of Iggy's stream-of-consciousness lyrics. I don't know if he'd thought about it prior to the sessions but it seemed very spontaneous.

Wild Style was a labor of love that was made possible by our friend Charlie Ahern, who produced and directed the movie for around fifteen grand. The approach to the soundtrack was very clever. I got called in to put some guitar lines and rhythms on already existing drum and bass tracks at some small, very funky midtown studio. After I was done Freddy put down some sound effects like motors and electric razors and sirens and such and laid down some phrases. We did a bunch of these tracks very quickly and Charlie had them pressed up. Then for the scenes in the film the various DJs used these in house records. Most of them gravitated to this one track, "Down by Law." I worked on two more detailed tracks with Grandmaster Caz. I did some weird stuff, like trying to sync a synthesizer to the scratching on the track. No one knew *Wild Style* would be as crazily influential as it turned out to be.

Among all the odd stuff I bought was a Bearcat scanner radio. This thing was portable and could pick up police and fire department calls. There was a big Diana Ross concert in Central Park that got partly rained out, leaving some four hundred thousand kids roaming around bored and making trouble. I sat in the town house listening to the cops trying to contain roving bands attacking Tavern on the Green. One night I accompanied some friend downtown to get some drugs at the usual tenement apartment of the dealer. I had to wait in the hall so I sat on the stairs listening to local police calls that beeped and clicked with their secret numerical code language. Some dude came into the building and went into the dealer's apartment. When my friend came out he was very amused and told me that the person who'd arrived said, "There's a cop in the hall!"

In later years I started listening to car-phone conversations. The first car phones were developed in the midforties but by the eighties and nineties, to a limited extent, they were out there in the hands of the masses. The conversations were all pretty mundane and fell into two categories: regular guys (it was all men) on their way home asking wives if they could pick anything up or, alternatively, what was for dinner, and guys who were attempting to impress their dates by calling to let them know that the call was indeed coming from a car and that they *had* a car phone. "I'm in front of your building" was a typical ploy. I did finally hear one guy in a discussion with what seemed to be a female sex worker that consisted of them negotiating a price for some upcoming gathering but that was a one-off.

I was reminded of a weird episode from years prior when I was still on the Lower East Side. Somehow I stumbled onto a combination of phone numbers that connected my telephone to whoever else was privy to the same entry numbers. It was some fluke thing, like dialing a number with a Staten Island area code then hanging up after one ring and then dialing a short combination, say 966 or such. My phone would then be connected to a bunch of kids chatting away on this sort of party line. I made a date with a girl but she didn't show up. At one point a telephone worker came on the line and ordered everyone off. The people who were talking of course said "Fuck you" and laughed. This went on for a month or so before being shut down. People today might have a hard time with the concept of the single central telephone as a focal point.

"Island of Lost Souls" was released as a single from *The Hunter* in the UK. The media was wrapped up in the Falklands conflict and decided that the song was somehow a commentary on the war between Britain and Argentina over territory in the South Atlantic. One of the final cheerful Blondie projects had been shooting a video for "Island of Lost Souls." We traveled to Tresco, one of the Scilly Isles, a small group of islands on the southernmost tip of the UK off Cornwall. I was starting to feel a little spaced out and weaker than usual but I just assumed it was from getting high. The island itself was crazy-beautiful. It's so far south that it's semi-tropical, replete with palm trees and exotic flora. Tresco was renowned for shipwrecks and in the small, picturesque town we found a guy selling prints made from old glass negatives of ships that had been cast up on the coastal rocks, these amazing images of antique schooners and multi-masted old boats with the sails ripped and blowing, the hulls broken, and people standing on the windswept beaches watching or salvaging.

We spent a few days being filmed running around in the woods and bushes of a parklike area. We sat on a beach and went in a rowboat. At the quaint hotel we were at, I had a great out-of-body experience where I simply was on the cobblestone path to our room looking at the various astral versions of objects along the route.

Debbie and I were in the UK and Europe doing promo and we were in trouble from having drug habits. We had a dealer in the U.S. mailing us dope in cassette boxes. We canceled a couple of appearances, a German TV show, and Shep was getting concerned, though he didn't say anything. There was a moment when we had some heroin on a dressing-room counter. Denny, our tour manager and handler, came into the room and tasted some on the tip of his finger. He didn't say anything and left. Again, these guys were flooded with cocaine, but we had crossed some line and gone over to the dark side, as it were. We weren't the only ones in the band getting high on the hard stuff.

Debbie and I bumped heads with Frankie frequently and when we were planning the Tracks Across America tour we replaced him with Eddie

Martinez, who went on to play all over Run-DMC's Rock Box and other rock hip-hop crossovers. Eddie was a very nice, easygoing, sober guy. The tour itself was upscale; we had a small horn section and were doing larger venues. It was dark, though; we had a tour manager who was actively scoring dope for us on the road. Heroin is a stupid drug. It offers constantly diminishing returns on the great amount of energy required to keep up with it and the window wherein it actually acts as a buffer or antidepressant is tiny and decreases throughout the relationship. When this was going on I didn't see it as creepy. I had this view of various heroes who were addicted, of course the image and glamorous facade taking precedent over any consideration of the inner aspects: depression, mental turmoil, immune system repercussions, et cetera.

I lost weight. I have some degree of body dysmorphia and didn't mind. I don't recall too much of the tour. Duran Duran opened for us and we did a version of the Rolling Stones' "Start Me Up" that was fun to play. A couple of shows got canceled and the last one was at JFK Stadium in Philadelphia. A European leg was also canceled.

We got back to our place in New York and got into deeper shit. The guy who had mailed us dope while we were in the UK presented us with an exorbitant bill for services and product. When we questioned it, he turned the debt over to some actual gangsters that we had to pay off to get rid of.

We were friends with a guy, Patrick Geoffrois, who we knew from his playing guitar with James Chance and the Contortions. Patrick was a self-styled dark magician and downtown dealer. A lot of people knew him. He would do tarot readings on St. Marks Place. The cops called him Frenchie. He was always straightforward with us. We scored from him and a few other downtown people but we had a degree of celebrity, which opened us up to a lot of bullshit and weird manipulation from other sketchy people we were dealing with.

Our lawyer Marty Silfen called and asked us to come to his office as the FBI wanted to talk to us. Seems the feds had been watching the goings-on at My Father's Place, a big club on Long Island we had played at many times. We had opened for John Cale for a week there. The office of the club was bugged and we were on tape saying, "Thank you for these nice drugs," or something to that effect. We met with two agents in

Marty's conference room. We were stoned and had to act surprised when they told us they were investigating heroin traffic. That was it for that; I don't know if they busted anyone from the club. We also had been buying heroin from this older guy who Debbie knew. He was a friendly dude with a nice art collection in his downtown apartment. An NYPD detective called Debbie and asked to meet with her. She sat in his car that was parked down the block from the Chelsea Hotel. He only wanted to talk to Debbie and ask her if she had a sexual relationship with our dealer friend. He'd been murdered in his apartment in a particularly grotesque way and her number was in his book. I sat on a stoop waiting while Debbie talked to the cop in the car. She was shaken afterward.

Burroughs sent a doctor friend around and he gave us Klonopin and some other meds to help us kick but it didn't take. Knowing that you can end up feeling awful by prolonging your habit is a constant factor of addictive personality that reaches beyond drugs and is just a component of habitual behavior.

We started running low on funds and Shep just ghosted us. I'm pretty sure he'd helped some of his other acts with rehab. I don't remember the last time I spoke to him but we never heard from him again. Not "I have to quit"; nothing. I guess the reasons were obvious. On top of that we discovered that Bert, our business manager, hadn't paid our taxes for the two years we were making the most money. He got extensions and had gotten us into a dodgy tax-shelter scheme, something about real estate, housing, in Texas that tanked. Chrysalis sent us a little sometimes but that dried up soon. I sold the timpani and a bunch of guitars, among them the Gibson Trini Lopez Custom and my '56 or '57 maple-neck Fender Strat that I had used for everything. I sold the Basquiat canvas that I'd given him the two hundred dollars for. Diego Cortez, who'd founded the Mudd Club with Anya, brokered the deal. It sold for ten grand. I should mention here that another guy we bought drugs from was a good graphic artist and did some early Basquiat fakes that I bet are out there in some big collections.

I was amused that I could fit into Debbie's pants. I got down to a hundred and twenty or thirty pounds. I had a cocaine habit too and eventually my nose and sinuses were wrecked. Then very quickly I got bad sores in my mouth and my diet got very restricted. I ate a lot of tofu ice cream. The last act of deterioration was getting gross sores on my legs that didn't heal. We made the rounds of a few doctors and finally one young guy we'd been put in touch with came over and said, "It could be pemphigus," which was the first I'd heard the word. He said I should really be in a hospital and called an ambulance. I got carried out in the middle of the afternoon on a sunny day. I said I was going to be okay to the doorman of the building next door who seemed concerned and got taken to Lenox Hill Hospital and put on the burn ward.

I had a little corner room with views of Park Avenue. If it were a studio apartment at that location, it would have been an expensive one. The first weeks were very fever-dream. Treatment involved high doses of the steroid prednisone, which is used for a lot of things, including skin diseases and inflammation. This plus my generally wrecked state, bad diet, and drug habits combined to really put me into an alternate reality. Debbie was out scoring drugs to bring back to the hospital. I was frequently in a half sleep where I would see her in different countries with strange landscapes, walking around and searching. I gradually must have adjusted to the steroids and I settled into a vague routine.

Initially I was quite scared and I can only imagine what Debbie was feeling. Lenox Hill was close to our house and Debbie would sometimes stay on a cot in the room and sometimes go home for the night. It took a while for me to get an official diagnosis. I had a lot of tests done, including a spinal tap, which is a really miserable thing that must be what getting shot is like. I was very glad to deaden the post-tap aftermath with dope. I wondered how people did it otherwise. After a while I started hearing that I had this thing called pemphigus vulgaris. I thought I would have liked to have a condition with a better name; I didn't like that one at all. Some young nurse pulled Debbie aside and told her what I had was potentially fatal. It was a hundred or so years ago. Debbie was needlessly terrorized.

I was irrationally scared and very resistant to even leaving the room at first but they sent two really cute nurses to convince me to get into a large vat of chemicals—Betadine and whatever else made the water in this huge steel whirlpool bath a rust-blood color. My whole back was covered in sores, and getting lowered into this tank was after a while an okay experience.

Days drifted by. I had my own bathroom with harsh neon lights. When I looked in the mirror it would bring back fragments of dreams I'd had of looking into a mirror in the same cold blue-white light. My mouth calmed down and I was able to eat normal food again. I gained some weight back. The doctors figured out that I was on drugs and tried giving me some methadone but my main physician was a skin guy and really didn't know about addiction so he just gave me twenty milligrams of it or such and it didn't make a dent. Maintaining a habit was difficult enough in the real world, but the hospital situation exacerbated everything. Supplies would dissipate and I'd go through stages of withdrawal.

About a month in, Jerry Hall was at the hospital having a baby and some camped-out media people spotted Debbie. The story was quickly all over the place. A photographer got a shot of Debbie in a supermarket looking disheveled and that was printed with accompanying mournful tidings in several places. One afternoon a kid who was around thirteen appeared at the door of my room and said hello. I talked to him for a minute and then he suddenly pulled out a camera and attempted to take my picture. I looked like a mess and just pulled a blanket over my head and yelled for security and the kid ran off. I figured he had probably attempted to get a picture of Jerry as well. I couldn't tell if he had been encouraged by an adult or was just a fledgling paparazzi. Weirdly, this same kid called my room a few days later to apologize but I told him to fuck off and hung up on him.

Most of the people we knew assumed I had AIDS; the first cases had been mentioned in the media a few years earlier. I don't think that I was ever worried about dying and after a while the doctors kept repeating that I was improving and must be doing something right, either praying or thinking positively or something. I got to know this one orderly kid and we would sit around smoking pot late at night. I had a TV and got very invested in watching *General Hospital*. This was the Frisco and Felicia period for anyone old enough to know what that means. *General Hospital* was very weird, the producers inserting action scenes into this dumb sentimental absurdly complicated storyline. I built a few Star Wars model kits and discovered that I could get mail at the hospital. I began getting the great event invitations that Area sent out, a new downtown club that I never went to. A Halloween party invitation that was a rubber knife with fake blood neatly packed in a cardboard container, boxes filled with fake money and confetti, et cetera. I ordered stuff from an antiques and oddities company that I'd dealt with for years. I got a really great old African drum, swords, and a couple of masks and knives that were placed around the room.

A particularly severe winter descended. Major blizzards hampered Debbie's efforts at procuring drugs and I kept dealing with withdrawal. I was in Lenox Hill for three months. I missed a whole season. I finally was discharged in the early spring. Prednisone made me heavier and inflated my face a bit. Debbie brought a supermarket shopping cart to the hospital because I had accumulated so much crap. We pushed it back to the house.

I began hanging out with Patrick more and started shooting up. He had an apartment that was right across from my old place on First and First. One day he and his girlfriend, Melanie, were awakened by guys with big dogs on chains. They gave him a few minutes to vacate the apartment. Patrick owed rent or the landlord was down on the cops coming to the building or both. They showed up at our town house and since we were getting dope from Patrick, it seemed like a mutually beneficial arrangement to let them stay with us. They moved into the upstairs section of the building where Chapman had stayed. Melanie had a job with an escort service, taking phone calls and booking visits, and she spent hours daily just talking on the phone. Patrick had some connection that would front him quantity and he'd come back to the house with large packages of hundreds of those little dope bags. Both of those guys had clients coming through the house occasionally but they were all nice enough and never caused any problems for us.

One weekend was a drug drought and I went out with Patrick and Melanie to score on the street while we waited for Patrick's usual connection to come through. Patrick knew where to go and we went back to his abandoned apartment to fix. He climbed up the fire escape and opened the front door. Getting stoned in an abandoned empty flat in the middle of the afternoon still wasn't apparently enough to convince me to knock it off. Many hours later Patrick showed up at the house where Debbie and me were miserably withdrawing with a bag of the little envelopes that he'd picked up on a street in Brooklyn. I'm amazed and lucky I only got hepatitis C. Patrick had become HIV-positive while on Rikers Island and it finally killed him about ten years later.

In the midst of addiction throes, Debbie did a Broadway play that also starred Andy Kaufman. *Teaneck Tanzi: The Venus Flytrap* was a weird musical-and-wrestling sort of rom-com that had been successful in a previous incarnation over in the UK. The theater was converted into a round environment with a full ring in the center. There were musical numbers that I don't recall and a climactic male/female match. Andy was the referee. I think this was after Jerry Lawler gave Andy a piledriver that resulted in Andy being seen around town wearing a big neck brace. I had a buddy who worked in a music store. Andy appeared there with the brace and after somebody wisecracked at him Andy stood in the street pounding on the window for a while. Look up *kayfabe*.

The play ran for two weeks in previews and then closed on opening night. Everybody blamed the director but I suspect it was ahead of its time, wrestling still being fringe in the early eighties.

We had another set of visitors at our town house near the end of our stay there, a certain very successful art gallery owner and his partner, who was the son of a rich diplomat. These guys would come over and engage in a strange power dynamic where the gallery guy would command his friend to do our dishes and clean up a little. This felt like some weird BDSM role-play thing presented in the guise of being helpful. We saw them a bunch of times before the story broke about the dead body of a male model being found on the estate of the diplomat's son. The victim had been shot twice and was wearing a black leather bondage-style mask. The Mask Murder headlines were all over town for months in the aftermath. The gallery guy beat the rap but later got put away for five years for tax evasion. His buddy is still up the river as far as I know. Amazingly, gallery dude did get back into the art world as a successful dealer although his lavish estate with some seven million in art mysteriously blew up, supposedly because of a gas leak. Debbie says that their visits with us were right after the murder.

As a result of Bert Padell's help with our finances I didn't have a credit card or any savings and what I owed the IRS that had started out as a hundred grand or so soon became a million bucks with penalties and interest.

Debbie found a lawyer, Stanley Arkin, who wanted to manage us and he at least hooked us up with a good accountant who didn't have any criminal tendencies. The house went next. Darren McGavin, the actor, came by and looked at it, he was very nice but didn't buy it. It sold to some rich family and we moved to Twenty-First Street, where we got the top two floors in a brownstone. Actors Michael O'Keefe and Meg Foster, who were living together, were the landlords. They were great. Meg was how we later visited the set of John Carpenter's *They Live* in downtown LA and saw her shoot Keith David. We got to meet Carpenter but not Roddy Piper.

We still pursued the dope thing and kept dealing with more sketchy people. There is this weird sort of addict's code. Generally junkies are greedy and self-absorbed but occasionally they will help each other out by supplying drugs (that's really the only way to offer help) and then feel like they are sainted in their beneficence, all exaggerated by being stoned. I succumbed to these Stockholm syndrome-like effects in regards to people we dealt with and I felt the same occasionally coming in my direction from them. Al, the guy who'd shown us how to chase dragons, reappeared. He had a sample of some super-pure heroin that he'd gotten from a downtown gang. It was called Number Three. I don't know why it wasn't Number One, but it wasn't. A bunch of us got money together and gave it to Al to go score a larger quantity. Al didn't show up again for several days and when he did, he looked like hell. He'd gone to buy the dope with his friend but the gang guys had just taken the money, held them down, given them hot shots—that is, shot them up with enough dope to kill them—and left them for dead. But Al's habit was big enough that he was able to stay awake and drag himself and his buddy to an emergency room. By the time he reappeared, he was quite sick and I gave him some money to go score. I think that was the last I saw of him.

Eventually anyone would get tired of the drug-habit grind. I would be out walking around and see people doing their day-to-day stuff and I would feel separated from any sense of normalcy. We got hooked up with a social worker at New York Hospital and made plans to go into detox there. Debbie and I were lucky to be able to afford help. A lot of people, no matter how exhausted, can't get into private programs, and city and state programs are always low-priority and underfunded.

I went in first, for around two weeks. The treatment involved feeling shitty and lying in the dark while being shot up with methadone. After less than a week, the bad feeling dissipated and by the time I got out I felt a little stable and almost upbeat. Debbie did the same deal but stayed on methadone for only a few months. I started going to a program at New York Hospital and had to deal with the red tape and daily appearances. I had a great and memorable doctor, Elizabeth Khuri, a charming older woman who was very encouraging. She advised me to stay on the program so as not to shock my system, since pemphigus can recur in some cases. I was still in treatment with another great doctor, George Hambrick, who was an old-time heavyweight in the dermatology field. He gave me shots of sodium aurothiomalate, which is basically a gold compound that is an anti-inflammatory. More is known about pemphigus now than when I was dealing with it, and over the years I've spoken to others who've had it, but luckily I never had it come back.

We settled into a post-heroin tenuous lifestyle. I must have had a profound psychological release because I had a long series of lucid-dream/ out-of-body/astral-projection experiences. I've always had them but this period was very intense and I was able to keep at it for a long time. The neighborhood we were in had been the farm of Clement Clarke Moore, the American poet and writer who's mostly known for "The Night Before Christmas." Across Twenty-First Street was a huge seminary, and the psychic climate of the area was pretty peaced out. At night and in the early mornings I would find myself in this disembodied state traveling around the local streets and rooftops in a kind of flight mode, all the while being self-aware and not disconnected as in a dream. A couple of times I was able to hold my waking consciousness into this trance state with no break. Generally the technique for me was entering into the sleep-paralysis place and, rather than resisting, relaxing and sinking into a deeper place, whereupon I would find myself in the disembodied awareness of whatever this condition is. I don't know if there's a supernatural component to this or if it's just an altered mental state but I filled up a small journal with notes and descriptions.

I'd spent some time struggling with Jung's essay on flying saucers in which he attributes the appearance thereof to what he terms a *collective archetypal vision* (*vision*, he emphasizes, as opposed to *hallucination*, which implies pathology, or disturbance). He wrote that people seeing UFOs was an unconscious reaction to a situation of danger—in that case, the Cold War. Interestingly, the book was written in the fifties when the UFO phenomenon was only some fifteen to twenty years old. It's too bad we don't have his views today, now that flying saucers, UAPs, whatever, have been around for some seventy years, and the abduction scenario, which didn't quite exist in Jung's day, is established. I wonder if the astral experience might be a similar unconscious reaction to cultural anxieties, the conflict of being technically free yet tied down to so much. I'm inclined toward the validity of the occult version of the experience, but that's just me.

Debbie and Andy did a presentation for Commodore and we were given an Amiga computer. I think the starting amount of RAM was 256 KB. I was intrigued and would screw around with it for hours. It was even capable of taking a primitive color photograph. One would use a black-and-white video camera with a red, blue, and yellow transparent color wheel in front of the lens. Then the subject would hold still while you took one shot with each color, and an algorithm would create the image. It was easier to go with a black-and-white image and just do one shot. There was no kind of music software at that point, but it had some very old-school games.

CHAPTER 12

Debbie and I had grown out of sync. Maybe in part because of her going off methadone and me staying on it, maybe lots of stuff, but things ran their course and she moved out. I was upset for a week or two but got into a new relationship with her. After all this, we were still friends. Maybe you want more details but there aren't many. I've heard her say she was afraid of us getting back into the drugs and other things. But it just went the way it went. I'll always love her, she and my wife, Barbara, and my kids are kind of my only immediate family.

The methadone program was very strict but I was a model patient for a while, and pretty soon I didn't have to go daily. I hadn't left Manhattan for something like three or four years. I called Burroughs, who had moved away from New York and spent more time in Lawrence, Kansas, and asked if he could tolerate my company for a while. I stayed there for two weeks. Bill lived in a very normal house on a very normal suburban-type street. He knew all his very normal neighbors and they all liked him. In his basement, he had this big tube set up on a stand to more quietly shoot guns through. He had a bunch of cats and I think this was around the time he wrote his short book *The Cat Inside*, which discusses his relationships with felines and their effect on his spiritual and psychic life. He didn't like dogs much and said the cane he carried was in part for dog defense.

At this point in his life Bill had been on methadone for years, so we had that in common. We would drink it together in the morning and then have coffee. His environment and decor was very spartan. All I remember on the walls was a calendar and terrific Brion Gysin calligraphy. There was fading wallpaper in some of the rooms and a general old-farmhouse atmosphere. I brought him a custom dagger; I forget the maker.

Bill had previously given me a great early shotgun painting. He did a series of these things that involved him putting containers of paint on a board and blasting them with buckshot, resulting in a Pollock-esque effect. Jean-Michel saw it and liked it. He sent word to Burroughs to see if he could trade some art for another one. I went to see Jean on Great Jones Street, where he was living in the great Warhol-owned old carriage house. I watched him put the finishing touches on an amazing piece he called *Red Nod*, a sculptural assemblage of a box attached to a stylized head by a piece of wood. The whole thing was painted white and red with black lettering and sigils. I hand-carried it on the plane in a paper shopping bag. I recently discussed this with James Grauerholz, Bill's longtime associate, and he told me they sold the thing for eighty grand later on. I picked out one of Bill's shotgun pieces to bring back to Jean-Michel.

A local punk venue near Burroughs's location was this club called the Outhouse. This place was epic in its outsider-fringe sensibilities, being an old storage garage, a cinder-block bunker in the middle of a cornfield. I'm not sure anyone even paid for electricity. There was a cable coming from a nearby telephone pole. Bill had the run of the place and was known as the Old Man to some of the kids who didn't exactly know who he was. We went one afternoon to shoot guns in the cornfield near the place. Bill had done some of his shotgun paintings in and around the Outhouse. The interior walls of the club were densely painted with graffiti and band names. I saw one show and afterward got friendly with a young couple from a band called Unseen Force. Greta Brinkman was the bass player and went on to play with Debbie and me, Moby, and various others. Her boyfriend, guitar player Dewey Rowell, later became the original Flattus Maximus in Gwar. The crowd, as expected, was enthusiastically nuts and threw themselves around appropriately. After the gig, everyone sat outside and smoked pot and drank beer. I asked the kids what happened when the cops came, the place being so outlaw and all, and they said they just ran into the cornfield. I think the Outhouse is a strip joint now.

I brought Jean-Michel to my methadone program. He wore a really nice tweed suit to the meeting with Dr. Khuri. We went to a fancy lunch afterward and he seemed all about trying to kick. He only stuck with it briefly. Andy thanked me for trying to help him. Jean was a very ornery character. He had a tendency to lean into confrontations. Once, Debbie and me were at some fancy restaurant that overlooked Times Square with Iggy and a bunch of people, and Jean arrived with a few others. He was holding a huge bucket of Kentucky Fried Chicken. He sat down with us— there were at least ten people at this table. Jean pulled out a big baggie of weed and started to roll a joint, and when Iggy asked him to put it away he got performatively annoyed and started a beef with Iggy, which was pretty funny; Iggy arguing for the rule of law was somewhat absurd. Jean put the weed away after they yelled back and forth for a couple of minutes but he definitely would have lit up if Iggy hadn't said anything.

A friend of ours, Kerry Riordan, had an old iron front-loft building downtown that her parents had left her, and she told us that the ground floor was vacant. After a long prep period I moved into this fantastic huge space on Greenwich Street in the area that was soon to be known as Tribeca. The space was a whole floor and basement with a street entrance and loading dock. I slept on a mattress on the dusty floor for a few days, then moved stuff in from Twenty-First Street. I still had all my recording gear and set it up in the basement, where I discovered I could make as much noise as I wanted, as the walls were thick and there weren't any neighbors to speak of. There was a giant skylight and only one other window aside from the ones in front. The second small window opened onto an airshaft and was filled with layers of the generations of pigeons who had been living there since the late nineteenth century, no doubt. I sealed up the small window and put bars under the skylight, as the area in the mid- and late eighties was indeed sketchy. It was filled with artists and bikers and had a population of street cats. There was someone around the corner who fed the street cats and they would hang around this cellar door where the cans of food were. It was an exciting time; I loved the environment. It was still a number of years before gentrification began in earnest and I remember being surprised a few years later by seeing well-off women pushing baby carriages around the industrial streets.

There was a great bakery around the corner on Hudson Street that would throw out large quantities of baked goods. Exotic breads, pastries, bagels, everything they didn't sell in a day would go in and around a dumpster that was in an alley behind the place. There would be stacks of boxes of fresh doughnuts. I would get enough stuff to last a week in a few minutes. I asked them why they didn't donate it and they said they had tried, called up various church and civic groups, but nobody wanted to deal with picking it up. I wasn't the only one from the neighborhood who frequented the dumpster; the sweet stuff would always go first. You had to get there on time.

I was still basically broke. I had a deal with the IRS that since I wasn't working, I paid them five hundred bucks a month not to kill me. Somehow this was okay for quite a while; I just never had any actual income or insurance or credit cards or anything.

Steve Sprouse opened a store in SoHo on Wooster Street in what had been the Firehouse, a very early men's club. SoHo was on the cusp and the store didn't last long. If it were around now, it would of course be a big-deal success. I still have a bunch of Steve's clothing but after the store closed, he gave me a pair of huge speakers that had been part of the sound system and I hung them in the basement over the old console. I recorded a lot of people and stuff, a lot of things that weren't released into the world. The loft developed a museum-like style with all my weird oddities and voodoo collecting.

I was with Steve and a couple of others watching a jazz band in the basement of a squat building in the Lower East Side. The Lower East Side had always been fertile ground for activism and borderline anarchy. Back in the sixties, I'd been at a small, spontaneous anti-police demonstration right on St. Marks Place that included people throwing garbage cans off a roof. Squats were pretty common before gentrification, but as the city was coming out of a long slump in the eighties, the squats became a sore point; a lot of squatter groups resisted eviction after they'd developed and fixed up the city-owned abandoned buildings that they were occupying. In the sixties and seventies when the city was struggling financially, services to poor neighborhoods had been cut back, leaving a lot of homelessness and destroyed, empty living spaces.

On that particular night we'd been watching this trio of horn, bass, and drums in a concrete room that was decorated with Christmas lights. They, somebody, charged a dollar to come into this space. At dark we emerged into the middle of the Tompkins Square Park riot. The police had proposed a 1 a.m. curfew for anyone in the park, which seemed designed to reduce the large numbers of people who were living there in tents. An anti-curfew rally was planned for midnight and the cops showed up en masse. From what I saw, the police totally overreacted. Skirmishes were taking place all around. We found our way to Avenue A and observed for a while. I saw the cops jump some poor guy who was just riding past on his bike. It was obvious that this dude wasn't involved in what was going on—he was dressed in a white sports outfit and was driving a racing bike—but the cops dragged him off and hit him with nightsticks. I might have stuck around but Steve said, "Fuck this, I'm leaving," and we walked out of the area.

I met a lot of fringe people that I mightn't have encountered in the aboveground music scene that Blondie had existed in. Artists and musicians and just fucked-up drug people. At a little storefront community arts and crafts center that was very rugged, I met a guy who had forged some knives out of Tompkins Square metal fence posts.

I was still in touch with Patrick and around this time he got involved with the major weirdness surrounding Daniel Rakowitz, the East Village alleged cannibal murderer. The Lower East Side had also always been a possessed place. I remember the local witches' covens in the sixties protesting outside McSorley's bar on Seventh Street for its unwritten rule of not welcoming women. I had dearly loved the local paper that existed for a while, the *East Village Other*. I'd spoken to Rakowitz a few times, once when he appeared at one of our gigs with his pet chicken.

In 1989 Rakowitz told various people in and around Tompkins that he'd murdered and chopped up his roommate and possible girlfriend Monika. More than one of the people he burdened with this information went to the cops, and Daniel was arrested. It's always been disputed whether he actually did the murdering but he undoubtedly did the chopping up, as he led the police to a locker in the Port Authority in which he was storing Monika's skull in a plastic bucket of kitty litter. The lurid story hit big-time together with all kinds of rumors surrounding the events. That Daniel had made cadaver soup that he served to homeless people in the park most probably didn't happen but made it into the media. Somehow the assistant DAs working the case dragged Patrick into the glare of public madness and speculation. Maybe the cops knew and resented Patrick from his heavier dealer days or maybe he was just a likely suspect and they were enjoying the weirdness. Whatever, he wound up being described as a cult leader by the media. Patrick got tossed into jail at Rikers Island for a while and I have some nice drawings and poems that he mailed to me from there. Patrick knew Daniel and had read his tarot cards on St. Marks and I don't think Patrick really had much of anything to do with Rakowitz prior to Daniel being busted. But Patrick loved drama and he kept up a correspondence with Rakowitz after Patrick got out of jail. Patrick definitely wasn't any kind of cult leader. He might have liked to have been one, but most of his fans and notoriety came after he died from HIV-related causes in 1994. Patrick would self-publish these little *Magick Warrior* pamphlets that he'd make at home with a printer and I would give him drawings I did that went into a couple of issues. I see them online selling in the two-hundred-dollar range. Rakowitz is still locked up in protective custody; he'll never get out.

A little later, another victim of the Satanic Panic phenomenon was someone I knew from the UK, Genesis P-Orridge. Gen was the singer and founder of industrial band Throbbing Gristle and later Psychic TV and the related group Thee Temple ov Psychick Youth. Thee Temple wasn't an organized cult and Gen never considered themself a cult leader, but media exploitation being so surface, I guess it was only a matter of time before they had various journalistic elements jumping down their throat. A TV special denounced Genesis as a ritual abuser and the cops raided their home and confiscated their stuff. I can attest that when I visited them in the UK I saw Gen interact with their kids as a very positive, affectionate parent. The whole deal was remarkably stupid.

Genesis and I had a mutual interest and affection for Austin Osman Spare. Spare was a particularly gifted UK artist and draftsman who identified as a magician. He had been an associate of Aleister Crowley but became disdainful of organized ritual magicians who he saw as phonies. He went off on his own and developed his own magical language and systems that are closer to what's deemed chaos magic. When I started seeing his work in the late seventies at what was my favorite bookstore, the Magickal Childe on West Nineteenth Street, Spare was quite obscure, and only a few of his drawings and writings were being cheaply reproduced. Jimmy Page, who also was an early fan, grabbed up a lot of Spare's major pieces. Genesis had one of these major late paintings, a great self-portrait with accompanying spirit heads.

When Gen got raided they were off in Thailand apparently doing some famine relief work. They were of course concerned about returning to the UK and instead came to New York. They somehow were able to get the Spare painting out and I bought it. Gen cautioned me not to look at it in a mirror.

Debbie and me started doing some solo shows. Blondie's stopping had never been addressed; it just faded without much comment in the media. Madonna and others filled any cultural gaps that Debbie and Blondie had left. We never got heavy support from MTV, probably because we stopped working as the channel began but also possibly because MTV wanted to be able to claim responsibility for the success of various new acts and we'd been making videos for years.

Andy had moved his headquarters from Union Square to a massive thirty-thousand-square-foot building on Thirty-Third Street that used to be a Con Ed substation. Sprouse took over the old Union Square factory loft. The new Warhol Factory was an amazing space with huge windows and entrances on three sides. Andy and one of his crew, Don Monroe, had been producing a TV show for MTV called *Andy Warhol's Fifteen Minutes*. I gave them a piece of experimental music that I'd done in the basement, and Andy liked it and used it for the show's theme. They started filming in the basement of the new Factory building and I conducted two interviews for the show, one with Burroughs and one with the Ramones. Both are on YouTube now. Burroughs and I shot a little .22 derringer into some boards and then discussed war as models strolled in the background, Bill saying that we lived in a war universe, that the Hindus suggested that war was a natural force. The Ramones interview was a few months later and involved them complaining about the state of rock music and Joey playing with a dried lacquer-covered piranha that he later gave me for a birthday present. Andy wasn't around for the Ramones segment, and people told us he had a cold.

I think it was the next day that I heard something had happened to Andy. I called Vincent and Shelly Fremont. Vincent had worked with Andy for years. Shelly answered the phone in tears; Andy had gone into New York Hospital for gallbladder surgery and died. I think everyone in the city was on the phone by midday. It was shocking. If he hadn't gotten shot, I think he would have lived longer. He was fifty-eight. Steve Sprouse told us he had a very vivid dream where he was in a white room with Andy, who was telling him not to feel bad, everything would be okay. A month and a half later there was a memorial at St. Patrick's Cathedral. We sat near Jean-Michel, who was very sad; a year later Jean died from a heroin overdose at the Great Jones studio. Andy's last Factory building is gone now too.

I was coming back from a party or something in Brooklyn around this time and thought it would be a good idea to walk to Manhattan over the Williamsburg Bridge. I realize now that I wasn't on the actual footpath but on some kind of small workers' walkway that was on the southern edge of the bridge. At first it was just a narrow path but by the time I was half-way out, it had turned into an Indiana Jones–type suspension bridge that was composed of a series of sections of three planks of wood that were laid over whatever metal framework was there. In places there were only two planks because one had fallen off. Miles below was the East River. The subway would roar past and the whole deal would vibrate. I persevered, all the while clutching onto rails that ran alongside. Finally the path became solid near the New York City side but when I got to the actual exit there was a large gate that was locked and plastered with No Trespassing signs. There hadn't been any warnings on the Brooklyn side and the path was completely open to the public. I climbed over the gate. My hands were blackened from holding on to the sides.

In 1990 I had a solo Christmas dinner that I got from a street cart in Chinatown: chicken fried rice. It cost three bucks; there was something awesome about that. I quite enjoyed being disconnected from the normal world. Funny thing is that I remember that Christmas more than others.

We'd hooked up with Gary Kurfirst, who was an epic manager and promoter who'd worked with the Ramones, Tom Tom Club, Jane's Addiction,
B-52s, and others. Gary was one of the nicest people I'd dealt with in the
music biz. We went on a tour together with the Ramones and Tom Tom
Club with Jerry Harrison that was dubbed Escape from New York. It was a
very fun and crazy-long tour. One of the main themes was who went on in
what spot, what the running order would be. The Ramones fans had a tendency to leave after those guys went on and nobody wanted to go on first
unless they were in a hurry to leave the venue early. Also, whoever went on
first played to people arriving and a potentially half-empty house. So every
few days there would be a meeting of the tribal elders and the spots would
be negotiated: "If you go first in Chicago, we'll go first in Columbus and
Cincinnati." And of course everybody wanted the second or third spot in
LA and New York. It all worked out and the tour finished with some wild
scenes that included me being aggressively pursued around our tour bus
by the Cramps' drunken bass player who later fell asleep in the bathtub in
Debbie's hotel room.

After the tour, I think this was the period where, for a month or so,
I was the only one who had Johnny Ramone's phone number. None of
them were speaking to each other and I would get calls like, "Call John
and tell him this . . ."

We did a bunch of tours and Debbie began doing some touring with
the Jazz Passengers. Meanwhile, my loft space had evolved into a kind
of salon and I received a lot of people. I was home alone one afternoon
and the doorbell rang and it was Val Kilmer. He was shooting in the area
and he'd heard I lived there. He gave me a Goldie bass and drum CD.
Sofia Coppola came over; Claire Danes came over with Ben Lee. Giger
and Jello Biafra came over. We knew Robert Williams from LA and I
entertained a bunch of artists after a Zap Comics show at the Psychedelic
Solution gallery on Eighth Street. Robert Crumb came with an adult-film
star who was his date. I asked him for an autograph and he got weird and
said he couldn't sign just anything. John Holmstrom was there and started
going through my record collection, saying, "You've got to have it," and
finally pulling out a copy of Big Brother's *Cheap Thrills* with Crumb's
cover art that Crumb couldn't refuse to sign. Iggy came over and we were

shooting an old Luger in the basement. He shot a hole in one of my gold records and I got him to sign it: *This hole made by I Pop April 22 1989.*

I was approached somewhere on tour by this kid, Barry Kramer, who had taken on the role of massive Blondie enthusiast and fan-club advocate. Barry was a complete computer-geek genius and we hit it off. He helped me build a new computer and get online for the first time. This was early dial-up days, and once again, maybe if I hadn't been so stoned, I would have seen the ramifications. I did enjoy the weird early internet. I remember spending time looking at the site of some college in Japan that had somewhat mysterious English-language descriptions of its environs. There were a lot of sites dedicated to weirdness, one on how to build etheric plasma generators and a long piece of writing that I particularly liked and printed out about mental exercises that were designed to help you remember after aliens picked you up and wiped out your memory. I eventually even talked to a couple of people on primitive message boards. I watched some home sex antics on a site called Netmeeting that had obviously not originally been intended for amateur porn. Then I heard about a method of connecting that was superior to dial-up. I called a local service provider, which was a Russian guy who was probably sitting in a loft somewhere, and they sent over a crew to install a DSL line. The guys who arrived asked me what the thing they were installing did. I would sometimes call this Russian guy and bullshit with him about the virtues of the latest iteration of Windows or something similar. This was a far cry from Spectrum or Verizon.

Jeffrey Lee Pierce came and stayed with me for a while. He was drinking a lot and was in bad shape. I gathered he was partially messed up about some girl, some relationship that had fizzled out. The neighbors would call and I would go collect him from wherever he'd passed out. He pulled himself together enough to go back to California, but in a few weeks I started getting calls from him in a hospital and soon after that he was gone. I gave his tape masters of the stuff we'd worked on to his mom and sister.

All the while I was still dealing with being on the methadone program. I don't know exactly when, but of course I found out about smoking cocaine, what's called freebase, basically crack. I had always done a little coke but smoking it was much more insidious and less painful. Also, the methadone was a perfect buffer for it. Dr. Khuri at my clinic swore by the idea that methadone was an antipsychotic and was potentially an almost complete cure for schizophrenia. She told me that she'd seen life-long schizophrenics turned around because of methadone. I completely believe this. It's just the narrow-minded establishment and idiotic war on drugs that won't allow for any testing or trials, in the same way psychedelics aren't investigated. Also, the laws on methadone are so stringent—one must prove one is an addict to have it prescribed. For quite a while when I was on a high dose of methadone and was buzzed out of my brain on coke, I would never get paranoid or anxious and I found out that a lot of people at the clinic were coke addicts.

But going to the clinic required that I give them urine samples and pretty soon I was relegated back to the daily program, which was a pain in the ass. Plus I was in with a bunch of kids and we got treated badly and lectured at. I heard about another clinic nearby that was more adult and it turned out that Burroughs's New York doctor, Harvey Karkus, ran it. This place was very nonjudgmental and I liked it better. Dragging myself all the way uptown daily in the early morning wasn't too great, but a habit was a habit. I would take cabs or sometimes get a lift up to Ninety-Second Street every day, pee in a cup, get a dose of methadone, and leave. For those who may not know, methadone is long-lasting. For me it took about thirty hours to leave my system and then the withdrawal was particularly crummy, maybe worse than heroin; I'm not sure how to quantify something like that.

My clinic experience was inexorably linked to taxicab rides to and from there. Earlier, my best cab event was when I got into one while leaving the Forty-Eighth Street music block with a friend. When we got near the diamond district, suddenly a guy opened the door, got in, flashed a badge, said, "Police! Get out," and told the driver to pursue somebody that we couldn't see. But during my clinic period I had a few interactions that were memorable. One was an old dude who told me he was very excited to be going to something in Florida called the Gathering of Eagles that was an air force reunion. He said in World War II he'd been a tail gunner on a B-52 and on a bombing raid over Germany, he watched a factory exploding, and the huge fireball looked like "a giant rose." He said when he was firing the guns, his hearing would just disappear after a while. This guy was a poet-warrior.

One morning, leaving the clinic, I got in a cab that was driven by a youngish woman. I started talking to her and quickly surmised that she was seriously crazy. She told me that she was married to the actor Steven Seagal, that he was a CIA operative, and that shadowy government forces were keeping him from her. This morphed into a discourse about Mick Jagger being two Mick Jaggers—one good and one evil. Probably some other similar stuff I don't remember. A few years later I found out that this person was a regular caller to Howard Stern's radio show. Howard encouraged her and she communicated her Steven Seagal fantasies to the nation.

And one day when I was in a cab going uptown and passing through Columbus Circle, the cabdriver told me that years ago he had been in the same place, following a similar route, early in the morning, and a naked girl ran out of Central Park, ran across the street, and dove into the fountain. He thought it might have been a college hazing event; it had been his first day on the job. (Also in the wealthy neighborhood of the East Nineties near the clinic, I found all three volumes of the first edition of *Lord of the Rings* that were in the garbage, tied up in a bundle with some wine magazines.)

I went on tour with Debbie in the throes of coke addiction and had a difficult time procuring drugs in the UK. We steered away from Blondie material and I don't know how successful the shows were. I did acquire a ton of British methadone, which was oddly easy to get hold of, requiring only one doctor's visit in London. During one of the last shows we were staying at an old priory that had long ago been converted into a golf club and resort hotel. I returned to my room at night, late, and briefly opened the window. It was cold, humid, and misty. Suddenly, bloodcurdling screams: *"Stop, stop! Don't come near me! Leave me alone!"* Maybe someone in the crew was abusing some girl. At the same moment, the old radiator in the room began clanking and hissing. I expected all the lights in the place to go on and the police to arrive, but nothing. Now, I was somewhat stoned, as usual, but I don't think this was an auditory hallucination. The next day we left and I spoke to a friend in New York City about what I'd heard and they said to ask the hotel for verification, see if

I'd actually heard anything. I called the hotel from the car we were in and the guy at the desk was very casual, saying that my room had been next to the haunted one and that many years ago a girl had killed herself over a stable boy and the next time I was there I could stay in the haunted room if I was so inclined.

The excess British methadone only messed me up. I was taking extra and when I ran out I went through more miserable withdrawal symptoms in spite of being on an already high American dose. Cocaine withdrawal is sad and shitty: lethargy, feeling suffocated and depressed. I'm not sure why it was ever considered nonaddictive by many. I did a lot of creeping around the streets procuring. By the early nineties, the city, especially the Lower East Side, was in the throes of various drug epidemics. I knew all these little bodegas and grocery stores that sold coke. There was a strip along Allen Street below Houston where almost everyone was selling drugs. There was a small candy store that was on St. Marks, right in the midst of things between First and Second Avenues, that sold coke. I was always amazed at the brazenness of these guys. Much earlier, in the seventies, I'd been passing a small store on First Avenue and I saw a policeman, a guy who had the gold braid and officer uniform, go in and quickly emerge carrying a small brown paper bag that I was pretty sure didn't contain coffee. Payoffs were part of the landscape. So I would go into one of these stores, ask for "un grande" or whatever the phrase was, buy a couple of generic cupcakes that were collecting dust on the sparsely stocked shelves, and that would be that.

Where I was on Greenwich Street was still weird and dodgy. One night very late I was, of course, awake and went out to get stoned further in "nature." The neighborhood was still rife with decaying abandoned shells of old warehouses (which are now very expensive condos and co-ops), and I settled down in the weeds in front of one of these big dark structures to smoke more coke. This place was across the street from a little parking lot and loading dock and I wasn't there too long when two cars pulled into the lot. Two guys in fancy suits got out of the cars and bodyguard dudes got out and stationed themselves on the curb, being observant. These two guys had obviously decided that the best time and place to have this meeting was at three a.m. in a parking lot in an alley in the middle of nowhere. I had the feeling that none of these guys should know I was there so I lay down in the grass and waited till they were done, which seemed like a long time but was maybe only fifteen minutes. They all drove off and I went home unscathed.

Some friends who lived in Chinatown introduced me to a local guy who they said I could buy coke from. This fellow, Chuck, was the leader of a small crew of cocaine fans who had their headquarters down on Pike Street. They had a candy store and around the corner from that was a kind of social club housed in what I think used to be a small storefront laundromat. I became friendly with Chuck and we hung around together for more than a year. These guys weren't affiliated with any of the actual Chinese gangs but they were on the fringes of the gang milieu. The Ghost Shadows and the Flying Dragons were still at it up until the midnineties when the feds finally broke them all up with the RICO Act. I ruined these guys by showing them how to freebase coke. Up until then they were happily sniffing it, and my influence was dire. I would walk across town and spend the day hanging with Chuck and his people. I was the only non-Asian participant in this scene. The candy store had a big one-way mirror mounted in the wall of the rear office and we would sit there observing the comings and goings. They didn't sell anything at the store except candy and cat food and the like, though. At six o'clock or there-abouts the store would close and we would adjourn to the little storefront around the corner and get high and play cards. I would sometimes show up at the storefront and be told that Chuck was off having a meeting. It was many months before I was let in on the secret, which was that he was just up on a mattress that was stuck on a dropped ceiling that could only be reached by climbing up the corner of a small closet. Chuck and company, not being dosed with methadone, were more prone to coke-induced paranoia. Chuck was certain that somebody was stealing newspapers that were delivered to the candy store in the early morning. We spent a couple of nights sitting around in the dark waiting to see if a culprit appeared. Later, toward the end of our relationship, Chuck would get high and complain of seeing ghosts on the street observing him as he drove around the city.

I suffered from my own paranoia too, and in the midst of my hanging with these guys, things occurred that I'm pretty sure were actually not totally hypnagogic in nature. There was a lot of back and forth between my loft and Chinatown and there's a possibility that cops noticed some of this activity. I don't remember much of the first World Trade Center bombing but there were odd activities in the neighborhood that might have induced and been related to surveillance. People on top floors told of flashlights shone into skylights and footsteps on roofs at night. For several days the whole neighborhood had streets cordoned off while guys in hazmat suits conducted some drill. Debbie was at the loft one night and Chuck gave her a ride home. I watched them get in his car and when they left another car pulled out of a spot down the street and followed them. I thought I saw a guy going through my garbage on a couple of occasions, and the phone would have suspicious clicks and odd sounds during calls.

One afternoon I was walking across town again and just as I emerged from under the Manhattan Bridge on Henry Street I saw a young guy lying on the ground who'd obviously been shot in the head. A crowd was standing around looking at him; there wasn't any excitement or distress, just people looking. It must have just happened and I later thought that I should have heard a shot. I kept going and never found out anything about what had happened.

At the end of our relationship, Chuck, who was a good guy, said philosophically that he'd been around to help me during this period and that our time together was done. He believed in fate and the inexorable forward motion of our time here. I heard from one of his cousins who was part of the crew that he was okay but I never heard from him again.

The loft had mice. I think I knew all along but maybe it took time for them to adjust to having a human roommate, and they gradually got bolder. I sometimes slept in a raised platform area that had been there when I moved in. It was close to the old tin ceiling covering and at one point I got the bright idea to see if there were wooden beams under the tin that might look good exposed. I pulled off a bit of the painted tin and was immediately covered with a flood of what was probably half a century's worth of mouse shit. It took a while to clean up. One night I did an experiment. I put a quarter-full bag of corn chips on the floor, turned the lights off, and waited. I didn't wait too long; there was a frantic scuttling and crinkling, and when I turned the lights back on every crumb of corn chip had been consumed or carried off and there were no mice to be seen. I tried some of those traps where the mice would get stuck inside and I'd take them out and release them, but it didn't make a dent in the population. The last straw was when I was lying in bed and one dropped on the pillow next to my head and ran off. It was time to get cats. Debbie found two at a deli on Twenty-Second Street that was near where she was living. Coincidentally there was an empty lot surrounded by a chain-link fence on the corner across the street from this deli and somebody had hung a very official-looking sign on the lot that said CHELSEA RAT FARM. The sign remained for a long time. These two tabby cats were Shadrach and Black Back. Black Back was nuts but Shadrach was a genius.

One night I went over to Chuck's candy store to hang out and he had two little kittens tied by pieces of string around their necks. He said a neighborhood kid had sold them to him for ten bucks. He'd asked the kid their names but they were nameless. He then asked the kid his name and was told Benjamin. Chuck told the kid, "These cats will be named Ben and Gee!" I didn't take them right away but after a few days of seeing them I couldn't handle it and brought them back to the loft. I tried to place them with my mother, but she couldn't deal, so now I had four cats. They did defeat the mice, though. The last mouse I saw somehow got stuck behind the glass in a picture frame and was squeezed in there while being surrounded by the cats. I let him loose.

I think Johnny Thunders came by the loft only one time. It was right before he was taking a trip out of town and we sat around in the studio talking for a while. Johnny and I had crossed paths many times over the years and although he had a reputation for being very intense, I always found him to be pretty low-key and measured. He left New York a day or so later and never made it back, dying under mysterious circumstances in New Orleans.

When Dee Dee Ramone started his rap career as Dee Dee King, I recorded a track with him in the basement studio. The track was called "The Goon" and seemed to lyrically be Dee Dee throwing shade at Joey.

Earlier I had been visiting with Stiv Bators and his girlfriend Carroll Ayache in central Paris and Stiv told me the story of the final battle in the Dee Dee/Johnny Thunders war. Johnny was staying at Stiv and Carroll's apartment when Dee Dee appeared unannounced. I don't recall any backstory on why these two were at odds but Dee Dee held them all sort of prisoner; he barricaded the front door and proceeded to pour bleach on Johnny's clothes and demolish Johnny's famous Les Paul TV model guitar. I don't know if these guys ever resolved their conflicts, and Stiv died as the result of a traffic accident soon after my visit.

On Twenty-Third Street one day I ran into Allen Midgette near the Chelsea Hotel. I knew Allen from around the scene and the periphery of the Warhol crowd. In 1967 Andy had been booked on a college lecture tour and he'd sent Allen in his place. Allen successfully negotiated several lectures until somebody figured out it wasn't Andy and a small scandal ensued. Allen was in a bunch of films by Bertolucci and others and he even had a small part in the first film version of *West Side Story*—he's the kid the Jets take the basketball from in the opening scene. Allen said he had just come from seeing Vali Myers, who was staying at the Chelsea, and that I should go up and see her. I'd known about Vali since the sixties when I'd seen those flyers around the West Village for a film called *Vali: The Witch of Positano*. Also I'd heard a lot about her from Carol Thomson. I didn't venture into the hotel then but a day or so later I saw Vali on the street and introduced myself. She didn't hesitate and invited me up to her room and I went a day later. Vali was just an amazing creature who was surrounded by a universe of magical significance. She spent time receiving in her rooms, salon-style. There were always people around her and she saw no distinctions between them. Soon after I met her she invited us to a party being thrown for her at George Plimpton's fancy East Side duplex that overlooked the East River. Vali had been the first graphic artist to be published in the *Paris Review* and Plimpton was a major fan and supporter. Vali was comfortable and accepted by these rich art types. At the same time she was friends with a bunch of wild guys who drove horse-drawn carriages in Central Park. These horse dudes would rage all night with her at the Chelsea, drinking gin. One of these guys fell five flights down the Chelsea central stairway and cracked the marble floor with his head. They sent him off in an ambulance and he came back a few days later and drank more gin.

She was sixty when we met and she'd seen everything. I was looking at an old copy of *Orpheus Descending*, the play by Tennessee Williams that

The Fugitive Kind is based on. In the short intro Williams states one of the main characters, Carol—played by Joanne Woodward in the film—should be presented "by a style of make-up with which a dancer named Valli has lately made such an impression in the Bohemian centers of France and Italy." I asked her about this and she held up two crossed fingers and said, in a slightly twangy Australian accent, "Oh, me and Tennessee were like that!" I'm fairly certain that not just the Carol character but also the lead, who's named Valentine Xavier—played by Brando in the film—is based on Vali and her dark freewheeling ethos.

Vali was a very unselfconscious work of human art; her whole being was integrated into her drawings and freedom and personal style. She dressed in these great flamboyant outfits that suggested folk costumes from various European locations, and she'd sometimes hit the streets without shoes. By the time I met her, I think she'd spent a few seasons at the Chelsea already, spending part of the year in her valley in Positano, Italy, amid many animals. She traveled with a portfolio of drawings that she would work on for years in some cases. Her notebooks were written in her distinctive calligraphy and included inserts like fur from a pet fox, leaves, and ribbons. Vali painted her room and the atmosphere was rarefied, to say the least; going there was an oasis experience. When she and some cohorts were initially painting the room they found a note hidden in a crack in a wall over a door. The message was from a previous tenant who had stayed in the same room and included a phone number that Vali of course called; she invited the note people to have drinks with her.

She had a dark side and demons that pursued her and made her party very hard at times but she remained unflinchingly optimistic. An oft-repeated motto of hers was about being like a shooting star that burns very brightly as it falls.

Through Vali I met Ira Cohen, who was one of the original Beats. Ira was a poet and photographer and I'd seen his psychedelic photos in *Playboy* when I was younger. In the sixties Ira hung around Tangiers with Burroughs and Gysin and company; he was a lovely guy who I was friends with for many years.

CHAPTER 13

I was getting worn out from cocaine use. Crawling around looking for drugs is annoying and stupid. The drugstores on Allen Street started getting raided, and a few times while walking around near there I thought I got eyeballed by plainclothes cops. Once, riding my bike to a dealer's apartment, I wiped out taking a turn and still went and bought the coke with my leg scraped to hell and bleeding. Drug dealers are usually hard-ass but the guy helped me clean myself up.

I don't recall how, but Debbie and I got an offer from some Russian gangster types to go to St. Petersburg and play in a club. In exchange for the two of us sitting on their small stage and doing a half hour of acoustic versions of a few Blondie songs, these guys put us up for almost two weeks and paid us. I was stoned on Russian dope most of the time but we did get to see the city. Turns out Peter was the Andy of his generation and there were beautiful examples of art and architecture everywhere, although a lot of the architecture was of the decayed, crumbling variety. My favorite thing was the Kunstkamera, which was allegedly the first museum in Russia. This place had a massive collection of oddities that Peter had put together: skulls, weird misshapen body parts, fetal anomalies, heads floating in jars, the whole nine yards. For a dollar they let me take pictures of the weird objects.

The Russian gangster guys were very nice. I don't know if they were actual gangsters but they did their best to play the part; they had the de rigueur leather jackets. They took us around and we even got into a friend's very Russian high-ceilinged apartment complete with exposed wiring and an awesome Cold War vibe. One of the guys gave me a naval dagger but I couldn't get it through the border check when we were leaving; I think they considered it state property. Weirdly, they left me the fancy scabbard when they took the knife.

Finally, as time passed and things got more sophisticated in New York, I was able to just get coke delivered by some enterprising individuals who operated a phone service. One would call the number and tell the operator how many tickets one wanted, and some innocent-looking kid would show up an hour or so later. This was a bad situation and I started succumbing to paranoia and obsessive behavior. The cats would knock something over and I would assume that the loft had been invaded by robbers, stuff like that. I visited a guy I knew on Canal Street and got stoned with him on occasion. He had a used-electronics place that was packed with old retro gear. This guy would smoke some coke then get completely paranoid and crazy, huddle in a corner moaning about rats coming for him. The terror of imaginary rats didn't stop him from getting more stoned, though, and I took this as a warning. I found a shrink uptown and began seeing him twice a week. He put a lot of emphasis on dreams and inner states and I liked his approach.

I was still broke, getting paid off the books, and selling knives and things I should have held on to. I answered an ad in the *Village Voice* that was placed by a rock-memorabilia collector. This guy, Ed Kosinski, turned out to be a good connection. I sold Ed the *Autoamerican* cover-art painting, among other things. Debbie and I sold him our passports from the 1977 period. Ed was married to Jackie LeFrak, who was the daughter of Samuel LeFrak, the New York real estate developer, and we found out to our synchronistic surprise that "Denise," the Randy and the Rainbows song that we'd had our hit with, was in fact written for Jackie's older sister Denise LeFrak, whom songwriter Neil Levenson had had a crush on.

Ed and Jackie introduced me to a guy they knew named Harry Sandler, a music-business dude, and he asked me if I'd considered getting the Blondie band back together. When Blondie stopped working, there weren't many immediate repercussions, but over the years I did see an increase in people, other musicians, referencing us. Well, sure I'd considered it. It was like that quote from *The Matrix*: "You don't know what it is, but it's there, like a splinter in your mind." I just wasn't sure how to implement it. What struck me, though, was something else Harry said, which was that if I didn't do it soon I might never get around to it.

I called Debbie and asked her what she thought about reforming the group and she said I was crazy. But Harry asked us to meet another guy who he worked with, promoter and manager Alan Kovac, and we had dinner with Alan at the neutral territory of Ed and Jackie's fancy apartment. Everybody hit it off and we agreed to meet again.

I persuaded Debbie to take it to the next level and proceeded to call the others. Everyone was in different places. I called Gary and Jimmy and Clem and they all agreed to come meet in New York. Debbie and I had been working with bassist Leigh Foxx for about ten years by then, and we didn't consider Nigel. Leigh had been onstage with various people and bands for a long time; he'd even done some shows with Muddy Waters. When we met him he was playing with Yoko Ono.

The guys were enthusiastic and we did a couple of shows, a showcase at a small, crowded studio in midtown and a big radio festival gig at RFK Stadium in Washington, DC, as we discussed doing a record. We had collected some material and as we were going over things, I again banged heads with Gary over elements of songs. I'm really sorry that I was so much of an egotist and couldn't just let Gary do what he wanted in regards to his material without my somehow feeling slighted and wanting to put in my two cents. The result was that he didn't do the band. I've seen him say that after feeling put off, he was okay not to go into the heavy touring, but I also know that I didn't handle the situation well.

A friend steered us to guitarist Paul Carbonara. He came to the loft and I listened to him play for five minutes and asked him to join us.

We went into a studio with Chapman and did a couple of demo versions of songs but it didn't pan out with Mike, and those tracks remain unfinished. Clem had done some work with Craig Leon in the intervening years and we talked to Craig and then went forward with him as producer. We set up in my basement studio on Greenwich Street. Again, my environment was intense. It was filled with my weird stuff. I had an original copy of the *New York Post*'s most famous headline—"Headless Body in Topless Bar"—pasted on a wall, things like that.

A few years prior I was with Debbie doing shows in San Francisco and we went to the Ripley's Believe It or Not museum on Fisherman's Wharf. When Gerald Gardner's Witches' Mill museum on the Isle of Man closed, Ripley bought the collection, much to the dismay of some of Gardner's followers. A lot of material was on display, including Crowley objects and a little winged figure that looked like it was intended to reference a mandrake root. I'd seen these things in 1969 when I visited the museum on the Isle of Man and this time I was more drawn to them and fascinated. The figure was called the Root Demon and accompanying information said it housed the spirit of Beelzebub. There are pictures of Gardner posing with it.

The next time I was back in San Francisco, the museum was gone. I asked people in the area and they weren't able to provide any information. The Ripley museum is back there now but was closed when I'd gone.

A few years later I was in New Orleans and I went into a gallery in the French Quarter called Barrister's. This place dealt with a lot of oddities and weird stuff and was run by Andy Antippas, who I immediately liked and started talking to. He said he had some skulls that he wasn't able to display publicly and would I like to see them? We went up to a storage room and there sitting on a shelf with skulls was the Root Demon that I had seen on the Isle of Man all those years ago. I was pretty amazed that it was there and I said, "Wow, that's Gerald Gardner's Root Demon," or something to that effect. Andy was equally surprised that I knew what the hell it was. He said he'd had people from the OTO up there and I was the only one who'd recognized it. Andy had bought it from a warehouse in Florida where the collection had wound up after its time with Ripley. I was able to buy the figure from Andy and it was shipped to New York.

Patrick was very excited about the arrival of the figure that he dubbed Pazuzu. We had an impromptu ritual that starred Patrick and Pazuzu. Patrick drew some spiraling diagrams on my floor under the big skylight and we concentrated. I don't think anything much happened then but the day I received him from New Orleans and took him out of his box, it had gotten quite windy downtown.

I still have Rooty, and with the help of friends in the UK, I've spent a few years trying to research him. As far as I can tell Rooty was made by Arnold Crowther, the husband of Patricia Crowther. Patricia was an early proponent of Wicca, and Arnold was a puppet maker and stage magician before he met Patricia and became interested in witchcraft. These two were buddies with Gardner and apparently they gave Rooty to him.

As I've been writing this I've been looking at a few other Blondie-related books and articles and I came across a quote from Craig Leon regarding my old loft space: "You'd be stepping over original Warhols and the dog would be pissing on them." I never had a dog and I was careful with the art in my collection. I did have a few Warhol paintings that I sold off when I was broke but they were all carefully hung, and this makes me question Craig's powers of memory and observation. Maybe he was being hyperbolic.

Craig brought in an Atari Radar unit that was an early digital dedicated twenty-four-track recorder and we were in the relative future. The Radar was able to cut and paste, which was a leap ahead in tech; digital recording platforms were around but not ubiquitous, and also the Radar sounded great.

We recorded a lot of stuff and developed a few things in the basement studio. Then Jimmy came in with a pretty complete demo for this song called "Maria" and I remember thinking it really had that something special that people would like. We did a song I wrote about Jeffrey Lee and we put in some samples of Jeff singing at the end. All in all, the record went pretty smoothly with only enough power struggling and tension to keep it interesting. Somewhere in this Clem came up with the idea to call it *No Exit* and he spent a half hour repeating the phrase loudly. We all liked it and told him he didn't have to sell it that hard.

I wasn't a big club person but one that I loved and did go to frequently was called Jackie 60. It existed as a Tuesday-night party in a funky bar space, first floor and basement, on the corner of Fourteenth Street and Washington Street in the meatpacking district. The name, Jackie 60, derived from a dominatrix's client list wherein the clients were each assigned a name and number.

The area around the club then was run-down and shady. The cops and the local LGBTQ community were constantly at war. In cold weather, guys would gather around flaming oil drums and the whole atmosphere was appropriately bleak and colorless. Today it's ridiculously high-end and sanitized; the old Jackie space, last I looked, is an industrial-art store that sells mass-produced, hotel-room-type, overpriced mediocre art. Jackie was developed by Chi Chi Valente, Johnny Dynell, Richard Move, and Kitty Boots, all people we knew from the downtown gene pool. It ran for almost ten years and evolved into Mother and an offshoot called Click and Drag that was run by a kid named Rob Roth. The Jackie milieu was fabulous and in the basement room was a small stage where eclectic shows would happen. There was something wonderfully old-fashioned about the whole environment; the Christmas shows, where all the stops were pulled out, were very magical. For me it was like being in a past era, the 1920s, perhaps. Anyway, we got close to Rob Roth, the Click and Drag promoter, and he shot the *No Exit* album-cover images at Jackie's one afternoon.

A couple of things happened around this time that would have an impact on my trajectory. Debbie and I spent a couple of summers sharing a funky rental cottage out on Dune Road in Westhampton on the beach. At that time, in the nineties, the area was less impenetrably monied and one could get a cheapish place even in what's now the fancy part of the strip. I would take the cats. Gee, or Geepee, Benjamin's sister cat, was brilliant. I would walk on the beach and she would follow along like a doggy.

Benjamin Cat was a big guy; he was overweight and would actively complain and push objects around if he wasn't fed in accordance with his eating plan. One time at the loft he went missing for several days. I was distraught. I finally asked the guys at the corner garage if they'd seen him. Dude with an Eastern European accent: "Oh, fat cat? He is here." He had just been lounging around in the garage getting fed by the guys who worked there. After that, if it seemed like Benjamin was heading for the street, Geepee would stop him. I saw her actually drape her arm around his shoulders as if to say, *Hey, man, be reasonable.*

So for a few days at the beach I saw this feral black cat hanging around. Geepee was also a black cat though Benjamin was a tabby and one night I heard a lot of cat screaming and howling that sounded like it was coming from under the house. Geepee got impregnated by a wild dune cat. She delivered only two kittens and I took her to a vet, where they induced labor. Two more were stillborn. All of the kittens were black.

Romy Ashby is a close friend and writer who's supplied lyrics for about ten Blondie songs on *No Exit* and *Curse of Blondie:* a countryish excursion called "The Dream's Lost on Me," another called "End to End," one called "Hello, Joe," which is a Joey Ramone tribute, a song based on a traditional Japanese melody called "Magic," and others as well as the opener for this volume. She's one of my favorite people. I knew her from the downtown scene and from Vali, who she was also close to. Her mom had sent her to a girls' school in Japan for acting out. She learned to speak Japanese while acting out more. One evening Romy and I went to see Penny Arcade do a show at the Knitting Factory when it was on Leonard Street. Penny is another downtown icon who came from the Warhol and John Vaccaro crowd and she would do stand-up shows that touched on numerous radical ideas and ideals. Penny is one of those people who know everyone in the world. That night two girls who were sort of dancers but also actors who highlighted and emphasized parts of Penny's dialogue accompanied her onstage. I was quite smitten by a beautiful brunette whose moves were clever and communicated a lot very simply. After Penny was done I expressed my desire to meet this person to Romy. Romy encouraged me to go say something to her. I approached this girl, whose name was Barbara. In spite of my shyness I have discovered it's best to attempt to at least politely speak to someone that you're attracted to; the worst that'll happen is they'll tell you to fuck off—you won't die. So I did what any guy might: I approached her and asked her if she wanted to come see my new kittens. Later I called Penny and asked her to lobby on my behalf and after a week or so, Barbara came by the loft and saw the kittens and we spent the afternoon talking and wandering around by the river.

An early date we had was in 1998. *XXL* magazine did a photo shoot in Harlem of 177 hip-hop artists and influencers on the same spot Art Kane had photographed fifty-seven jazz greats in 1958. The great Gordon Parks took this new image, and Debbie and me were invited and are right in the middle of the shot. Barbara came with us as we mingled with all these legendary hip-hop stars. Great moment.

In the intervening years I'd had several longish relationships that were based on drugs or sex or sex and drugs. Barbara and I were just friends for I guess almost a year; she watched the cats while I went on the road with the band at the beginning of the Blondie re-up.

Barbara Sicuranza grew up in Queens in a rough environment and went on to act, dance, and plug into the CBGB's hard-core scene: Cro-Mags, Bad Brains, et cetera. We eventually had a romantic night at Jackie 60 that eventually led to us going to Vegas and getting married. We'd gotten into a cab at our hotel and asked the driver if he knew a nice wedding chapel. He probably got a kickback but he took us to the Silver Bell where Dorothy Stratten got married to the guy who shot her and Angie Dickinson married Burt Bacharach. The cabdriver was the witness. Back in New York we had a big marriage party at the Angel Orensanz Foundation on the Lower East Side, which was then a very funky and decaying old synagogue. It's more fixed up these days. Joey Ramone and Debbie and my mom and Barbara's sisters and the Dazzle Dancers came. We had so much food that it didn't all get eaten so we managed to donate it. It was very hot and we walked down the aisle to the "Imperial March" from *Star Wars*. Miss Guy, an old friend and Toilet Boys singer, was the DJ.

The band started a new touring cycle but just as we were beginning, Nigel and Frankie decided it would be a good idea to sue the rest of us. I think they wanted tour income going forward or wanted to participate or both. Now, those guys got paid for everything they were involved in. This was a pain. The whole case came down to a very obscure point about our intention in initialing a certain paragraph in the Blondie band agreement. At least that's what I remember. I may be wrong but it was something small like that. After weeks of preparation we found ourselves downtown in front of a judge. When Nigel and Frankie appeared in court they had Peter Leeds in tow. This was like if you were on trial for weed possession and the prosecution came in with Harry Anslinger in the entourage (look it up, this is a very funny reference). I'll never know his reasoning, but the judge somehow immediately caught something was up with this guy and threw Leeds out before he sat down. The courtroom ceilings were very high and had spotlights aimed straight down. Debbie said, "The lighting makes everybody's cheekbones look great." Our eternally great lawyer Marty Silfen went on last in cleanup position and I don't think anyone else really needed to testify; it could have just been him. The judge didn't leave the bench, said, "I can rule on this now," said we were "more credible," and that was it. A huge waste of time and energy and those guys still get paid. Everyone, including the lawyers, stood around on the court steps crying because we actually got some systemic justice.

"Maria" went to number one in the UK and was in top chart positions all over Europe. I heard that it went to number one three times in Spain but I can't verify that. We did a whole world tour. An early gig was at an iHeartRadio festival in California that also had Will Smith and Britney Spears. This was five months after Britney's first album was released and she was still a little unknown. Will Smith, who was the headliner, did a whole *Men in Black* dance number and rap.

Endless rounds of media ensued and I kept finding myself in existential crises over the endless repetitive questions and forced answers and the feeling that we were pursuing some sort of incarnation of ourselves.

We did a couple of shows in Australia and this was the last time we stayed at the Sebel Townhouse in Sydney. I loved the Sebel; it was like the Chelsea in New York. It had this great dark brown drawing-room atmosphere and coming from the bright sun and hot streets into this cool place was dramatic. Everybody from Bowie on stayed there. Elton John had his wedding reception there. But it was also a very weird place. There was a story that a guy lived there for months with a goat in his room. On the corner of the block was a very funky little old gift-shop type of store that was where I first learned about the Rosaleen Norton saga. The store sold large photocopies of some of her paintings.

Norton was known as the Witch of Kings Cross. She was a fantastic character; her paintings of demons and pagan entities having sex were, needless to say, very controversial in Australia in the forties and fifties. In 1949 a show of hers in Melbourne had paintings declared obscene by the local cops and seized. It went to trial and Rosaleen won. She was awarded four pounds, presumably from the police. Vali told me that she'd known her.

Kings Cross, where the Sebel Townhouse was, by 1999 was exceedingly sleazy in a great sad way. There was a long strip of "adult" stores and the area had a large population of street people, addicts, and sex workers out and about at all hours. There was a little park at the end of the road that was the home of a colony of big fruit bats that hung upside down from the trees. It's all been gentrified now and the Sebel is closed, replaced by an upscale restaurant.

We played the "No Exit" song on the American Music Awards. Coolio is on the record and he, Mobb Deep, U God, and Deck from Wu Tang joined us. Amazingly some of these guys told us that "Rapture" was the first rap song they'd heard as kids.

Barbara came with us for a lot of the touring. We were walking around in Porto, Portugal, which is a beautiful old-fashioned place. We were on some main street when I heard someone calling my name and Glenn O'Brien pulled up in a little sports car. Glenn had just gotten married and he and Gina were on a honeymoon. There's not much to this story; we went to lunch in a small café, but it was just so cosmically weird running into each other out in the world like that.

We were to receive the Silver Mask Award in Campione, Italy. The following is from my notes at the time.

The award ceremony/dinner went like this. It was a very legitimate affair, the awards themselves being really nice pieces of work housed in blue leather satin-lined cases. Roman Polanski as well as various other notables of the fashion and art world were in attendance. Previous winners included Dizzy Gillespie, Fellini, et cetera. Blondie is the first rock and roll anything to be presented with this honor so we have to sit listening to interminable Italian songs and speeches. I start getting a headache from champagne and restaurant phobia sets in. Several courses of rich food later, we are about to get our award and I can only think of hiding in the bathroom. Meanwhile Clem is getting more and more hammered. When we finally mount the stage, the view shifts and I'm struck with the surreality of the moment and reminded of the Fellini short film *Toby Dammit* that stars Terrence Stamp as proto–Johnny Rotten. We are supposed to conduct the absurdist ritual of lip-synching "Heart of Glass" in front of an audience without even a live vocal. This is fairly embarrassing and the crew offstage provides jeers and obscene gestures. As the song progresses Clem begins hitting his drums louder and pulls off the protective covers that keep the volume down to mimic level. The small audience is actually paying rapt attention and one must picture this crowd to appreciate what happens next. Earlier, my delicate radical interest was piqued by a magazine in the hotel titled *Happy Few* that was full of images of rich people at parties, and the group here was indeed that "happy few," gray-haired impresarios and their bejeweled female companions. When the song ends, Clem, now regally bombed, attempts to leap out over the drums off the fairly high riser platform. He, of course, miscalculates and winds up diving headfirst, followed by drums and cymbals, onto Leigh and Paul. Paul narrowly escapes but Leigh goes down and I look over in time to see Clem and Leigh sprawled facedown on the stage covered with drums and guitars. Cries of "Oh my God" erupt as Clem lifts himself up and careens drunkenly down the stage stairway and is about to demolish our table with a chair he's raised over his head when for some unknown reason he thinks better of it and lets me guide the chair safely to the floor. All around old guys with white hair in tuxedos cringe and look appalled. Clem staggers out mumbling something about breaking things. Luckily, no bystanders were even grazed, so the whole thing takes on some measure of a great existential moment, though I'm pretty sure Clem's intention was merely to land coolly on his feet. Jimmy and I have to negotiate a peace, since Paul and Leigh were already plotting Clem's demise. Clem has been known to achieve many punk moments but this might have been his finest hour. Everyone talked about it for days.

The *No Exit* touring was extreme. It went on for over a year. In 1999 we played shows every month. I went through a brief period of drinking too much on the road but that was short-lived as I've never been inclined toward alcohol and I'd find myself going into hangover mode very quickly. I still was on methadone that I was trying to gradually decrease and had completely knocked off any other drug use. Barbara was an enthusiastic supporter of my drying out.

Now we were on the receiving end of a lot of accolades. At times it felt odd being hit with all the "legendary" labels. We would do a show and the audience would sing along to everything they knew. They would start singing when they recognized the intro to a song before the vocals came in. Blondie picked up a whole layer of generational energy. I kept hearing the same things: "First album I ever bought"; "I was too young to see you sixteen years ago." I was very appreciative of the renewed fan support but was conflicted about having to spend these large amounts of time sitting in hotel rooms and dragging around airports. I found it really hard to write music while intensely traveling and would get discouraged by this. Barbara would stick it out for long periods but she must have found it even more challenging without at least having the boost of doing the shows.

We played millennial New Year's Eve on South Beach in Miami with the Dazzle Dancers being dazzling and dancing in various states of undress (mostly undressed) to our version of KC's "Get Down Tonight." The feared Y2K crisis didn't happen, nothing broke down, and we entered the twenty-first century. Blondie took some time off the road.

I'd heard that something was wrong with Joey Ramone, though I might not have been clear on exactly what. He called me from the hospital. It was emotional. I later heard that he'd also called Debbie. I wanted to go see him but he wasn't receiving people. I think I understood that he was saying goodbye to his friends, though I probably didn't want to acknowledge it.

We saw Joan Jett and Tommy Ramone and many others from the old CB's scene at Joey's funeral in Forest Hills, Queens, his old neighborhood. He was buried in Lyndhurst, New Jersey. The attendees were able to throw some dirt on his grave, which made for a personal connection. It's something, a moment, I still see clearly. Joey was the best.

I had been seeing media about this thing called Burning Man for quite a while and when I met Barbara, it was one of the first things we talked about. In 2000 we went for the first time. We just went with a couple of sleeping bags and a Kmart tent. At Reno airport Barbara's credit card was maxed out on its three hundred dollar limit and we couldn't get a rental car. But we met two guys at the rental place who were going and they took us. We got to the site at night and it was a very entertaining magical environment, all these lights sparkling out in the middle of this vast desert expanse. We discovered that every year had a theme—this year's was the Body. A huge sculpture was composed of three massive masks that comprised the walls of a three-sided pyramid. A giant copper face cried tears of fire; a driftwood face cried water; and the grass-covered one wept sand. Cars and all kinds of illuminated vehicles buzzed around like insects and there were people dressed in spectacularly inventive outfits.

Our tent blew away within a couple of nights and we slept in the two guys' rental car. One of these guys we were with was a very gung ho corporate type who was all about shooting some shampoo commercial while he was out there. This guy's conceptual materialism quickly dissolved as, within a couple of days, he got stoned on molly or mushrooms or something and was running around in a Batman costume, apparently having forgotten about filming commercials. We didn't have proper clothing either and by the end we'd punched holes in the sleeping bags and were wearing them. We went into the local radio station one night and when we were asked if we wanted to say anything on air, I said, "Can I plug my band?" The DJ asked what band and when I said Blondie they thought I was crazy and threw us out. It might have been the dust-covered-sleeping-bags outfits. Finally the Man burned. We hitched out with some people in an RV and got to a hotel. We put the sleeping bags in a dumpster. The next day we had a great cabdriver who took us to the airport and said we smelled "like cowboys." We went to Burning Man for seven more years and it kept growing. The last year we were there the Man was huge, twice as tall, motorized, covered with neon tubes, and standing on a gigantic flying saucer that was also a wooden building. In 2000 the Man had been relatively small and just stood on a bunch of hay bales. I recommend it to everyone. In later years we'd rent an RV in Las Vegas and do the nine-or-so-hour drive to Black Rock City, Nevada, which is what the site is called for the weeks surrounding the event.

The next year, 2001, the Burning Man theme was the Seven Ages and it was the first year the Man was hoisted into place by a crane, not pulled up by a bunch of people with a big rope. Banksy was supposedly doing murals around the big central camp tent. This time we were slightly more prepared, having rented a U-Haul van that was equipped with an air mattress. The van got covered with dust but it was preferable to sleeping on a car seat. We flew in and out of Reno, Nevada.

We'd been back for less than a week. It was earlyish morning and I'd just come back to the loft from walking Barbara's big dog Flapjack. He was a goofy guy and the cats would terrorize and corner him in spite of his size. I heard a louder than usual airplane engine pass overhead, the big skylight in the rear of the loft being open to the world. The engine sound was followed by a dull explosive sound that I took to be a sonic boom. Not long after that the phone rang and someone, I forget who, was yelling that we should turn on the TV. The loft was some fifteen blocks, about a mile, uptown of the World Trade Center Twin Towers. A plane had crashed into the North Tower. We ran out to the street; crowds were forming and a stream of people were walking along Greenwich Street away from the World Trade Center site. There was a huge smoking hole in the side of the North Tower. It was surreal. The sky was bright blue and clear; it was a beautiful day by New York standards. We got our video cameras and took pictures and talked to people on the street in front of the loft, the neighbors and strangers. A delivery guy told us he'd been up in the North Tower a half hour ago. The sky around the tower was filled with floating debris, maybe glass, definitely paper that came from destroyed offices. The delivery guy said it might be terrorists but was probably an accident. As we were standing there, there was another huge explosion accompanied by a massive fireball. I had been filming in a different angle and didn't see the second plane. From where we were it could have been another blast from the North Tower. All the birds took off from all the roofs and a fire started on a roof that seemed much closer to where we were. More and more people were walking up the street away from the site, hundreds of people. A corporate-type guy stopped after a while and explained what we hadn't seen, that planes had hit both towers, the North Tower by a plane going south and the South Tower by a plane going west. He knew it was terrorists; he seemed really angry and disgusted at the same time.

Debbie had gotten a kitten somewhere and we had intended to go see it, so we started walking uptown. All along the route there were people huddled around cars that had the doors open and their radios playing news stations. News that the Pentagon had been attacked was especially creepy and added a whole layer of grim paranoia. The whole country had been put on some high-alert level. We got to Debbie's apartment in Chelsea. Her power was out; she said she'd seen one of the planes out her window. We saw the kitten; it was very nice. On the way back downtown we passed St. Vincent's Hospital. There was a line around the block of people waiting to donate blood. A guy from the hospital was telling people to leave, as they were overwhelmed with donations. Fire engines were still racing downtown and when we got near Canal Street, there was a crowd looking up at some fighter jets that blasted past overhead. We saw a large group of police just standing around under the Houston Street overpass looking very directionless. These people wanted to do something but whatever that something was remained undefined. When we got onto our block, a huge dust cloud had replaced the towers. They were just gone. The area was much quieter now with just police and fire vehicles coming up and down the street. Some of them were covered in dust that was falling off them as they drove. Everything was hazy with dust. We spoke with a neighbor who had talked to firemen. These guys had told him that there were likely thousands of people killed.

During the next week the whole of Greenwich Street became encamped with media. Tents were set up all along the route toward the smoking pile of wreckage. Bored journalists would be lounging, half asleep, on folding chairs that were on top of media vans. I guess that people still thought that someone might be rescued and the scene had taken on this aspect of waiting. Jimmy Destri told me that a couple of nights after the event he'd just walked onto the site itself and looked around; nobody stopped him.

The attack was on a Tuesday and on the following Sunday, Canal Street erupted into a crazy party carnival atmosphere. Tourists were all over the place and street vendors were selling food and 9/11-themed merch and T-shirts. Maybe it was a way of dealing on a mass level. The event had created a lot of camaraderie; people all seemed to relate to each other differently for a while. The area was still full of first responders and some of the bars were distributing free meals and drinks to the cops and firemen.

One of Barbara's childhood friends, John Jacovina, was a working fireman. He'd told us not to go closer to the site early on. One afternoon he showed up at the loft in his complete uniform and sat on the front loading dock in a shell-shocked state. He'd been at the Ground Zero location for days, crawling around looking for survivors. His hands were scraped up and he was covered in dust. Barbara tried to get him inside but he wouldn't come in and went back down to the site. I don't know exactly when they realized there weren't any survivors.

After another week or so the National Guard appeared along Canal Street and we had to show them our IDs to get onto the block. That went on for a month or more. The debris at the Trade Center site burned for a hundred days and the neighborhood smelled acrid and weird. I rarely have dreams that correspond directly to waking but I had a couple of vivid repeating ones of pairs of planes, full-on 747s, falling out of the sky just straight down as people scattered.

After a while I grew more grossed out by what I considered disaster tourism, the weekends loaded with people hanging around the area in a forced patriotic celebratory mode with cameras and recording devices. Maybe it was a coping mechanism for some, but many aspects of the aftermath struck me as false fascinations. The camaraderie only lasted for a couple of weeks and was replaced by heightened suspicious interactions. I wasn't a big George Bush fan and I was fairly sure that the powers that be wouldn't be happy without starting some sort of armed conflict related to these attacks.

We continued touring with the band and began working on a record. The recording took forever; it was filled with disputes, lost tapes, and long delays, and the album title, *The Curse of Blondie*, reflected that. It was a phrase that we'd bandied about for years that referenced a lot of the jams and convoluted nonsense that we got involved in.

A little more than a year after Joey died, Dee Dee was found dead of a heroin overdose in his LA apartment. I hadn't seen him much since he was living at the Chelsea Hotel. Dee Dee was a terrific witty writer and I spoke to Arturo about something I'd seen that Dee Dee had written about Joey. Artie emailed this to me:

> *Hey Chris this is exactly the way Dee Dee wrote it, he did not care much for grammar*

JOEY

I LIKE DRAGONS SO MUCH THAT I LOOKED UP AT THE SKY TO TRY AND SEE ONE. I SPOTTED ONE IMME-DIATELY IT WAS A SEA DRAGON DESGUISED AS THE TIP OF A CLOUD FRAMING ITSELF IN A BEAUTIFUL BLUE SKY.

IMAGINE ONE FLYING OVER ONE OF THE MEADOWS HIGH ABOVE NEW YORK CITIES CENTRAL PARK ONE CROWDED SUNDAY AFTERNOON. MAYBE THIS DRAGON COULD BE JOEY RAMONE.

HE'D HAVE TWO FLASHING AND LOVING EYES AND WOULD WINK DOWN AT EVERYBODY STAIRING UP AT HIM IN AMAZEMENT. THEN HE WOULD SPREAD HIS FIRERY WINGS AND FLY TOWARDS THE SUN TO CALIFORNIA TO BE WITH ME AND JOHN.

I DON'T SEE WHY NOT. HE COULD BE A BEAUTI-FUL GOLDEN AMBER ONE WITH A SILVER LIGHTEN-ING AMBIANCE RADIATING FROM HIS BODY AND HIS WINGS.

DEEDEE RAMONE

Barbara is an actor and she had gotten hired for a TV spot for what was then called the Sci-Fi Channel, later the Syfy network. The ad was an early example/attempt at viral marketing that depicted Barbara as a tourist on a helicopter ride in New York. The helicopter is flying near the World Trade Center when suddenly Barbara points to an object that's hovering behind the South Tower and says, "What is that?" Indeed, it's a flying saucer, and it shoots out from behind the building, buzzes the helicopter, and zooms off, leaving a vapor trail. She said they were in the thing for an hour, her pointing at empty sky in numerous takes, enough time to make her throw up the bagel she'd eaten in the greenroom. The commercial is a kind of masterpiece. It's a little over thirty seconds and looks great. I suspect that the UFO isn't completely CGI but is in part some old-school optical effects that heighten the whole deal. I guess people reacted to the spot when it first aired in 1999 but after 9/11 it got really popular since the Word Trade Center towers are prominently featured. Different international UFO groups, ones in Mexico and Japan, et cetera, contacted us. People really wanted to believe this and happily overlooked the TV advertisement context. I tried to address it on YouTube comments on the main version of the ad. At the time I didn't realize that the YouTube comment section is like speaking to the dead, and the great thing was that the more Barbara and I tried to communicate the notion that this wasn't an actual UFO encounter, the more we were accused of disseminating false information, covering up for whoever knew about flying saucers attacking the towers. This went on for years and the clip still has supporters.

When I first met her, Barbara had an apartment in central Williamsburg and we watched as the whole place transitioned from a cheap seedy fringe area to this weird upscale urban fantasy. She would come home at night and step over people who were nodding out and shooting up in the hall in front of her apartment. Orthodox dudes in big cars would cruise the local sex workers who waited on the street corners under the streetlights. It was all very picturesque and romantic to me. The place she was in, as well as much of the neighborhood, had been built as working-class lodgings and the old Depression-era vibe still lingered.

We made a zero-budget movie that Barbara directed and I shot that took place in early Williamsburg. It was called *Drive*. This was ten years before the Hollywood movie of the same name. The story of the film was based on an allegedly true set of events that befell friends of Barbara's. A crew of guys went to get high at some isolated spot. During their revelry, one of them passed out and was left for dead by the others but not before his best friend removed his gold chain since he wouldn't need it, being dead and all. Of course the deceased guy woke up a bit later, found his buddies, and was perturbed to see his friend wearing his chain. The end.

Some of the acting might be a little questionable but everyone did his or her best. Debbie had a cameo as a street person. One day while shooting we came upon a dude in a full rabbit suit. We worked him into a hallucination scene. All this was framed by the city and sections of Williamsburg in the period just prior to full gentrification. The waterfront was still full of abandoned buildings and desolate empty lots. We even had a screening at what's now the Tribeca Cinema where the film festival is. The movie exists now as a poorly rendered lo-res ghost on YouTube.

After 9/11 there was a big shift in many aspects of American life. It marked the end of the old New York City milieu. The floodgates of rampant consumerism and gentrification opened. The neighborhoods fell. Even before the attacks, there'd been a push to hold the 2012 Summer Olympics in the city. After 9/11 this ramped up and resulted in a lot of corporate focus and investment. I suspected that the quest to host the Olympics was in fact just a ploy to pull money into the city. Giuliani made the most of his tough-guy-mayor role, and Times Square and, to a lesser degree, the Lower East Side were repaired or ruined, depending on one's perspective. At the same time as Elmo costumes and singing M&Ms made their appearance, a ludicrous musical called *The Life* that dealt with the excitement of the good old seedy Times Square, sex work, strip joints, et cetera opened on Broadway. Everybody wanted to see it but not be in it. The city turned a corner. All through the 2000s the clubs gradually lost ground, and boutique hotels became the place to go hang.

Barbara was walking the dog one morning and came back saying she'd seen a tiny kitten in a hole at a construction site in the middle of the West Side Highway near Canal Street. She left the dog and we headed back toward the hole that was right in front of a gas station. We passed a group of kids and they were holding this same tiny white kitten. They had just wanted to rescue him and were happy to turn him over to us. We named him Moby since he'd been found in front of a Mobile gas station. He was very cheerful and integrated quickly into the cat community at home.

CHAPTER 14

The rent on the loft went up and although it really wasn't that much, I couldn't afford it. The taxes had gone up on the building and our landlord, Kerry, had trouble affording it. I had four Warhol skull paintings. I'd sold two earlier and now I sold the remaining two for much more than the first ones. The Andy market had increased considerably over ten years. Barbara and I, after much looking around and many road trips, found a house upstate near Woodstock and left the city for a while.

Unloading the years of residual junk that was in the loft was challenging. There'd been a couple of major floods at the loft; one was caused by the main building water pipe exploding. Stuff in the basement floated; I remember a cat afloat on an object but I'm not sure if that's a false memory. I left another pile of debris in the basement.

We were in the middle of the woods upstate. I would go off with the band and come back during a snowstorm and the car couldn't make it up our dirt road and I would walk for a quarter mile through drifts carrying a bag. It was very nice to be up in the country even if the winters had elements of isolation.

We would take trips to the city and stay at the Chelsea Hotel occasionally. We were in a room there when Barbara announced that she was pregnant. I don't know how surprised I was; I'd always had recurring dreams of taking care of small living things. I'm told that these dreams are more common in women but I think that notion is more patriarchal bullshit. I said, "Congratulations," which she still thinks was weird.

Vali Myers had returned to Australia after not having been there for many years. The country had undergone quite a cultural renaissance over time and she was embraced and accepted where once she had been an outsider. I hadn't seen her in several years and I got word that she wasn't doing well and was living in Melbourne. She called me one night from a hospital that she was in. When I asked her how she was doing she said, "I'm fine, love, only I'm dying." We talked for a while; she was excited that I was going to become a dad. At the Chelsea Hotel she had a child's fancy red quinceañera-style dress hung on the wall that she said belonged to a spirit daughter. I spoke to her briefly one more time a week or so later and she didn't sound as strong. She would always admonish people not to say "I love you"; she didn't want to hear it: "We don't say that, love."

Finally I heard that she was gone; she'd done it all.

Growing up, I never drove a car. I'd been practicing driving and finally passed the road test and got a temporary license. The very next morning Barbara approached me, all slumped over, and said that she'd been having contractions since seven a.m. and that this was it. So I was able to legally drive her to the hospital. Our obstetrician was a local guy named Ira Jaffe. Barbara was in the middle of labor when he came into the room and said, "I just remembered! I met you with William Burroughs at the Warhol Factory!" Ira was one of Bill's buddies, and as we were reminiscing, Barbara growled, "Shut the fuck up," as she was distracted by having the baby. We shut up and Akira emerged very rapidly at 4:44. (Since I began writing this, a distant relative in Germany supplied us with a copy of my father's birth certificate, and he was born on the same day as Akira.)

My mom spent her last year at an assisted living place near us. She was able to see Akira a few times before she died, a few days prior to her ninety-fifth birthday. She'd done it all too.

The baby reality is a strange kinetic state that changes in waves of difficulty based on the kid's interface with reality and age—easy, then hard, then easy again, et cetera. Akira stayed cheerful through it all and put up with our attentions.

The band was touring a lot and I was coming and going frequently. We were in an airport lounge somewhere in the world, coming or going from someplace, when I noticed a guy weirdly moving around the periphery of the room, as if he were feeling the walls for some unseen vibrations. I pointed him out to Debbie and said something like "Look at this alien." Then he approached us and it was Uri Geller. We'd met him briefly years ago and everyone exchanged pleasantries. I told him the story about staring at his picture in Australia and the person dropping the tray of utensils in 1977. He asked us if we wanted to see some "parlor tricks" and told me to go get some spoons from the buffet area in the lounge. I brought him three spoons. Now, regardless of how accepting I might be of UFOs, ghosts, Bigfoot, et cetera, my innate skepticism kicked in and I watched very closely as Uri did his bit. He seemed to rub the spoons very gently. If he pressed hard, he was a master at disguising the effort. The spoons bent. But best of all, he said that they would continue to bend after he handed them to us, and lo and behold, they certainly seemed to. Was this suggestion or an actual phenomenon? Then he told me to draw something simple that he would copy by mental connection. I was carrying two Martin Amis novels, *Money* and *Time's Arrow*, and I gave him one and drew on the first page of the other. I thought to myself, *I bet everyone draws a house.* I drew a cat face—two big circles with a double J shape as the nose and mouth, lines as whiskers, and inverted Vs for ears. He thought about it for a minute, drew something in the book, and handed it to me. It was a crude car with two big circles for wheels. Then Uri said, "Many people draw a house." I was sufficiently impressed. Was this a great cold reading? Was I a circle guy as opposed to a house guy? I kept in touch with Uri for a while; he sent me some books . . . nice guy.

Around 1974 or 1975 Debbie and I had met with a psychic named Ethel Myers. I think Debbie found her either through a personal recommendation or maybe from an ad. Ethel lived up near the Beacon Theater in the West Seventies. She had been an opera singer. Her husband, a musician named Albert, was accidentally killed by a pharmacist who gave him the wrong prescription. Ethel was grief-stricken and as she attempted to drown herself in the sea, the spirit of Albert appeared and dissuaded her from self-harm. After that she connected with the American Society for Psychical Research and became a medium. She even got involved with the *Amityville Horror* house, being one of the first on the scene there with paranormal investigator Hans Holzer. Ethel apparently "calmed" the house for a while, though not long enough to prevent its being represented in a movie franchise.

Ethel's place was awesome. It was on the ground floor of a prewar building and somehow had a sitting room that was an atrium with glass walls and ceiling. The atmosphere was like the apartment in *Rosemary's Baby* when Mia Farrow and Cassavetes are first shown it. Plants, living and dried, were everywhere. There was a brown and yellow haze that covered the environment. Old books about ectoplasm and yoga that were placed on end tables looked like they'd been there for many years. We sat down with her, and Ethel encouraged us to tape the session with our little cassette machine. She did what might have been a great cold reading or a look into other realms and the future. She told Debbie that she saw her onstage, traveling and being fulfilled in life. At the time we hadn't known about Ethel's musical background and I don't recall if we volunteered the info about ours. But what did happen was after a while she told me that a man was "watching" from the other side and he was making fun of me, saying, "I wouldn't touch him with a ten-foot pole," a phrase my sarcastic father used frequently. Maybe she was just in touch with the vernacular that my parents' generation used, but it was a close hit. We would sometimes listen to the tape we made and it seemed like her voice grew fainter and farther away over the years.

When Akira was three weeks old Blondie did a couple of shows in Japan and an Australian tour. I opted out of the dates and only traveled to Japan with the band to hang out and do press for a few days. In Den Den Town in Osaka, I wondered if the lack of a drug epidemic in Japan was due less to strict laws than to the level of participation of the cool kids. The arcades were filled with the cool kids, who were full speed ahead with the intricate electronic games. I saw kids who brought their own drumsticks to play on drum video games. There was a total involvement. The craft and creative world was on another level. I hit a lot of model stores, the kind that sold little Gundam and anime figures. There would be a single super-expensive two-inch-high figure all by itself in a glass case. I wasn't able to tell why this one cost a lot more than other ones but the kids in the shop all knew.

In Tokyo this massive craft store called Tokyu Hands is like nothing that exists in the U.S. It had a whole section devoted to umbrella repair as well as a million types of pens and markers. Best thing was they had miniature T-shirts that were intended as models for your T-shirt-related projects and I was able to get Akira tiny black T-shirts that weren't available anywhere else in the world as far as I could tell.

I was amazed at how much energy Akira could spend doing not much, just wiggling around and picking things up and putting them down in other places. After a while she was big enough to bring out on the road, and the lights and activity that surrounded touring would impress her. We'd put the little headphones on her to keep her ears from blowing out.

Jimmy, who had shared my fondness for overdoing it with cocaine, left the group and was replaced by his keyboard tech Kevin. This was another difficult personnel change but Jimmy needed to address his demons.

The Blondie situation was in a sort of mid-level working-class position. We were always on tour and I spent a lot of time looking for DVDs of Asian movies in Asian neighborhoods we visited. I became a huge Takashi Miike fan. We did a show in Panama City at a club in a multistory mall that was the essence of cyberpunk sensibility. Little stalls sold CDs, Hot Topic–style clothing, video games, primitive tech, and Magic trading cards. The place had an appropriately decayed ambience and the club itself was decked out in funky old strips of neon and dingy mirrored plastic. There have always been a lot of rock music fanatics in Latin America, and the crowd was enthusiastic. Just as we finished the set and were about to come back out for an encore, the neighborhood lost power and the place was plunged into darkness. At least we got to finish the show. Guys with flashlights led us down many flights of stairs.

A few days later in Lima, Peru, I watched the U.S. election results in the hotel room. George W. Bush won his second term and I was dismayed at the amount of polarization and discontent I was seeing in America.

In the late eighties I started noticing and being somewhat appalled by the use of dramatic musical soundtracks inserted into news stories on TV. I don't know that I specifically saw this as presenting real-world events as entertainment but I instinctively wasn't fond of the trend; a story about a kid in a hospital didn't need sentimental music to emphasize the sadness. By 1990 the culture was being subjected to a fresh and more cheerful type of mass hypnosis or mind control. From some 2002 notes: "The breakdown of this generation making way for the easier conditioning of the next. We rush towards an indirect kind of collective mind whereby the masses all share the same thoughts desires and perceptions, a 'false hive mind' that doesn't benefit from any actual connectivity. Maybe coming to this point could force a jump in thinking and awareness but while steeped in materialistic pursuits and the trappings of experience can the sense of time be changed?" I have a few big notebooks filled with this stuff. There's also a bunch of space in these same notebooks devoted to whining and complaining about Bush and the post-9/11 environment.

I watched a lot of kids' TV with Akira. I'd never paid any attention to *Sesame Street* and was amazed by its Freudian aspects. The monsters run the gamut of weird human emotional states and mental conditions. Big Bird is some sort of depressive; Bert and Ernie share a sadomasochistic relationship in which Ernie is a total passive-aggressive control freak. Elmo is borderline psychotic, reminding me of the type of person who when you run into and say, "What's happening?" screams back, "You are! You are!" Oscar is completely negative; Grover grovels, hence his name; and the Count is obsessive-compulsive. The Cookie Monster was the only one who seemed well adjusted, clear about his goals, and with a sense of humor. Even weirder, all the real people on the show were bereft of any psychological traits; they could all be the same person. There were a couple of other shows that left an impression. *Bear in the Big Blue House* seemed to have a Celtic witchcraft subtext, and *Oobi*, which was made up of hands with eyeballs that talked to each other, was a surrealist, somewhat nightmarish dreamscape.

We (mostly Barbara) had a second baby daughter who was named Valentina but who is mostly known as Vali. The baby thing was all-encompassing and I wondered how single mothers could do what they do. The sleep deal was its own category of stress-inducing comportment. We finally arrived at methods of tying them up . . . that is, swaddling, tightly wrapping them up in blankets. For a few months Vali would only go to sleep while bound up in an electric swinging baby thing. Akira's first word was *Batman,* and Vali kept asking for somebody named Al Gold, who I assumed was her agent. They rapidly increased. At a show in the UK, Akira was watching from the side of the stage and then in the middle of a song wandered out and started talking to me.

Barbara and I started renting apartments back in the city. An early one was actually in the same building as the Knitting Factory on Leonard Street, where we'd met. Now, about six or seven years later, the place had descended into hipster semi-chaos. Kids ran around all night in the halls and this activity was amplified when there were shows going on at the Knitting Factory. One night there was a knock at the door. We were used to the bell ringing randomly, as people in front of the building waiting in line to get into the show would lean against it or just press it for amusement. At the door was a young girl who said that she was staying at an apartment upstairs and when she got there the door was open; someone was inside and she was scared and would I accompany her inside? I went with her back to the apartment in question and we went in. This place was filled with bunk beds like a weird camp or dormitory. It was set up for maybe ten people to stay in this small space. The beds were hung with cheap curtains, so the overall effect was like a Japanese coffin hotel. The source of the scariness was an even younger girl who was in one of the cubicles. She seemed to be the only one there. She said she'd just arrived from Europe and had fallen asleep. I just left. We didn't last too much longer there and the next apartment we got was back on the Lower East Side on Eighth Street between Avenues B and C.

Unlike some of our contemporaries, like six-time nominated Kraftwerk and the still unrequited Devo, Blondie got into the Rock & Roll Hall of Fame the first time we were on the ballot. It might be my imagination but I felt like more people congratulated me about that than about having children.

The induction event was at the Waldorf Astoria hotel in the same place where the Dolls had done their Halloween gig years ago. In 1973 the ballroom was decaying and funky, and now, in a great example of time being a flat circle, the fixed-up renovated stage was decked out to resemble an old decaying funky space. The Sex Pistols, who were also getting in, just sent a handwritten fax that said *Piss off, we're not coming* and complained about the expensive admission, charity or not. Jann Wenner read their message and announced that the physical awards would be held in Cleveland if the Pistol members ever wanted to come and smash them.

Playing songs in front of a crowd composed of music-business heavyweights was daunting but we rose to the occasion and found our way onto the stage. I saw Jimmy and we said hi; he was looking well. Gary was still pissed at me but we talked and I didn't say anything to the other guys as we went to the podium to say thanks. I said my bit and went over and took my guitar-playing position on the stage. Debbie said her stuff and came over to where I was and we briefly discussed thanking Paul, Leigh, and Kevin, who were onstage with us, whereupon Frankie, who followed Debbie, decided that the best use of his time was to complain about not playing that evening. From where I was, I couldn't hear what he was on about, but Debbie went over to him and said something about having her band already in position. Afterward I got the gist of it all and I never have been sure if he actually wanted to play or just complain. I've thought that if he'd called me once over the prior twenty years and said he wanted to play, I would have considered it. That's probably bullshit but I might have. Maybe if he hadn't tried to sue us . . . the only time I'd seen him in twenty years was in court.

After we played, Elvis Costello pulled me aside and told me that he had something similar with one of his bandmates when he was inducted. The upshot was that Blondie eclipsed the Sex Pistols in providing soap-opera drama at the event; most media had reports of "Blondie Mayhem at Hall of Fame" and several people asked how much we paid Frank to pull this stunt.

Akira was bigger, and while living on the Lower East Side, we would wander around what used to be sketchy streets that now were "benefiting" from rapid gentrification. One afternoon we passed CBGB's while a hard-core show was going on. Akira was disappointed that we couldn't wheel the stroller inside but we went in and watched for a while. By this time CB's was surrounded by cleaned-up renovated buildings and the club reminded me of the gap left by missing teeth in an open mouth. Pretty soon thereafter CB's closed. Hilly couldn't keep up with the new high-value neighborhood. There were some disputes about rent and I wonder how much more than the nineteen grand a month that Hilly paid in 2006 is paid now by John Varvatos, whose flagship clothing store occupies the space. Blondie played a sort of unplugged semi-acoustic set on the final Saturday night and Patti performed on the last night and that was that.

We went back a few times after the closing and watched the place being deconstructed. The kids came and sat around on the stage. Over the next few weeks the place got completely pulled apart, revealing layers, strata of debris and stickers that had been pasted to the walls over the past twenty years. By the end it was all just rubble in a long narrow space. I'd never noticed certain repairs in the floor, pieces of metal nailed in place over what presumably were holes or fault lines, the effect being very Frankensteinish. The last time I was there the old murals were still where they always had been. I don't know if they're still there at the Varvatos store; I've been in there a few times but I forgot to look. There was a lot of talk about a CB's opening in Las Vegas but that never happened and there's a sanitized diner version at Newark Airport. Hilly died about ten months after the club closed. The last time I saw him was when we were on some panel discussion together.

Matt Katz-Bohen joined Blondie in 2008 as keyboardist and programmer. We knew Matt from the Jackie 60/Mother milieu. He'd worked with Miss Guy and others and became an essential and elevating part of the modern Blondie era. Matt's parents both divorced and remarried so he has eight grandparents and two surnames.

In the modern era, touring was a different animal than it was for us in the 1970s and '80s. It was industrialized and streamlined and decidedly less frantic. Any fondness I'd had for airports was long gone but bus travel was borderline enjoyable. The buses were all equipped with DVD players that soon evolved into hard drives and I watched probably hundreds of movies while lying on faux-leather benches in rear compartments.

Somewhere in here I finally stopped methadone after twenty-odd years of dealing with it. The band had arrived in a Scandinavian country, I don't recall which, and I discovered that I'd left the methadone in New York. The only other time this happened we had arrived in Seoul, Korea, and I discovered to my horror that I'd left the stuff in my Singapore hotel room. I called the clinic in New York and they said, "Sure, just go to the methadone clinic at this hospital," and gave me an address. I was actually quite curious about what a Korean methadone clinic might look like but when I got there, they didn't know what I was talking about. A worker had to look up what methadone was on his computer and he seemed shocked that it was used for addiction. He told me, "There aren't any drugs in Korea," and gave me some Valium. I did the Korean show in an uncomfortable blur and the drugs caught up to me in Hong Kong, having been sent from Singapore by DHL. By now I had gotten down to five milligrams so I didn't bother taking it and after a week of feeling a little spaced out, I was finally, at least technically, done with the remnants of opiate addiction.

CHAPTER 15

Barbara and I kept going back to Burning Man. We went for eight years all told, the last three times with the kids. We would stay in Kidsville, which was a child-friendly camp that one could stay in only if one had kids. At first Akira and Vali seemed to consider the whole thing the world's biggest sandbox, but by the last time we all were there, they had made friends with other burner kids and adopted a burner fashion sensibility. We spent several years "working" at the post office and were there when they finally got an actual postal code for the period of the event. Before the code, mail was taken en masse to the nearest town to be postmarked.

Burning Man always had a bit of a class divide—that is, there were always rich dudes with elaborate setups—but it seemed like every year there was more complaining about it and more of a wealth gap. Even the first time we went, in 2000, we ran into high-end camps: massive tents that had couches and little refrigerators. By 2013, mega-celebrities and DJs were in regular attendance, and one year when we were leaving in the mass of traffic that caravanned out after the burning of the Man, we found our RV behind a dust-covered stretch limo, something I hadn't seen there previously.

I loved the bleak desert areas and towns out in Nevada. So much of it was this forgotten frozen world. Goldfield, Nevada, an old gold-rush town, is particularly awesome. It was the biggest city in the state in 1907 and now has a population of around three hundred. The atmosphere there is densely haunted and secluded but every year during Burning Man season, there's a stream of young hipster types that pass through and buy bicycles and water bottles from the few locals. The small main street has deserted old destroyed houses next to a new firehouse and gas station. The place is full of spirits; the big old empty Goldfield Hotel is frequently on various supernatural ghost-hunter TV shows. I keep seeing that the hotel will be revived but as of now, it's still closed. If anyone wants to get away from it all, this would be a good place.

Blondie toured incessantly up to the present. We did two more records, both with Jeff Saltzman producing. I liked *Panic of Girls* and *Ghosts of Download* a lot but they didn't get much attention. Paul Carbonara quit and was replaced by Tommy Kessler, a good-looking kid who'd been work-ing in *Rock of Ages* on Broadway. Tommy completed the current band incarnation. Tommy's first performance with us was at the eighth annual TV Land Awards, where we got an Icon prize. Ann Coulter was there and asked me if she could take a picture with Debbie. I asked Debbie, who said, "No fucking way." I took a picture with Ann that I have. Barbara told me she'd kill me if I posted it online. We also met David Hasselhoff and the GEICO insurance caveman.

You know that old joke: The guy is shoveling elephant shit at the circus and another dude approaches him and says, "Why don't you get a decent job instead of shoveling elephant shit?" and the first guy says, "What? And quit show business?"

So gradually, over twenty years, Debbie, the band, and me developed more and more credibility. I got in with the Morrison Hotel Gallery and began selling photos and put out two photo books with Rizzoli. We kept getting honorary awards and invitations to events. With the addition of new manager Tommy Manzi, I actually started making enough money to be able to afford to live in Manhattan again. Upstate is bucolic and charming but the winters do indeed get like *The Shining* and Barbara and I wanted the kids to get onto the streets a little. On one trip to New York City we were staying again at the Chelsea and the kids were crawling around under the bed. We heard a tinkling sound and they emerged hold-ing a crack pipe, so maybe not that much street but some.

After a lot of looking around, we found a place we liked in the West

Village. Coincidentally it was downstairs from Lou Reed. Early on Barbara and Vali, who was still little, went down in the elevator and of course Vali pushed all the buttons before she left. Lou, who must have recognized Vali's distinctive wild pink-and-blue fluffy monster hat, caught up to them on the street. He approached Vali, pointed his finger, and in a stern but amused manner said, "You sent me on a ride." I saw him a few times in the building. He said he was happy to have me in there. But within a couple of months of us arriving, Lou died. I'd had many encounters with him over the years. A girlfriend and I had gone to a pizza place with him. When she went to the restroom, Lou looked at me with a wry grin and said, "If you don't kill her first she's going to drive you crazy." At the time I thought this was weird but that's exactly what happened. She's alive but she did drive me pretty crazy during our drug-fueled relationship. Lou's demise was partly what inspired me to seek treatment for hepatitis C, which I was thankfully able to get rid of completely with the new protocols available.

Debbie was invited to the *Saturday Night Live* fortieth-anniversary show. It was NBC's most watched non-sports event, with twenty-three million viewers. Everybody in showbiz, from Rihanna to Prince to Christopher Walken, was at this thing. When I talked to Debbie the next day and asked how it was, she said, "You can't imagine what a skank Sarah Palin is in person." That was her takeaway.

The kids' school upstate was very hippie-style peaceful. I was off on tour for the kids' first day at New York public school and distressed Barbara called me saying, "It's so chaotic!" And indeed, in the early morning, all the kids collected in a large cafeteria and ran around like maniacs. Walking the kids to and from school was a task but now, a few years later, I remember that time and the walks very fondly.

We still had our house upstate and we'd go back and forth and spend summers there. The kids' old hippie school also doubled as a summer camp and they'd spend some time there. The camp was the last place I saw David Bowie. He had a house in the area and his daughter, Lexi, attended the camp. I would sometimes run into him on warm summer afternoons and we'd spend a few minutes talking under big shade trees. I remember his expressing concern for Lou Reed right after Lou got a liver transplant.

After many years Blondie pulled it together to make another record. We collected a bunch of songs from other writers, who seemed happy to donate, added a few of our own, and hooked up with producer John Congleton. As we were getting started with the recording phase, Bowie died. We'd all looked up to him and it was a shock. He'd kept his illness secret and the news was quite sudden. His leaving a final project of music and video that addressed his death was sublime. I couldn't think of anything like it except maybe Mishima's public end, which, unlike Bowie's *Blackstar*, was aligned with the sensibility of the nobility of failure. It was as if Bowie had created his own hermetically sealed pyramid-style resting place that would preserve him while launching his spirit into the next world. I saw Laurie Anderson a day or two after we heard about David and she said, "It makes me proud to be an artist."

Recording was done at the Magic Shop in New York's SoHo. Coincidentally, this was where Bowie had just recorded his final project. It was a month or less after he'd gone and his presence was felt. The Magic Shop, run by founder Steve Rosenthal, had been going for almost thirty years and had this great old-school atmosphere. It was like someone's home loft that had a ton of recording gear in it. The studio was fitted with funky old furniture: a massive beat-up old couch, et cetera. On a little table in the main studio room was a paperback copy of *Simulacra and Simulation* by Baudrillard that engineers said Bowie had been reading: "the concept of mass reproduction and reproducibility that characterizes our electronic media culture." Under the book on a pile of old *Village Voices* were four dollar bills, change from a food order from one of Bowie's sessions. We were the last band to record at the Magic Shop, which closed a few months after we were there.

The record, called *Pollinator*, was well received and garnered more attention than the previous efforts. We did some memorable shows during this period. The one at Madison Square Garden with Morrissey two days after the Marriage Equality Act passed was a nice event. At the finale our friends from What Cheer? Brigade, a great manic marching band from Rhode Island who had played their horns on the record, joined us for "Tide Is High"; Debbie wrapped herself in a big rainbow flag and everyone went home happy. Our second time at Glastonbury there was a huge crowd and the promoters said it was the biggest for a Friday afternoon. Another vast crowd was at our gig with Phil Collins in Hyde Park, London.

I hadn't heard from Glenn O'Brien for a while when I got a call from Amos Poe saying, "You'd better go see Glenn, he's not doing well." Freddy and I went to see him and he was very weak. Only a few people around him knew he'd been in decline. A day later, Debbie and I went to see him and say goodbye and he was gone soon thereafter. Glenn's passing left a hole in my group of friends. We were off on tour and missed his memorial. Somebody, I can't recall who, said, "How unlike Glenn to die."

When we moved back to Manhattan, Barbara and I needed a doctor in the city. One of our neighbors upstate, fashion and glamour photographer Russell James, referred us to the guy he saw. Harold Bornstein was an older, very sweet eccentric guy who had an office off Park Avenue in the West Seventies. That area is rife with old-school doctors' offices in these upmarket big old prewar apartment buildings that were built with the blood of the workers. When we first started going to see Harold, he was obsessed with Italian culture and fancy cowboy boots. On the wall of his office was a picture of two young boys wearing suit jackets and ties sitting in an audience surrounded by screaming girls. The two boys are smiling broadly but not screaming. This was Harold and his buddy at the Beatles rehearsal (I guess sound check) during their first appearance on *The Ed Sullivan Show* on February 9, 1964. Harold said that every few years when the media latched onto the anniversary of the event, he'd get a lot of calls.

Much to a lot of people's surprise, Donald Trump, the New York City real estate guy and TV host, was elected president, and soon after that Barbara and I woke up one day to see Harold all over the news. There were pictures of him being pursued by paparazzi on the street in front of his office with his wife, Melissa, running interference. It seemed that a few months earlier, Harold had written or signed off on a letter stating that Trump was the healthiest individual who'd ever walked the earth, let alone run for president. We'd had no idea of his connection to Trump and when I asked him about it he said he'd "inherited" Donald from his father, whose practice Harold had taken over. He went to the inauguration and came back annoyed that he hadn't gotten a seat. He had a bad back and complained about having to lean against trees.

I think that to Harold, this whole thing was a lark, and he was surprised by the backlash that crashed down on his head. He briefly had a photo of him and Trump hanging in his office but his patients started to bail on him and he took it down. One afternoon we were there and I suggested that given the chance he should dose Trump with LSD. His wife, Melissa, was with us and said, "That would be illegal!" loudly enough to make me wonder if his office was in fact bugged.

Harold came to a few Blondie shows and hung around with the band. He was a really great diagnostician and nothing like the weirdo portrayed in the media. He was aware of being represented on *Saturday Night Live* and told me he would happily go on the show. I thought about getting in touch with someone from the show but never followed up. Eventually, men in black from the White House or CIA or something raided Harold's office unannounced and removed all of Trump's paper files. Harold was really put out by this, said he felt assaulted, and gave up on Trump. He publicly said he'd had the initial letter dictated and merely signed it. It was too late to rehabilitate his public persona, though, and Harold will always be seen as an eccentric. Barbara and I had become quite friendly with Harold and Melissa. I really liked them. They were great old-school New York characters. Not long after they visited our house in the city, in the early virus days, Melissa called and emotionally told us that Harold had died suddenly. As of this writing, everyone, humanity, is still somewhat in the throes of the COVID-19 virus and pandemic. Harold had gotten and recovered from a bout of COVID, so maybe it was related; it's not clear.

My old friend writer William Gibson suggests a creeping dystopia, a long-term apocalypse that he calls the Jackpot. The Jackpot arrives gradually and is largely self-inflicted; it's not like the asteroid.

I used to think that the intelligence of the masses was greater than that of the individual. I've seen a lot of stuff but I'm impressed by the depth of stupidity that has politicized this virus situation. The first time we were in Japan and I asked why people were wearing surgical masks on the street I remember being told that they were just being respectful of others and that it was common practice during cold and flu season. This was in 1977. Watching this bottomless well of pissed-off complaining about freedom and masks and vaccines is both fascinating and awful.

I'm grateful to have grown up in the 1960s. There was no struggle to create what was creating itself. As a segment of the macrocosm, I'm caught up in a pursuit of nostalgia. The whole of Western culture is drenched in nostalgia constantly being mined. At best it forms a bridge to where I am now. Conversely it's a trap that negates the modern and makes me suspicious of the onrush of the future. So much forfeiture is involved, it sometimes feels like everything is a sacrifice to some idol of loss.

I also used to foresee a jump in human consciousness in which everyone would, I don't know, suddenly exist outside of time and be able to enter into their collective dreams and such. But I suspect that things like Twitter have screwed that up for the time being. Everyone is so outside of their heads and plugged into this neural network of misinformation and partisan personal opinion that the real is dispossessed and equaled by the imitation of the real (to suggest Baudrillard again). Recently we even had the government volunteer feeble information about the nature of the UFO phenomenon. There was little to it and of course there was nothing about the Jungian model where the flying saucers are presented as in part stress-related psychic archetypes that are both internal and external simultaneously. Maybe it's always been a trade-off.

At a Blondie gig somewhere in America, many of the kids were naturally recording with phones, something we never discouraged. A few rows from the stage was a girl sitting on a guy's shoulders and filming herself with a big iPad. I guess she was doing a video of her face with the crowd in the background. As a result, the screen was facing the stage and we were looking at a disembodied video head on a human body swaying to the music. I wonder how I might have explained this phenomenon to my younger self. I like that everybody runs around with an easily accessible small high-end camera and video recorder but there are a lot fewer if any occult bookstores in Manhattan now.

It was a really hot summer this year but the fall seems to be rapidly approaching, having been ushered in by a big-ass hurricane that soaked New York City, producing many hours of video recordings depicting flooded streets, basements, and hallways. Naturally the fragile subway system completely failed and shut down. Videos from the underground realm showed trains that seemed to be moving under waterfalls. One particular video of a swimming subway rat was especially entertaining, as the rat seemed to be enjoying himself immensely. This video circulated widely until it was revealed that the happily swimming rat was actually swimming in a puddle in the Philippines and not in a New York subway.

The COVID thing has been challenging. The final event before the virus messed up the world's momentum was a party at Jimmy Webb's downtown clothing store I Need More that had Debbie and Iggy putting hand- and footprints in concrete inside the place. A lot of people turned out for that and Jimmy died of cancer soon after the event. When we would go on tour Jimmy would frequently take care of our dog Teddy. Teddy loved him so much, he would see him through the car window and start jumping up and down.

The kids didn't like two-dimensional-screen school. Akira graduated high school online. We spent most of the year upstate in the woods. Vali, who had just turned sixteen and had recently started running around with a crew of friends, really didn't like being isolated.

I did quite like the empty-city period, though; I kept flashing to the Will Smith zombie movie with the deserted streets. I never saw any deer in Manhattan but we did see a raccoon uptown near the West Side Highway once. All this was playing out against a backdrop of new social upheaval and tumultuous stupider-than-ever miserably bitter politics. I can't say enough about how badly the current political climate fucking sucks, ridiculous culture wars distracting from any semblance of actual debate.

The city still marches to its own ridiculous layered rhythm. People are going to concerts and clubs and bars. A lot of restaurants in our neighborhood, which is filled with restaurants, have succumbed and closed, and the many outdoor-eating-booth things all over the streets have screwed up traffic even more and encouraged the rodent population.

I saw Debbie the other day. She'd driven in from New Jersey and when she got to our apartment with some old clothes for the kids, she complained about having been stuck in the Holland Tunnel for an hour or more as the traffic stood still. "A parking lot!" Later that evening I saw that the standstill had been the result of some idiot opening fire with a handgun at the entrance of the tunnel during a road-rage incident, so business as usual.

I was alone upstate recently, everyone else having gone into the city for a day. I wandered around the house and sometimes out amongst the trees. We had recently discovered that the upper eaves of the house were inhabited by a large colony of bats. Barbara was out in front at the right time of early evening and saw a bunch of them emerging from a hole right at the point of the roof. We had to hire some guys to plug up the holes in the roof and replace the destroyed insulation that the bats had been pooping on for several years. I like bats, but they had to go, and I assumed that they just relocated.

Vali's girlfriend Isabella had mice, and Vali coveted mice. We tried to discourage this but Isabella had a lot of mice, and Vali got two. Vali tried to sneak them in but was quickly discovered. The mice are two males named Al and Spoon. They coexisted happily for a while in a big bin in Vali's closet but after around two weeks, Al started beating up on Spoon. Al bit Spoon's tail. They had to be separated into two big bins in Vali's closet.

Barbara called me. She told me about a dream she had of "visiting an Italian artist." This person had been making a full-size model of the Duomo Cathedral, presumably the one in Milan, out of lollipops that he licked into shape. As she spoke to him, he was busy licking a buttress on the elegant glass-like edifice he'd created.

I was alone wandering around the house and I passed Vali's room. It was the evening and I had just turned off the light in her closet. Everything was very quiet and I heard the sound of the mice running on their little exercise wheels, just a faint whirring sound. I found it tremendously comforting.

EPILOGUE

Going into writing all this I hadn't considered writing about so much addiction and death, but it was unavoidable. We lost our older daughter, Akira, nineteen years old, to an accidental overdose a few months ago as of this writing. The family was crushed. It was the hardest thing I've ever dealt with, and am dealing with. There's a tendency to present tales of personal addiction as colorful "war stories," art produced by pain and being hooked. I know I glamorized the addictions of artists I looked up to: Lou Reed, William Burroughs, et al. Through it all, many people I knew died, and this was decades before the fentanyl epidemic that's currently killing hundreds a day. I thought that I presented my own drug experiences in a negative light to our kids, but I'm wracked with guilt that any discussions might have been misconstrued.

I miss her terribly. We miss her terribly.

In the 1915 novel by Russian author P. D. Ouspensky, *Strange Life of Ivan Osokin,* as I recall, Ivan, the protagonist, goes to a magician and tells him, "Listen, if I can live my life over again I won't screw it up, I'll correct all my mistakes." The magician sends him back and he does everything exactly the same.

Two other literary themes that intertwine for me are F. Scott Fitzgerald's declaration that "There are no second acts in American lives" and a favorite book, *The Nobility of Failure,* by Ivan Morris. I'm not sure that Fitzgerald adhered to his phrase, and seems to disavow it, in spite of his using it in a couple of places. The band and I are well into the third act.

In *Nobility of Failure*, Morris presents and discusses the Japanese notion that a wholehearted attempt that fails can be equal or even superior to a great success, an idea that I identify with and one that is antithetical to Western thought.

Barbara and I were recently watching a well-hyped TV show about Andy Warhol, and Debbie is sprinkled throughout and presented as a superstar, assuming that her superstardom would be taken for granted by the audience. The show delved into how Andy and Basquiat and others of the time period always questioned their fame. I remember that back then, Debbie and I never felt we'd quite succeeded, that we'd only attained some cult status; it's only now in the rearview mirror that people consider Blondie as part of some grand showbiz hierarchy.

It's always the best and worst of times; those guys back then didn't have any kind of exclusive.

—New York City, Autumn 2023

INDEX

INDEX 283

ABOUT THE AUTHOR

Axel Dupeux

CHRIS STEIN is the cofounder, songwriter, and guitarist of the iconic band Blondie. Stein's photographs have been featured in galleries around the world, and published in *Chris Stein/Negative: Me, Blondie, and the Advent of Punk.* He has collaborated with numerous other writers and artists, including Andy Warhol, Jean-Michel Basquiat, William Burroughs, Devo, Glenn O'Brien, and Shepard Fairey. He lives with his wife, Barbara, and daughter, Vali, in New York City.